The Pregnancy Police

REPRODUCTIVE JUSTICE: A NEW VISION FOR THE TWENTY-FIRST CENTURY

Edited by Rickie Solinger (senior editor), Khiara M. Bridges, Laura Briggs, Krystale Littlejohn, Ruby Tapia, and Carly Thomsen

1. *Reproductive Justice: An Introduction,* by Loretta J. Ross and Rickie Solinger
2. *How All Politics Became Reproductive Politics: From Welfare Reform to Foreclosure to Trump,* by Laura Briggs
3. *Distributing Condoms and Hope: The Racialized Politics of Youth Sexual Health,* by Chris A. Barcelos
4. *Just Get on the Pill: The Uneven Burden of Reproductive Politics,* by Krystale E. Littlejohn
5. *Reproduction Reconceived: Family Making and the Limits of Choice after* Roe v. Wade, by Sara Matthiesen
6. *Laboratory of Deficiency: Sterilization and Confinement in California, 1900–1950s,* by Natalie Lira
7. *Abortion Pills Go Global: Reproductive Freedom across Borders,* by Sydney Calkin
8. *Fighting Mad: Resisting the End of* Roe v. Wade, edited by Krystale E. Littlejohn and Rickie Solinger
9. *Fatal Denial: Racism and the Political Life of Black Infant Mortality,* by Annie Menzel
10. *The Pregnancy Police: Conceiving Crime, Arresting Personhood,* by Grace E. Howard

The Pregnancy Police

CONCEIVING CRIME, ARRESTING PERSONHOOD

Grace E. Howard

UNIVERSITY OF CALIFORNIA PRESS

University of California Press
Oakland, California

Cataloging-in-Publication data is on file at the Library of Congress.

ISBN 978-0-520-39106-2 (cloth)
ISBN 978-0-520-39107-9 (pbk.)
ISBN 978-0-520-39109-3 (ebook)

33 32 31 30 29 28 27 26 25 24
10 9 8 7 6 5 4 3 2 1

Contents

Illustrations

FIGURES

TABLES

Acknowledgments

This book is the culmination of over a decade of work that started while I was still a political science doctoral student at Rutgers University and that eventually became the subject of my PhD dissertation. I would like to first thank my graduate school adviser and the chair of my dissertation committee, Professor Cynthia Daniels, a fellow first-generation college student who showed me how it's done while also making sure I had the practical support needed to succeed. I never could have finished my PhD without her. I would also like to thank my dissertation committee members (and professors who supported and mentored me through graduate school), Professor Lisa Miller, Professor Nikol Alexander-Floyd, and Professor Dorothy Roberts. Thanks to Professor Dana Britton, who taught me how to conduct research interviews and who offered so much first-gen grad school mentoring.

National Advocates for Pregnant Women (now called Pregnancy Justice) shared case data with me during my graduate studies and also during the book-writing process. Special thanks go to Lynn Paltrow, Farah Diaz-Tello, Professor Jeanne Flavin, Laura Huss, and Dana Sussman. Journalist Nina Martin also generously shared case data from her work. Professor Rose Corrigan and Professor David Cohen offered support and feedback of paper drafts that would eventually become book chapters. The

Rutgers Center for Race and Ethnicity offered graduate student support and feedback on early chapter drafts. Professor Wendy Bach, Dr. Orisha Bowers, and SisterReach offered insights for Tennessee arrest cases. I also must thank Professor Kim Mutcherson, Professor Michele Goodwin, Professor Carol Mason, Professor Johanna Schoen, and Professor Sarah Roberts for support, mentorship, and feedback.

Thanks also go to Professor Khiara Bridges, who encouraged me to submit my proposal for this book, who showed me what book proposals are supposed to look like, and who pumped me up through my writing struggles and crises of confidence! To Professor Monica McLemore, thank you for friendship, mentorship, good food, and practical support. Professor Dierdre Condit and Professor Chris Saladino, thank you for convincing me that I could go to graduate school and succeed. I never thought in a million years that this would be my life, and I never would have done it without your encouragement.

Many thanks go to Professor Edith Kinney, for friendship, support, and help getting me out of the apartment with the creepy neighbors. I am indebted to Professor Tanya Bakru, Professor Sara Angevine, and Jazmín Delgado for friendship and for hosting writing groups. I am indebted also to Professor Laury Oaks for her incredibly useful review and feedback. I would like to acknowledge Professor Molly McNulty, whose 1987 article inspired the title of this book. Thanks go to Nicole Carre and Stephanie McLemore Bray for keeping me going. I would also like to thank my family members, who were supportive of me in this outrageous, challenging process, and my dear friends, especially Geoff Taylor and Adrian Vazquez. Thank you for reading early drafts, for reminding me to go outside, for making sure I had things to eat, and for giving me the support I needed to do this. I'm also thankful for the many cats who kept me company during this process. I only wish they could read.

Introduction

In 2011 a twenty-five-year-old white woman named Heather Capps gave birth to a healthy baby boy via cesarean section.[1] Her newborn baby tested positive for opioids. Heather had opioid use disorder, which developed after she had been prescribed the drug to treat her chronic back pain. Heather lived in Alabama, in a small town in the northeast part of the state. She had heard about a local policy ordering the prosecution of women who used drugs during pregnancy on the basis that their drug use constituted a form of child abuse. She had also heard that the withdrawal symptoms from quitting oxycodone could be dangerous for her and for her pregnancy. She needed help. Heather was unemployed and relied on Medicaid and $200 a month in food stamps to support her family. She was referred to an inpatient drug treatment facility in Birmingham, nearly an hour-and-a-half drive away from her home. As a single mom with two young children, inpatient treatment was not an option—who would look after her little boys? Heather was trapped. Seeing no other solutions, she decided to gradually taper down her use of oxycodone and to take the lowest possible dose in an effort to protect her pregnancy.

Two days after Heather gave birth, and still recovering from her cesarean section, she was arrested at the hospital. She spent the next three months in jail, separated from her newborn and her two other children, unable to post the $500,000 bond.[2] Over a year after her arrest, Heather pled guilty to a charge of chemical endangerment of a minor, a class C felony. In Alabama crimes designated as class C felonies are punishable by one to ten years in prison. She was given a three-year suspended sentence—if she completed a rehab program, she wouldn't have to serve three years in prison. Heather was ordered to stay in a halfway house while she was in court-ordered rehab. During that time she was permitted to see her children once a week. So for Heather to finally access the drug treatment she wanted, she was forced to self-manage her substance use disorder through her pregnancy, forcibly separated from her newborn and two other young children, and arrested and forced to spend her first three months postpartum in jail. She pled guilty to a charge of felony child abuse and then was assigned to a halfway house to complete drug treatment, with the stress of a possible three-year prison sentence weighing over her.

The pregnancy police do not exist in a discrete agency or department. They don't carry pregnancy-police badges or wear special pregnancy-police uniforms, but the pregnancy police are all around us. Sometimes they wear scrubs or white coats. You can find them at the hospital or at the Child Protective Services office. Sometimes they are deputized to police pregnancy by law or policy. Other times they are acting only on the basis of their own beliefs. They are our neighbors, our partners, and our friends. They are nurses, doctors, and social workers. They are found in institutions of health care, of social services, and of civil and criminal law enforcement. Sometimes the pregnancy police may even exist in our own minds, when we see a pregnant person doing something we don't approve of, like lifting weights or drinking coffee or wine. Policing pregnancy is a process informed by politics and historical inequalities, developed over time by law and ideology. The pregnancy police are those who are involved in surveilling, reporting, prosecuting, and incarcerating pregnant people for pregnancy-related offenses.

Throughout the United States, pregnant and postpartum people have, for decades, faced charges for committing crimes against the fertilized eggs, embryos, and fetuses that they carry.[3] People who test positive for drugs during or immediately after pregnancy, people who survive suicide attempts but lose their pregnancies, and people injured in car accidents who have stillbirths or miscarriages, for example, face the possibility of lengthy prison sentences. These arrests have occurred in the absence of any declarative criminal law and even in the presence of statutes that explicitly *exclude* pregnant people from prosecution. Three states, South Carolina, Alabama, and Tennessee, have explicitly criminalized pregnant people's actions with regard to fertilized eggs, embryos, or fetuses, yet arrests of pregnant people for crimes against their own pregnancies have been made in almost every state. This includes blue states with more progressive abortion laws.[4] For example, in 2007, an eighteen-year-old Dominican immigrant was arrested and charged in Massachusetts for having an illegal abortion after she took she took misoprostol, a medication that can cause uterine contractions.[5] In 2011 a woman in New York City was arrested for self-managing an abortion.[6] In 2019 a white woman in California was charged with homicide when she had a stillbirth.[7] The widespread nature of these arrests and prosecutions suggests that webs of pregnancy police are already in place throughout the country.

The criminal prosecution of pregnant people for crimes against the fertilized eggs, embryos, and fetuses they carry relies on a legal understanding that pregnant people are legally distinct from and enjoy fewer rights than other similarly situated nonpregnant people.[8] Pregnant people occupy a different, lower space in the United States' system of law. I call this *pregnancy exceptionalism*—where pregnancy ipso facto reduces the legal status of pregnant persons relative to other similarly situated persons. Pregnancy exceptionalism is most useful in legal analysis, demonstrating the ways that people with the capacity for pregnancy have essentially already been defined as a separate and lesser legal class.

Typically, because of medical privacy laws, including HIPAA, a positive drug test at a doctor's office cannot be legally shared with law enforcement, but pregnant and postpartum people have been arrested after their healthcare providers reported a single positive drug test.[9] Generally, people who survive a suicide attempt are not criminally prosecuted, but pregnant and postpartum people have been charged with felonies when they survive but lose their pregnancies. Legally competent adults are allowed to reject a course of medical treatment, but pregnant people may be cut open against their will for cesarean sections by court order and may be criminally charged if they resist.[10] Pregnant people are being held criminally accountable for actions and behaviors that would otherwise be legal or at least nonprosecutable, like drinking a beer, testing positive for marijuana, or taking their legal prescription medication. Pregnant people have also been charged with crimes more severe than what their actual illegal behavior would typically warrant. For example, a pregnant person caught in possession of methamphetamine might be charged with unlawful neglect of a child or delivery of drugs to a minor (through the umbilical cord) instead of just drug possession.

These examples of differential treatment are not limited to the criminal justice system.[11] Pregnant people are treated differently and can face limitations on their fundamental rights in a variety of areas, because of the fact of their pregnancies. They can be forced to jump through state-regulatory hoops to access basic medical care, have medical treatment forcibly imposed on them, and even lose their right to medical privacy. Pregnancy *is* a women's issue but not exclusively so. Pregnancy is an issue of sex *and* gender but not exclusively so. Pregnancy is also an issue of class, race, religion, relationship status, ethnicity, and ability, among other intersections of identity and oppression. The reproductive justice framework acknowledges that reproduction is shaped by these intersections.

REPRODUCTIVE JUSTICE

Much of the mainstream reproductive rights activism has centered on the legal right to have an abortion, using the rhetoric of "choice." The prochoice-antichoice debate obscures the reality that the legality of abortion is not the same thing as the accessibility of abortion, and it does not take into account the complex social and economic factors that limit choices around pregnancy. What does it mean to "choose" abortion when you can't afford to have one? Or when you can't afford to have a baby, for that matter? Or when you are afraid that your child may one day be killed by a police officer? Or when you are worried that you might die if you give birth? The prochoice-antichoice debate also limits discussion about reproductive issues to abortion. While certainly important, the regulation and control of pregnant people is not limited to those who seek to end their pregnancies—it also touches the lives of those who want to give birth and parent their children.

In the 1980s and 1990s, organizations dedicated to the reproductive health of women of color, and of Black women specifically, noted the shortcomings of the "pro-life" and "pro-choice" framing of the fight over reproduction, arguing that it "masked the ways that laws, policies, and public officials punish or reward the reproductive activity of different groups of women differently."[12] Boiling down the entire scope of reproductive life and the way that law and culture shape reproductive life to a matter of being pro- or antiabortion is inadequate. Reproduction is so much broader and more complex than prochoice and prolife. Indeed, this overly simplified notion of reproductive rights may have led us to where we are now—no constitutional right to abortion, very limited government supports for families and children, and high maternal mortality rates, especially for Black women and birthing people, on the rise.[13] Black women–led organizations emphasize the importance of a more holistic and expansive view of reproductive health as more than the technical legality of abortion. This broad view includes issues of access but also aspects of life beyond abortion that disproportionately impact poor women and women of color, such as forced sterilizations, sexually transmitted infections, housing and wages, child care, maternal mortality, and state and intimate partner violence.

As historian Rickie Solinger and Loretta Ross, professor and cofounder of the reproductive justice movement, note, "Reproductive justice is a contemporary framework for activism and for thinking about the experience of reproduction. It is also a political movement that splices *reproductive rights* with *social justice* to achieve *reproductive justice*. The definition of reproductive justice goes beyond the pro-choice/pro-life debate and has three primary principles: (1) The right to *not* have a child; (2) the right to *have* a child; and (3) the right to *parent* children in safe and healthy environments."[14] In this book I adopt the reproductive justice framework to examine the criminalization of pregnancy. Beyond abortion people who intend to carry their pregnancies to term, give birth, and parent their children face obstacles in the course of laws and regulations that limit their reproductive autonomy and legal status. State regulation of abortion and of pregnancy and birth are two sides of the same coin.

As I write this book, the legal rights of people with the capacity for pregnancy are in an unprecedented amount of flux, in large part because of the overturning of *Roe v. Wade* (1973) and *Planned Parenthood v. Casey*

(1992), two Supreme Court decisions that defined and outlined the rights of pregnant women (in these cases in the context of abortion) against the state's interest in pregnancy and birth.[15] In 2018 Mississippi passed a law banning abortion after fifteen weeks of pregnancy, directly contradicting the US Supreme Court's precedents in *Roe v. Wade* and *Planned Parenthood v. Casey*. It was hardly the only state to do so. After 2010 a large number of antiabortion laws went into effect in the states, intentionally meant to challenge existing court precedents.[16] Passing such blatantly unconstitutional laws is an invitation for those laws to be challenged in courts and potentially by the US Supreme Court. Legislators introducing these extreme measures hoped that, with the conservative shift in the Supreme Court, *Roe v. Wade* would be overturned, leaving each state to form and enforce its own abortion policy. This is how the challenge to Mississippi's fifteen-week ban found itself before the Supreme Court in December 2021. Abortion rights advocates urged the court to use *stare decisis*—to maintain their own, nearly fifty-year-old legal precedent—and strike the Mississippi law down as unconstitutional. Antiabortion advocates urged the court to reject those precedents, saying past courts had erred and had gone beyond their legal authority when they made abortion a fundamental right.

On June 26, 2022, the US Supreme Court gave its opinion in *Dobbs v. Jackson Women's Health Organization*. It made no dramatic departures from the draft that had been leaked months earlier, overturning *Roe v. Wade* and *Planned Parenthood v. Casey*.[17] After the opinion was released, law and policy shifted almost immediately. Trigger bans, laws passed in the states that would become enforceable in the event that *Roe* was overturned, started to go into effect. Unenforceable state laws from the pre-*Roe* days *could* be enforced. Courts throughout the country tried to figure out if and how these state laws could be enforced. State legislatures began to introduce new legislation, to protect abortion rights or to restrict them. At the time of this writing, abortion is banned outright in fourteen states and is severely curtailed in four others. Abortion threatens to become mostly or completely illegal in a further eight states sometime in the near future, and legislators are introducing laws that attempt to restrict the movement of pregnant people; ban medication for abortions; define fertilized eggs, embryos, and fetuses as legal persons; and criminalize people thought to have endangered their own pregnancies.[18]

Soon after the court gave its opinion, a flood of news coverage featured harrowing stories about the real-life impact of restrictive, or even punitive, abortion law and policy, such as doctors afraid to provide care to patients with lethal ectopic pregnancies for fear that they could lose their medical licenses or even be criminally prosecuted; children impregnated by rape forced to flee their home states to access abortion care; and patients being told to return to the hospital only once their pregnancies became dangerously septic, because only then could their miscarriages be treated legally.[19]

However, even *with* the limited protections of *Roe v. Wade,* pregnant people and people with the capacity for pregnancy have struggled to have their full humanity recognized during pregnancy, in violation of their internationally defined human rights to life, health, equality, privacy, and bodily integrity. People were forced to jump through state-imposed, medically unnecessary hoops, like state-mandated informed consent, waiting periods, and compulsory ultrasounds before they could access abortion. Federal bans on the use of public funds for abortion care meant that poor people died from illegal abortions.[20] Pregnant people were denied medical care and had care imposed on them, on the basis of fetal protection. People struggled to access contraceptives, died from pregnancy or birth complications, and experienced violence when they gave birth or after they gave birth. *Roe* had carved out one area of reproductive life and promised constitutional protection for it: people could make their own decisions on abortion, with a health-care provider, with limited or no state financial support, before fetal viability. Though *Roe* also implied that the rights of pregnant people supersede the state's interest in future persons, it maintained that this was true only for the first two trimesters of pregnancy, and other reproductive issues remained a state by state or even county by county free-for-all.

The reproductive justice approach is fundamentally grounded in "the human right to control our sexuality, our gender, our work, our reproduction."[21] Though *Dobbs* had enabled new and dramatic state-level abortion restrictions, *Roe v. Wade* never guaranteed the human rights of people with the capacity for pregnancy and never achieved reproductive justice. Violations of the rights of pregnant people had actually been happening in some hospitals for decades, especially at private religious hospitals, which had legally permissible, ideologically driven antiabortion policies.[22] Obstetric violence and the criminal prosecution of pregnant and postpartum people for crimes against their own pregnancies were also nothing new.

In some part due to the stigma surrounding pregnancy and drug use and in part due to tunnel vision or issue blindness, mainstream organizations who fought to preserve the legal right to abortion often kept their distance from criminal cases involving pregnant drug users. Law professor Michele Goodwin explains, "As the criminal prosecution of women perceived as 'bad mothers' did not explicitly relate to abortion, many of these poor women were on their own. And because abortion legality frequently dominated much of the feminist discourse and lobbying, prosecuting pregnant women strangely was not perceived as, nor was responded to as, a woman's issue. Instead, the criminalization of poor, pregnant women of color was perceived as a race issue—something too remote for feminist discourse and activism."[23]

Carving out the criminal prosecution of pregnant people for substance use as separate from other reproductive rights or feminist issues is unfortunate for two reasons. First, the criminalization of pregnancy is a major issue all on its own, implicating many of the same issues as abortion legality, like bodily autonomy and medical privacy but also substance use and mass incarceration, and illuminating the roles that both the medical system and criminal system play together. Second, arrests of pregnant people for substance use were a bellwether for the further criminalization of pregnancy, including current efforts to criminalize abortion. By failing to address the unjust treatment of the most stigmatized and marginalized, many abortion rights advocates were blind to the decades of legal decision making that defined pregnant people as secondary to their own pregnancies.

Indeed, at the *Dobbs* oral arguments, Justice Clarence Thomas mentioned the *Ferguson* case, a Supreme Court case involving the criminal prosecution of pregnant people for substance use. He used the drug charges brought against a pregnant woman to challenge the legitimacy of the "liberty" argument for abortion, pointing to places where he thought a pregnant person's liberty *should* be limited. Solicitor General Elizabeth Prelogar, who was arguing in opposition to the Mississippi abortion ban, didn't know what case he was alluding to but seemed to agree with this limit:

JUSTICE THOMAS: You heard my question to counsel earlier, about the woman who was convicted of criminal child neglect. What would be your reaction to that as far as her liberty and whether or not the liberty interest that we're talking about extends to her?

GENERAL PRELOGAR: Well, Justice Thomas, I have to confess that I haven't read the specific case you're referring to, but, if I understand the question you were posing, it sounds as though the state is seeking to regulate for a child that's been born that was injured while it was inside the womb. And I think that we are not denying that a state has an interest there.[24]

My heart sank in that moment. Not only had Prelogar not read the case Thomas was referencing, but she also expressed agreement with Thomas's assertion that the state has an interest in children that were "injured . . . inside the womb." In reality the Supreme Court in *Ferguson* placed *limits* on the ability of health-care providers to gather criminal evidence from their patients and did not deal substantively with whether pregnant people could be charged with pregnancy-specific crimes. In this exchange Thomas actually departed from *Ferguson,* asserting that the state should be allowed to treat pregnant people with fewer rights than other similarly situated people, and General Prelogar, the attorney arguing in favor of abortion rights, agreed, essentially ceding ground on equality for pregnant people.

I include myself in my criticism of the mainstream reproductive rights movement's blind spots. I have been passionate about the legality of abortion since middle school. In college, as a first-generation student, studying political science and gender studies and cobbling part-time minimum wage jobs together to pay rent, I was involved in a lot of organizing and activism. I offered support for incarcerated people and for victims of sexual violence. On Sundays I participated with Food Not Bombs, distributing hot meals and groceries to unhoused people. I was the president of my college environmentalism club, working with people from the heart of Appalachia's coal country to stop the construction of a new, destructive coal-processing plant. I was a member of the college Students for a Democratic Society chapter and was involved in reproductive rights organizing on my college campus, sometimes even donning a barely recognizable mascot costume of a condom for free condom-distribution days. I marched to demand protections for undocumented immigrants and for gay rights, and I led workshops where people learned about sexual and reproductive anatomy and self-advocacy in medical settings.

I graduated from college during the financial crisis of the late aughts and didn't have the kind of social connections that can help land a job with benefits and a decent wage. So I figure modeled for art classes, went dumpster diving for groceries, split rent with a bunch of feminist housemates, and kept up with my activism, organizing, and education. While working as a bar line cook and a café baker, I learned about obstetric violence and trained and volunteered as a birth doula. I eventually got a job at an abortion clinic, where I did office work, patient counseling, and hand holding during abortion procedures. I studied for the GRE and eventually (at the urging of my undergraduate professors Dr. Deirdre Condit and Chris Saladino) applied to political science PhD programs. I was admitted into the program at Rutgers University and was awarded an Excellence Fellowship, which covered the cost of my education and provided me with a living stipend while I completed my work—the only way a PhD program was financially possible for me. Despite all this involvement and interest, I didn't learn about the criminalization of pregnancy until I was completing my political science PhD coursework. Professor Cynthia Daniels and Professor Shatema Threadcraft were coteaching a gender and public policy class and assigned legal historian Dorothy Roberts's groundbreaking book, *Killing the Black Body: Race, Reproduction, and the Meaning of Liberty*. Roberts's book reshaped all of my thinking about reproduction and the law and showed me some of the many blind spots I have as a white person. I was eager to learn more. I have spent the last twelve years trying to do that. My dissertation, "The Criminalization of Pregnancy: Rights, Discretion, and the Law," eventually grew into this book. Now, as a professor, I put my education to work inside and outside of the classroom.

Killing the Black Body has been hugely influential for my own work on the criminalization of pregnancy. In this foundational legal-historical text, Roberts skillfully locates the roots of reproductive oppression in the United States in the institution of chattel slavery and traces the continued reproductive oppression of Black people in general and Black women specifically. From forced breeding in slavery to sterilization to contraceptive abuse and the criminalization of pregnancy, Black women have been subject to a system that disregards their humanity and devalues their mothering ability, as it simultaneously defines them by their presumed procreative abilities. I am incredibly thankful and honored to have had Professor Roberts serve as my outside reader for the dissertation that preceded this book.

Professor of law Michele Goodwin and her brilliant work on the criminalization of pregnancy have also been instructive. Her most recent book, *Policing the Womb: Invisible Women and the Criminalization of Motherhood,* provides a compelling analysis of the rights deprivations experienced by pregnant women, including the criminalization of miscarriage, shackling during childbirth, and the use of sterilization in plea bargaining. Goodwin demonstrates, through in-depth legal analyses of notable cases across a breadth of areas, that by focusing on the most marginalized women, the conversation about reproductive oppression is necessarily broadened. Goodwin was present at my first-ever conference presentation, which took place at Rutgers-Camden in 2013, to commemorate the fortieth anniversary of *Roe v. Wade.* I presented my preliminary theoretical work on methamphetamine, reproduction, and white trash stereotypes. Goodwin offered mentorship and feedback on my pregnancy criminalization work at Law and Society Association meetings and through graduate school and my first academic position.

Law professor Wendy Bach gave a presentation about the criminal prosecution of pregnant people in Tennessee under the newly adopted fetal assault law at a meeting of the Law and Society Association. I presented some of my dissertation work on the criminalization of pregnancy in Alabama at the same meeting, which is how Professor Bach and I met. We traded insights and talked about the difficulties of doing work on this subject. She wondered if it would be worth pursuing an academic text on the work she was doing in Tennessee, and I strongly encouraged her to do so. Her book, *Prosecuting Poverty, Criminalizing Care,* explores the criminalization of pregnancy in Tennessee through the cruel and ineffective contradiction of using punishment to obtain drug treatment for impoverished pregnant women in Tennessee, with analyses of arrest cases and interviews with system actors such as judges and lawyers.

SAMENESS, DIFFERENCE, AND EQUALITY

The assumed biological distinctiveness of people assigned as females at birth, especially their potential (assumed or actual) ability to gestate a pregnancy, has been presented as a dilemma for the advancement of equality in law, generally in binary notions of male/female and man/woman. How can males and females be treated equally if they are biologically different? They are not considered both different from each other, but rather males are considered the standard kind of citizen, and females are *different* from them. Historically, *different* has meant lesser, weaker, or worse. Political theorist Zillah Eisenstein writes, "Man is never viewed as '*not pregnant,*' so pregnancy must be constructed as woman's 'difference' and not man's lacking."[25] She continues, "In this usage, being 'different' is the same as being unequal." Feminist political scientist Sally Kenney, who specializes in women and law, asserts, "'If women are different from men,' society 'can treat them less favorably.'"[26] Political scientist Gwendolyn Mink states, "Gendered rights are tricky business, as the differential treatment of women in law and policy has too often meant our unequal treatment."[27] Historically, these differences have been used to reduce the legal status of women as a class, either by legally addressing women and men identically and ignoring the material differences brought by the realities of menstruation, pregnancy, birth, and breastfeeding or by addressing them differently, reducing them to their procreative functions.

Sex-neutral laws may result in identical treatment with different impacts. Shackling both men and woman who are incarcerated will have a more punitive effect on women, because sometimes women are pregnant. A lack of a lactation room at work will have a more punitive effect on women because sometimes women are breastfeeding. A lack of bathroom breaks will have a disproportionate impact on women because sometimes they are menstruating. Sex-conscious laws can address these issues: because people of different sexes, especially when one experiences pregnancy, are not similarly situated, differential treatment on the basis of sex is not necessarily discriminatory. However, sex-conscious laws *may* open the door to a host of other inequities. A person may be forced to submit to invasive medical procedures that would be considered unconstitutional if not for the pregnancy. A pregnant person found to habitually lack self-control may be detained, without an attorney, a jury of peers, or a public trial, for the duration of the pregnancy.[28] A pregnant person who is brain-dead or in a persistent vegetative state may be kept on life support until the fetus has sufficiently developed to survive outside of her uterus, in violation of her advanced medical directive.[29]

This choice between sameness and difference in legal treatment is a false one. Whether defined as the "same" as men or as "different" from men, women keep getting the short end of the legal stick. Political scientist Judith Baer writes, "Our gender-neutral law of reproductive rights treats women worse than men, but so did 'protective' labor legislation. Conversely, both gender-neutral and gender-specific laws can promote sexual equality." Feminist legal scholar Catherine MacKinnon notes, "Affirming differences sometimes has, in any case, not overcome the imposed homogeneity and affirmation of privilege of the sameness mode. If 'same treatment' for sameness has offered an illusory equality, 'different treatment' for differences has been demeaning and dangerous, at times catastrophically so." She continues, "If the point of equality law is to end group-based dominance and subordination, rather than to recognize sameness or accommodate difference, a greater priority is placed on rectifying the legal inequality of groups that are historically unequal in society, and less priority is accorded to pure legal artifacts or rare reversals of social fortune." In other words, the focus of equality law must be ending oppression rather than technical legal wrangling over whether a subordinate group should be treated as "same" or "different" to the dominant group. Indeed, as Mink asserts, "policies or rights derived for the generic woman risk defining the experiences and needs of particular groups of women as the experiences and needs of all . . . but we don't need to claim rights for women only. We can draw from women's diverse gendered experiences to design policies that correct inequalities attached to those experiences. . . . We can consciously avoid assuming or requiring that all women conform to a single gender role, and avoid obligating *only* women to perform that role."[30]

Cultural anthropologist Gayle Rubin interrogates the very notion of binary biological sex categories in our debates over sex equality: "Sex is sex, but what counts as sex is equally culturally determined and obtained. Every society also has a sex/gender system—a set of arrangements by which the biological raw material of human sex and procreation is shaped by human social intervention and satisfied in a conventional manner, no matter how bizarre some of the conventions might be."[31] Eisenstein explains, "Sex is the realm of biological raw material, and gender reflects human social intervention. But we need to recognize that even what is thought of as raw biology is socially constructed."[32]

QUEERING REPRODUCTIVE JUSTICE

You may notice my use of non–gender-specific language when discussing pregnancy: "pregnant person" or "people with the capacity for pregnancy." This is intentional for two reasons. The first reason is that it reflects reality. People of many genders have the capacity for pregnancy. Trans men, nonbinary people, and cisgender women can become pregnant. Reflecting this in language is one way to resist the erasure of queer people who experience reproductive oppression and control at the intersection of sex and gender oppression.

In July 2022 Berkeley law professor Khiara Bridges spoke at a congressional hearing on pregnancy. Republican senator Josh Hawley asked Bridges, "You've referred to people with a capacity for pregnancy—would that be women?" Bridges explained, "Many women, cis women, have the capacity for pregnancy, many cis women do not have the capacity for pregnancy. There are also trans men who are capable of pregnancy as well as nonbinary people who have the capacity for pregnancy." Hawley responded, "So this isn't really a women's rights issue? It's a—" and Bridges interjected, "We can recognize that this impacts women while also recognizing that it impacts other groups. These things are not mutually exclusive, Senator Hawley." She went on, "I want to recognize that your line of questioning is transphobic, and it opens up trans people to violence by not recognizing them . . . because denying that trans people exist and pretending not to know that they exist is dangerous."[33] In the first three months of 2023 alone, antitrans bills have been introduced in all but three states: 452 introduced bills in total. At the time of this writing, 32 of these 452 bills have been signed into law, and 417 bills are still being considered in legislatures.

The second reason for my use of non-gender-specific language is built on the first and is central to the argument I make in this book. While pregnancy is certainly a cisgender women's rights issue and one that has been influenced by cultural definitions of appropriate femininity and motherhood, it is most definitely not exclusively a cisgender women's rights issue. By queering the discussion about reproductive control to include anybody with the capacity for pregnancy and anybody assumed to have such, my analysis is both more inclusive and more reflective of reality. It also allows me to engage more substantively with (however misguided) legal precedent that denies the rights of pregnant people because they are separate from the rights of cisgender women, as not all cis women are pregnant at all times or have the capacity for pregnancy at all.[34] Given this legal history, it is important to intentionally highlight how pregnant people as a class, regardless of their sex or gender, have been systematically held as an exception to otherwise fundamental rights and liberties and how pregnant people as a class have had their humanity devalued.

Legal historian Marie-Amelie George writes, "Queer people's exclusion from reproductive justice advocacy is not just harmful for sexual and gender minorities—it is counterproductive for nonqueer individuals. Queer reproductive rights may sometimes be different in form from their nonqueer counterparts, but they nevertheless implicate the same fundamental concerns as other reproductive rights—dignity, autonomy, privacy, liberty, and equality. What may mask their similarities is the vast jurisprudential disconnect between them."[35] As queer Cuban writer, doula, and activist Miriam Zoila Pérez explains, "Reproductive justice is not just about one's ability to reproduce. Its *[sic]* about autonomy, its *[sic]* about respect, its *[sic]* about shared principles based in the human right to health and a desire for real social change. . . . This isn't about feminists versus abortion advocates versus queer people; this is about building a movement within which we can all find a space."[36] In queering reproductive justice, the women's rights movements and queer rights movements lose nothing. Indeed, it opens the door to building alliances and coalitions based on shared struggles.[37]

As I've noted previously in another work, "There is a tension between current legal terminology and reality. Cisgender women are not the only people who have the capacity for pregnancy. Trans, nonbinary, and queer individuals also experience pregnancy and will experience the impact of regulations on pregnant bodies. However, currently [and historically], legislation and court cases do not generally acknowledge this, instead only referring to 'women.'"[38] As such, my use of gendered language in this book will be careful and intentional.

None of the defendants included in this study were identified as queer, trans, nonbinary, or gender nonconforming in news articles or in criminal case records, but that doesn't mean all of them were cisgender. Misgendering, or referring to a person by the incorrect gender, is not uncommon in media coverage and in other records.[39] While this study does not deal substantively with reproductive oppressions imposed on queer people as queer people, that doesn't mean such oppressions don't exist. This study engages theoretically in queering, or making strange and troubling cultural depictions of motherhood.[40] Much of the panic about the behavior of pregnant people is influenced by gendered thinking about appropriate and proper ways to be a mother or birthing person.[41] Poverty, racialization, and other forms of gender impropriety contribute to the disdain for and punitive responses to pregnant drug users.

Queering reproductive justice also allows us to think critically about the way that law constrains and separates intersecting oppressions, allowing us to remedy only one form of oppression at a time. This impacts the ability for the law to be a useful source of liberation or even to fully grapple with reality. Defining the criminalization of pregnancy as exclusively a cisgender women's issue, with cisgender women understood as a monolithic group, absent variation in wealth, ability, relationship status, location, race, or citizenship status, for example, obscures the complexity of what is actually happening.

INTERSECTIONALITY

Introducing the legal concept that she called "intersectionality," Black feminist legal theorist Kimberlé Crenshaw writes about how the court's insistence on using discrete legal categories limits the ability of Black women to make legal discrimination claims on the basis of race, sex, or race-sex. She explains, for example, that in *DeGraffenreid v. General*

Motors (1976) the court rejected an employment-discrimination claim brought by five Black women. General Motors didn't hire Black women prior to 1964. In January 1974 GM engaged in a seniority-based layoff practice that disproportionately impacted Black women. Crenshaw explains that, in the court's view, because General Motors had hired women before 1964—white women—there was no legally actionable sex discrimination. The five Black women were encouraged to join an ongoing lawsuit over racial discrimination (as it was experienced by Black *men*). An intersectional legal approach would recognize that Black women experience racism and sexism differently than Black men experience racism and white women experience sexism: "This focus on the most privileged group members [Black *men* and *white* women] marginalizes those who are multiply burdened and obscures claims that cannot be understood as resulting from discrete sources of discrimination. I suggest further that this focus on otherwise-privileged group members creates a distorted analysis of racism and sexism because the operative conceptions of race and sex become grounded in experiences that actually represent only a subset of a much more complex phenomenon."[42]

State reproductive control is frequently discussed in terms of women as a monolithic category, obscuring dimensions within that group and focusing on the most privileged members of that group—white women. The war on drugs is frequently discussed in terms of its impact on the Black community, with a focus on the most privileged members of that group—Black men. Framed in these ways, the interaction of race *and* sex is obscured. How does race factor into reproductive rights? And how does gender factor into the war on drugs? The criminalization of pregnancy, as it exists today, has grown out of race, gender, and race-gender oppressions—a collision of state reproductive control and the war on drugs. It is not surprising, then, that the first targets for arrest and prosecution were Black women.

In this book I examine *pregnancy exceptionalism* through the lens of pregnancy-specific crime. Several studies have identified and discussed the arrests of pregnant women for crimes against the fertilized eggs, embryos, and fetuses they gestate.[43] A 2013 study conducted by Lynn Paltrow, the attorney who founded National Advocates for Pregnant Women (now called Pregnancy Justice) and sociologist Jeanne Flavin, identified and analyzed 413 arrests or detentions of pregnant women for crimes against the fetus made from 1973 to 2005. They discovered dramatic disparities in the race and socioeconomic status of the women who had been arrested and found that arrests or detentions had been made in forty-four states

During the bracketed span of time included in the Paltrow and Flavin study, only one state—South Carolina—had explicitly criminalized a pregnant woman's conduct as it relates to the fetus. Subsequently, two additional states, Alabama and Tennessee, have also formally criminalized a pregnant person's conduct—Alabama in 2013 and Tennessee in 2014. The legal developments in Alabama and Tennessee allow for a further study of arrests of pregnant people over time and in varied legal contexts. This study contributes to the literature on the prosecution of pregnant people by engaging in a detailed analysis of all known pregnancy-related arrests prior to, and after, formal criminalization in the only three states to explicitly criminalize a pregnant person's actions with regard to their pregnancy. In this way it is possible to examine arrest and prosecution patterns under varied legal conditions and to study trends and shifts in motivations, tactics, and arrest behavior. By examining arrests of pregnant people before formal criminalization, and then in a context where the action has been explicitly criminalized, I can make comparisons about the impact of criminalization on actual legal practice. If pregnant people can be arrested in the absence of, or even in defiance of, existing criminal laws, this reveals a failure of the criminal justice system to act within the confines of the law and, indeed, a failure of the system of checks and balances supposed to prevent government overreach. I demonstrate the ways that the law fails to constrain the actions of police officers, prosecutors, and judges; how racialized drug panics and the ideology of fetal personhood drive punitive treatment; and the ways that these arrests and prosecutions rely on a long-standing infantilization or villainization of birthing people to justify the denial of their rights.

The criminalization of pregnancy and villainization of birthing people rely on the liberal philosophical position that a person's place in the world is a result of their individual choices. Political scientist James Morone's *Hellfire Nation* traces the strong influence of protestant Christianity in shaping politics in the United States, beginning with the Puritan focus on hard work and the idea that success is an indication of divine favor. This would eventually transform into the capitalist work ethic: "Work is virtuous, success smacks of salvation, poverty insinuates moral failure." Inherent as well in this religious framework is a hierarchy of authority and obedience used to uphold economic inequality, racism, and sexism: "Men must defer to their leaders, servants to masters, women to men."[44] Joining this particular strand of white supremacist, capitalist, Christo-fascist religious thought to the state would eventually provide a foundation for the criminalization of pregnancy.

This thought at work in US laws and policies relies on defining social and economic oppressions as individual moral failings and rejecting the need for a social safety net or the regulation of industry. Why provide a social security net, when doing so rewards bad choices and immorality? With its focus on birthing people as mothers and its moralizing around individual behavior, the demonization and punishment of pregnant substance users fits much more squarely within this framework than, say, expanding the social safety net and providing accessible quality drug treatment—even when these things have been shown to actually help. This philosophy is so embedded in United States political thought that it shows up across party lines. Mink writes, "I've heard feminists and patriarchalists alike argue that 'those people' are bad mothers who ought not to bear and raise children at all; that people should have children only if they can afford them; that motherhood is a choice, not a necessity. From this point of view, social provision for care-giving is a moral hazard, encouraging procreative irresponsibility and subsidizing lousy mothers."[45] This combination of capitalism and puritanism has prescribed women's ultimate role as that of mother. Birthing people who fail to behave in the prescribed way do so because of individual failings, not because of broader social or economic structures. Sociologists Sheigla Murphy and Marsha Rosenbaum write, "Mothering is a social role with tremendous responsibilities, little preparation, and ambiguous standards of good practice. People do not necessarily know how to tell a woman to mother, but everybody seems to know when she is doing it wrong."[46] Political scientist Julia Jordan-Zachery writes, "a 'good' mother is defined as self-sacrificing and protective of her fetus, and later, her child. Women perceived as falling outside of this ideal are portrayed as deviant."[47] If poverty is caused by bad choices, coded as immoral choices, then impoverished mothers are defined deviant and immoral. If quitting drugs is a matter of individual willpower, and good mothers are supposed to be self-sacrificial and nurturing, then pregnant drug users have failed on both fronts.

Lots of people use drugs: people of all racial groups, socioeconomic statuses, and professions. People use drugs for lots of reasons, and not everyone who uses drugs has or will develop substance use disorder. Some of these drugs are prescribed, some are legal, some are illegal, and some are considered more socially acceptable than others. I regularly used caffeine in the form of coffee while I wrote much of this book—with a generous dose of sugar added to it. Alcohol, cigarettes, and in some states marijuana can be purchased at stores, with fun brand names and packaging.

Sometimes people who use drugs become pregnant, and sometimes people continue to use drugs after they become pregnant. Use of certain substances by pregnant people has been a major concern for decades. The concern primarily lies in the fear that intrauterine exposure to these substances could harm a developing fetus. There is some evidence to support this concern. Drinking alcohol during pregnancy may increase the risk of miscarriage or stillbirth. Heavy consumption of alcohol during pregnancy is associated with a heightened risk of having a baby with fetal alcohol spectrum disorders, which can include lower birth weights and cause intellectual disabilities and organ defects.[48] Compared to 8.5 percent of pregnant women who drink alcohol, over 50 percent of nonpregnant women drink alcohol.[49] Smoking cigarettes during pregnancy has been linked to preterm birth, lower birth weight, birth defects, respiratory problems, and sudden infant death syndrome.[50] About 16 percent of pregnant women smoke cigarettes, while just over 25 percent of nonpregnant women smoke cigarettes.[51] Benzodiazepines may slightly increase the risk of having a baby with a lower birth weight or a cleft lip or palate.[52] Intrauterine exposure to opioids may increase the risk of having a baby with neonatal opioid withdrawal, symptoms of which can include irritability, tremors, sleep disturbances, difficulty feeding, and overstimulation.[53] Stimulants like amphetamine and dextroamphetamine (Adderall), caffeine, cocaine, and methamphetamine are associated with an increased risk of preeclampsia and the premature rupture of the amniotic sac.[54] About 6 percent of pregnant women use illicit substances, compared with the 11 percent of nonpregnant women.[55]

While certainly relevant to health and well-being, a narrow focus on substance use during pregnancy is puzzling when contextualized: 13 percent of pregnant people receive inadequate prenatal care (and 1.9 percent receive no prenatal care); 13 percent of unhoused women are pregnant; 3–9 percent of women are abused by intimate partners during pregnancy; about 17 percent of women pregnant between 2010 and 2016 experience obstetric violence—physical, verbal, and emotional abuse and rights violations.[56] While substance use during pregnancy can potentially have a negative impact on the health of the pregnant person and their pregnancy, it is only one of many factors that impact the health and well-being of pregnant people and their pregnancies.

All pregnant people, regardless of whether or not they use drugs, are also exposed to substances in their environment that could have a negative impact on their health: lead in drinking water, chemicals in the air and soil, microplastics in seemingly everything.[57] Medical racism has contributed to rising rates of infant and maternal mortality.[58] Violence at the hands of intimate partners is a leading cause of deaths of pregnant people.[59] Gun violence is the leading cause of death of children in the United States.[60] The male contribution to pregnancy outcomes, though potentially substantial, has been largely overlooked. Research has found that male substance use and exposure to environmental toxins contributes to miscarriage, low birth weight, congenital abnormalities, cancer, and neurological problems.[61] In light of the many factors that can have an influence on a pregnancy outcome, it is interesting that substance use during pregnancy has remained as a politically salient concern—and one that has been met with punitive state responses.

The so-called war on drugs, which started in earnest in the 1980s under the Reagan administration, is composed of shifts in criminal law and in police strategy that increases criminal penalties and primarily targets people of color, mostly Black people, for punishment. Hugely expensive and devastating to many communities, the war on drugs has been one of the major causes of mass incarceration in the United States. The US incarceration rate is the highest in the world.[62]

Though this study focuses on criminal laws and processes, pregnant drug users face civil penalties as well—including the loss of child custody. By 2022 forty-four states and Washington, DC, had adopted some kind of prenatal drug use policy, most of which defines substance use during pregnancy as child abuse in the civil system. Roberts describes the child welfare system, which handles cases of suspected child abuse or neglect, as a family-policing system: "In 2018 alone, 3.5 million children were involved in an investigation by child protective services (CPS).... Based on state child neglect laws, the investigators interpret conditions of poverty—lack of food, insecure housing, inadequate medical care—as evidence of parental unfitness."[63]

Annually, about 250,000 children are removed from their families by CPS agencies, and another 250,000 are removed informally. Roberts notes that foster care rates for children in the United States (576 per 100,000) are about the same as incarceration rates of adults (582 per 100,000), and Black and Indigenous children are disproportionately removed from their families and placed in foster care. She contends that the child welfare system's structure causes harm to children who are separated from their families, inflicts trauma, and fails to ensure care and safety from sexual and physical abuse.[64] Separating children from their family is commonly associated with elevated levels of "guilt, post-traumatic stress disorder, isolation, substance abuse, anxiety, low self-esteem, and despair" in the children.[65] The lack of oversight in the foster care system leaves children vulnerable to rampant abuse. One study found that foster families "had seven times the frequency of physical abuse reports compared to non-foster families. Moreover, foster homes had double the likelihood that a physical abuse report would be substantiated." Another study found that one in three children in foster care experienced sexual abuse by an adult in the foster home.[66] Many of the people included in this study, in addition to facing serious criminal charges, were separated from their children—in some cases permanently.

This book contributes to the literature on the criminalization of pregnancy, reproductive justice, and the policing of substance use, from historical, sociological, political, and legal perspectives. Using detailed analyses of 1,116 arrest cases, introduced legislation on pregnancy and crime, and interviews with prosecutors and law enforcement personnel, this book provides a much-needed update to the history of pregnancy criminalization beyond the crack cocaine crisis and its racist focus on Black people of the late 1980s and early 1990s and moves into the methamphetamine scare of the early 2000s and the opioid epidemic of the 2010s, which are more rhetorically focused on varied populations of poor and low-income whites, frequently described as representing degenerate whiteness. The mixed-methods analysis of original prosecution data provides a more comprehensive perspective to the arrest and prosecution of pregnant people for crimes against their own pregnancies, including the perspectives of the people who were arrested and the people responsible for their arrests and prosecutions. Excerpts from cases demonstrate the inhumanity and ineffectiveness of the legal system in its attempts to control pregnant people and illustrate the institutional networks that are already operating, in essence, as the pregnancy police. I conclude with strategies to resist the increasing criminalization of pregnancy and to push back against the pregnancy police.

Though the case files and news articles that I used for my analyses are on the public record, I have taken care to protect the confidentiality of those who were charged or arrested for crimes against their own pregnancies. The systematic collection of even public records that include sensitive identifying information requires an ethical approach that protects this sensitive information. As such, throughout this book, you will notice that case files and news articles are cited as being archived and on file with the author. I use real names and full citations of defendants only when a case has already received a substantial amount of major press coverage or when the parties involved have been named in major court cases.

ORGANIZATION OF THE BOOK

Chapter 1. The Peril of Protection

In this chapter I discuss my analysis of all bills introduced in the states that would create pregnancy-specific crimes from 1973 to 2022. I show how laws initially framed by the need to protect white pregnant women from brutal violence have ultimately grown into laws meant to punish pregnant people in the name of protecting the fetus and protecting society from the social and economic burden of fetal harm. These bills are divided into four types: (1) laws that criminalize abortion; (2) laws that create separate offenses or heightened penalties for pregnant victims of violence (3) laws that criminalize third-party harm to fertilized eggs, embryos, and fetuses; and (4) laws that criminalize the actions or inactions of pregnant people.

Chapter 2. Angels and Antimothers

I trace the legal foundations for pregnancy exceptionalism in US jurisprudence under two legal frameworks: maternal protection and fetal protection. I examine the role that maternal protection played in granting protective labor regulations to women during the Progressive Era. Next I examine the shift to fetal protection, showing how even as pregnant people gained the right to abortion, child abuse laws were being added to the criminal code, and the fetus was being elevated as a legal entity that would ultimately be used to eliminate abortion rights. I show that the state has long expressed an interest in pregnancy and reproduction and that it has sought to pursue those interests under the umbrella of protecting women from exploitative labor practices and later protecting fetuses from the people who gestate them. Indeed, even in court decisions that expanded reproductive rights, like *Roe v. Wade*, the state interest in regulating pregnancy is preserved, continuing the legal legacy of defining people with the capacity for pregnancy as legally distinct and in need of regulation and control.

Chapter 3. Bad Breeders

I discuss the twentieth-century eugenics movement in the United States in the lead-up to *Buck v. Bell* (1927), the Supreme Court case that found forced sterilization laws constitutional. Motivated by fears of being outbred by emancipated Black people and southern and eastern European immigrants, eugenicists of this era sought to shore up the strength of the white race by eliminating the reproduction of "degenerate" whites—disabled people, sexual "deviants," people who committed crimes, and poor people, among others. I analyze the role that "white-trash" stereotypes played in the early twentieth-century eugenics movement, arguing that they were depicted as biologically and racially distinct from "real" whites, thus threatening notions of white supremacy. I discuss the lingering impact of eugenic thought and eugenic sterilization laws at work in welfare reform and in the continued forced sterilization of people with disabilities in the United States.

Chapter 4. "The Dead Babies May Be the Lucky Ones"

I explore the collision of pregnancy exceptionalism, eugenics, and the war on drugs, showing how contemporary drug crises have held a specific focus on prenatal substance use and fetal harm. Judicial and legislative efforts to punish pregnant people for crimes against their own pregnancies in South Carolina, Alabama, and Tennessee correspond with three periods of racialized drug panic. South Carolina policy targeted low-income Black women during the crack cocaine crisis. Alabama policy targeted low-income white women during the methamphetamine crisis. Tennessee policy framed white opioid users as child abusers in need of state intervention. I present data on pregnancy-related drug arrests, showing that, while the drugs implicated in pregnancy arrests are out of line with drug use statistics and drug arrests unrelated to pregnancy, the pregnancy-related arrests align with contemporaneous racialized drug crises. Each of these targeted modes relied on the understanding that children born to certain kinds of (politically salient and highly racialized) drug-using pregnant people would be inherently and irreparably damaged by drug exposure. The mothers, having violated expectations of motherhood *and* having produced babies that the public perceives as irreparably broken, should be punished. One political pundit asserted that, if exposed to drugs in utero, "the dead babies may be the lucky ones."[67]

Chapter 5. "I Felt Like Nobody"

I share my analysis of 1,116 arrests of pregnant people for crimes against fetuses in South Carolina, Alabama, and Tennessee. I discuss the kinds of charges applied in arrest cases and describe the kinds of actions criminalized for pregnant people. I also discuss birth outcomes, how law enforcement became aware of pregnancy crimes, and how pregnant people attempted to evade detection. Notably, I document the first case of a crisis pregnancy center sharing information about a client with law enforcement to support a prosecution. I share how people charged with crimes against their own pregnancies experienced being arrested, jailed, and sentenced, with some people forced to give birth in state custody, and others giving birth outside of hospitals to avoid potential punishment. Finally, I share what life was like once their sentences were complete, showing that the impact of arrest and incarceration during pregnancy has a lasting negative impact on their lives. I find that high levels of prosecutorial discretion lead to dramatically different experiences, with some pregnant people offered treatment and others thrown in jail, some sentenced to drug court and others sentenced to twenty years in one of the most notorious women's prisons in the United States. From self-managed abortion to attempted suicide to substance use, 1,116 arrests were made for actions that, but for the fact of the pregnancy, would not have been considered criminal.

Chapter 6. Wielding the Velvet Hammer

I discuss the goals, tactics, challenges, and outcomes of policing pregnancy, using test, report, and arrest policies and focusing on the role that law enforcement officers, prosecutors, and judges have played. Prosecutors are left with a great deal of discretion over when and how to apply the policies and some degree of confusion over what they can get away with legally. Using evidence drawn from research interviews and statements in media, I show that prosecutors hope to use their authority to solve the problem of prenatal substance use in the absence of other resources, like quality drug treatment and a more robust social safety net. With cooperation between health-care providers, social workers, police officers, and judges, who together compose the pregnancy police, the introduction of official laws wasn't necessary—so long as the parties involved were willing to extend legal personhood to the fetus.

Conclusion

I draw out the potential consequences of the criminalization of pregnancy for women's rights and the rights of people with the capacity for pregnancy more broadly. I connect these rights deprivations to historical and current patterns of reproductive injustice, asking what it would mean to defund the police when social workers and health-care providers already function as systems of policing and in some cases are already literally working with law enforcement. I explore how the overturning of *Roe v. Wade* may facilitate the further criminalization of pregnancy, and I show how this criminalization process may unfold.

1 The Peril of Protection

Laci Peterson went missing on December 24, 2002.[1] She was thirty-two weeks pregnant. Her body was found four months later, as was the body of her fetus, who she planned to name Connor. Scott Peterson, Laci's husband, was charged with Laci's murder. The Petersons lived in California, one of thirty-eight states that define the fetus as a potential victim of crime. As such, Scott was also charged with causing Connor's death. He was found guilty of first-degree murder for killing Laci and second-degree murder for causing Connor's death. Peterson received the death penalty, which was later reduced to a life sentence, after the California Supreme Court determined that potential jurors had been wrongly dismissed for their beliefs on the death penalty.[2]

If Laci had been killed in, say, Colorado, instead of California, the loss of her pregnancy would not have been considered a crime. Laci's family supported an end to these state-to-state legal differences, and they campaigned in support of federal legislation that would legally recognize fertilized eggs, embryos, and fetuses as victims if they are harmed or killed during the commission of a violent crime within federal jurisdiction. Laci's mother, Sharon Rocha, explained, "What I find difficult to understand is why groups and senators who champion the pro-choice cause are blind to the fact that these two-victim crimes are the ultimate violation of choice. What about mothers who survive criminal attacks but lose their babies? I don't understand how any senator can vote to force prosecutors to tell such a grieving mother that she didn't really lose a baby—when she knows to the depths of her soul that she did.... There were two bodies that washed up in San Francisco Bay, and the law should recognize that reality."[3] While it is understandable for Rocha to grieve both the murder of her daughter and the loss of her daughter's wanted pregnancy, right at the cusp of her due date and with the fetus already named, the call to prosecute separately for the death of Laci and for the loss of Laci's pregnancy essentially defines the fetus as a legal person. Framing Laci and Laci's pregnancy as separate legal entities ultimately reduces the legal rights of pregnant people like Laci.

After Peterson's death a bill was introduced by Representative Melissa Hart of Pennsylvania, a Republican, and was signed into law by President George W. Bush in 2004: the Unborn Victims of Violence Act (UVVA), or Laci and Connor's Law. The UVVA creates a separate criminal offense for the death of or bodily injury to an unborn child in federal jurisdictions. The law applies to unborn children "at any stage of development" and includes exemptions for "conduct relating to an abortion for which the consent of the pregnant woman . . . has been obtained," "for medical treatment of the pregnant woman or her unborn child," and "of any woman with respect to her unborn child."[4]

The UVVA spawned a debate over the rights of pregnant people and the personhood of fertilized eggs, embryos, and fetuses. Some UVVA supporters felt that the recognition of a fetus was essential to recognizing the full scope of violence against pregnant people. In fact, homicide is among the leading causes of death of pregnant people in the United States.[5] Most frequently, pregnant women are murdered by their current or former intimate partners.[6] Supporters of the UVVA hoped it could do something about this pervasive violence.

Others expressed concern over the impact of the UVVA on reproductive rights. Though the law is named after both Laci and her unborn son, the UVVA legally addresses only the harm done to fertilized eggs, embryos, and fetuses, not the harm done to pregnant people. There was fear that by establishing fetal personhood in the criminal code, these laws would erode the right to have an abortion, or they might result in criminal charges against the pregnant people themselves. Some antiabortion activists opposed the UVVA because they feared, if it were used to prosecute pregnant women, it might have the effect of incentivizing abortion as a way to avoid criminal charges. Banning legal abortion may, in their minds, eliminate that concern, though the evidence tells us that banning abortion does not eliminate abortion.[7]

In this chapter I present my analysis of pregnancy-specific criminal law in the United States and discuss four typologies of pregnancy crime: (1) laws criminalizing abortion; (2) laws creating separate offenses or heightened penalties for pregnant victims of violence; (3) laws criminalizing third-party harm to fertilized eggs, embryos, and fetuses; and (4) laws criminalizing the actions or inactions of pregnant people.[8] Next I provide an in-depth account of the criminalization process in South Carolina, Alabama, and Tennessee—the three states to ever officially criminalize the actions or inactions of pregnant people. Providing this broad view of different types of laws creating pregnancy-specific crime in the United States and some of the frameworks motivating these laws lends social and legal context to the criminalization process in the three study states. My analysis shows that, despite a frequent rhetorical focus on the need to protect (white) pregnant women, the laws themselves have been focused on elevating the status of the fetus, often at the expense of pregnant people.

LAW TYPOLOGIES FOR UNDERSTANDING PREGNANCY CRIMES

Type 1: Laws Criminalizing Abortion

Laws that criminalize abortion work in a few different ways. They may make the performance of an abortion a crime akin to homicide, or it may exist as its own separate offense. Some laws criminalize only certain kinds of abortion procedures, while others define criminal penalties for abortion of all kinds. A state law may limit the provision of legal abortion only to obstetricians or criminalize any type of abortion provider. They may even move to make it a crime for a person to self-manage their own abortion. In the wake of the *Dobbs* case, which ended the constitutional right to abortion, more states are adopting laws that criminalize abortion or are allowing formerly unenforceable abortion bans from before *Roe v. Wade,* in some cases dating back to the mid-1800s, to take effect.[9] Criminal penalties vary, from fines to revocations of medical licenses to prison sentences. Some states include explicit exemptions for pregnant people. A Texas law comes with the most severe penalty: five to ninety-nine years in prison. Some state laws may not spell out the details on charging and sentencing, allowing for a great deal of prosecutorial discretion.

New versions of these laws should be expected in the coming months and years. In addition to laws creating penalties for abortion providers who fail to comply with state regulations for procedural abortions, introduced bills sought to criminalize the following: using telemedicine for abortion, using abortion pills or abortifacient plants for abortion, transporting minors across state lines to help them get an abortion, and distributing abortion pills. Some bills sought to extend state abortion laws to residents when they leave the state, in an attempt to eliminate travel for abortion. Several bills would punish state employees who do not comply with criminal abortion laws—for example, prosecutors who refuse to pursue abortion-related prosecutions. Another bill sought to make it a crime for a credit card issuer to run a transaction for the purchase of abortion pills. Bills introduced after the *Dobbs* case overturned *Roe* prescribed more elevated penalties for abortion, including the death penalty both for the abortion provider and for the person who has the abortion. Other post-*Dobbs* bills removed exceptions from older abortion crime statutes, like exceptions for rape and incest, and exceptions that prohibited the prosecution of pregnant people.

Type 2: Laws Creating Separate Offenses or Heightened Penalties for Pregnant Victims of Violence

This second law type specifically addresses harm done to pregnant people, regardless of its impact on the fertilized egg, embryo, or fetus and as separate from crimes against nonpregnant persons. A total of 145 introduced bills sought to create specific crimes against pregnant people. Laws of this type sometimes define pregnancy as an aggravating factor in a crime, but more often are defined as unique crime types. Some states include other persons in this penalty-enhancement victim category, such as police officers, the elderly, people with disabilities, minors under age twelve, and even sports referees. These laws are meant to provide additional legal protections for populations who are particularly vulnerable to or exposed to violence. Because these laws center on harm to pregnant people, the stage of the pregnancy is considered irrelevant, as is the actual outcome of the pregnancy. When these laws are applied to people with the capacity for pregnancy, their vulnerability to violence is given additional legal focus, without bestowing personhood on the fetus through the criminal code. States were more likely to pass "unborn victims of violence"-type laws than these laws that center pregnant people.

Type 3: Laws Criminalizing Third-Party Harm to Fertilized Eggs, Embryos, and Fetuses

The UVVA, the federal law described earlier, is an example of this type of law. If people, in the course of harming a pregnant person, harm the fertilized egg, embryo, or fetus the pregnant person carries, they can be held criminally culpable for that harm. These laws vary somewhat by state. Some include penalty enhancements for harm to pregnant people that results in fetal demise or injury. Others create separate and equivalent criminal charges for violence against pregnant people and "the unborn" as individual and separate victims, where the death of a pregnant person could trigger two murder charges—one for the pregnant person and one for her pregnancy. Some states create separate and unique crimes that are applied only to harm against fertilized eggs, embryos, or fetuses, for example, "feticide" or "murder of unborn child." Many of these laws contain "exception" sections. These exceptions commonly bar the application of the law in cases involving legal abortion, medical care, and actions or inactions by the pregnant person that could have a negative impact on a fertilized egg, embryo, or fetus, such as not receiving prenatal care or using a substance during pregnancy. Thirty-eight states have adopted this kind of law.[10] A total of 629 introduced bills created various crimes against the fetus. Laws vary from state to state in terms of the gestational age at which the criminal law would become active. In most states the law applies from the "moment of conception," a moment that is virtually impossible to pinpoint. In others the law would apply only to fetuses that had reached viability. Still others do not explicitly state at what stage the law would apply, as is the case in California, Maine, and Virginia.

States frequently linked their feticide legislation to specific and notable crimes against pregnant white women and girls, just as the UVVA was linked to Laci Peterson's murder. As the Republican state senator of North Carolina, Neal Hunt, explained, "Generally, the only way we get things like this is public outcry. . . . So if the public gets incensed enough and lets the legislators know, that's about the only way we'll get this heard."[11] Many of the bills were named after individual unborn victims, using the names they would have been given had they been born. Perhaps this is meant as a further recognition of the personhood that these laws essentially create. Kansas's 2007 feticide law, Alexa's Law, was named after what fourteen-year-old Chelsea Brooks planned to name her daughter, had she been born.[12] Brooks was nine months pregnant and had just finished middle school when she was murdered by the twenty-year-old man who had raped and impregnated her. North Carolina's feticide law, called Ethen's Law, was named after what Jennifer "Jenna" Nielsen had planned to name her son.[13] Nielsen was murdered while she delivered newspapers early one morning. The married twenty-two-year-old mother of two was eight months pregnant when she was found dead behind a convenience store, having been stabbed in the throat. Her murder remains unsolved. The murder of Heather Fliegelman was invoked in the passage of Maine's feticide law.[14] Heather was twenty years old and eight months pregnant when her husband stabbed her forty-seven times. She was discovered dead in her home, surrounded by the dead bodies of her four cats. Her husband was sentenced to fifty years in prison.[15]

Women who survived violent attacks resulting in pregnancy loss and families of homicide victims have advocated for the passage of these laws, sharing heartbreaking stories and sometimes shocking photographs. Tracy Seavers Marciniak, a white woman only five days away from her due date, had a stillbirth after she was beaten by her husband, who then prevented her from getting medical care.[16] She gave testimony before a US House Judiciary Subcommittee in support of the UVVA, showing a photograph of herself holding the body of her stillborn baby.[17] Chelsea Brooks's mother worked to advance a law to recognize unborn children as victims of crime: "Two lives were taken from us last week and we will do whatever it takes to make sure that the law in the future, recognizes all life, even if it is too late for our girls."[18] Jennifer Nielsen's family felt that the inability to legally recognize the loss of the pregnancy erased the "unborn child's" existence. Jennifer's husband, Tim, told reporters, "with [North Carolina] not having a fetal homicide law at the time this happened, I do feel like [Ethen] was overlooked."[19] Christina Alberts's mother presented a photograph from her daughter's open-casket funeral to the West Virginia Senate. It showed Christina and her dead fetus together in the coffin. When speaking on the floor of the US Senate, Heather Fliegelman's mother shared a photograph of the autopsy of her "unborn granddaughter" so that the audience would be forced to acknowledge how baby-like the fetus looked and so that they might understand why she was demanding that the law recognize the loss of the fetus as a second, separate death.[20]

These laws rely on frames of fragile, vulnerable white femininity—virtuous white women and their innocent "unborn children"—to expand the criminal justice apparatus *into the uterus*.[21] Meanwhile, these frames virtually ignore the fact that most of these women and girls were killed by the men who impregnated them. These laws do nothing to address the role that intimate partner violence plays in these tragic cases.[22] Additionally, while sometimes named after women and girls who are murdered, these laws ultimately do not center pregnant people and do not offer them any additional legal protection. Legislation that recognizes only the fetus, perhaps at the legal *expense* of pregnant people, invokes the names of pregnant people who have been attacked. I suggest that feticide legislation uses the veneer of the protection of pregnant women as a cloak, obscuring the reality that these laws concern only the fetus and that these supposedly protective laws have been used to punish pregnant people.

Type 4: Laws Criminalizing the Actions or Inactions of Pregnant People

These laws criminalize the actions or inactions committed by pregnant people against their own pregnancies. In other words, these laws create the crime of pregnant women, intentionally or unintentionally, harming or potentially causing harm to a fertilized egg, embryo, or fetus. These laws have a profound effect on the legal rights of pregnant or potentially pregnant people, including privacy and due process, and may have the effect of criminalizing behaviors that, but for the fact of the pregnancy, would not be considered criminal. Berkeley law professor Khiara Bridges puts the implications of this succinctly: "When pregnant women are arrested and face criminal charges after a positive drug screen, it is because pregnancy has transformed otherwise legal behavior into a crime."[23] Bridges spells out numerous legal implications of these kinds of policies: "Criminalizing substance use during pregnancy represents an expansion of the criminal law . . . creates a gender-based crime [, and] may open the door for the criminalization for otherwise perfectly legal activity," if it is thought to risk harm to a fetus.[24] Legal sociologist Katherine Beckett writes, "Prosecutions of women for prenatal conduct thus create a gender-specific system of punishment and obscure the fact that male behavior, socio-economic status, and environmental pollutants may also affect fetal health." Law professor Priscilla Ocen asserts that the use of these policies subject pregnant women to a "form of status offense." A status crime is an offense that is considered a crime only because of the identity of the person who commits it. Ocen explains, "status offenses, which criminalize the behavior of pregnant individuals within a select group of people that would be noncriminal if committed by persons outside of the group, have been utilized to regulate disfavored cases. Pregnant women, especially those who are poor and of color, are similarly constructed as a disfavored class and are therefore subject to unique forms of criminal regulation."[25]

States with this type of crime law *require* the violation of medical privacy, much in the same way that mandated reporters are required to report serious and imminent threats of harm to one's self or others. Most of these harms relate to substance use during pregnancy, but they may also include self-harm, failure to follow medical advice, and self-managed abortion. Laws of this type do not only criminalize the use of illegal substances but also can criminalize the use of legally prescribed and obtained medications.

THE LEGAL ROLE OF THE US SUPREME COURT

The US Supreme Court has heard only one case involving the prosecution of pregnant people for their actions during pregnancy. *Ferguson v. City of*

Charleston (2001) concerned women receiving prenatal and birth care at a public hospital who allegedly used cocaine during their pregnancies.[26] Nurses and doctors in obstetrics at the Medical University of South Carolina (MUSC) were concerned by the apparently increasing incidence of cocaine use among pregnant people and had heard many terrifying (if anecdotal and even blatantly false) accounts of the impact of cocaine on a pregnancy, signaling concern for fetuses and disdain for pregnant cocaine users.[27] They felt that not enough pregnant patients were voluntarily seeking substance use treatment and, rather than developing more workable treatment options, hoped to use what they called a "carrots and sticks" approach to push pregnant and postpartum patients into treatment. A white obstetric nurse named Shirley Brown spearheaded a collaboration between health-care providers, local law enforcement, and the then circuit solicitor, Charles Condon. Together they developed a protocol for drug testing pregnant patients and reporting them to law enforcement, called the Interagency Policy. Hospital representatives alleged that this policy was meant to ultimately help pregnant drug users to discontinue their drug use and was not meant to be punitive, but the thirty patients represented in the *Ferguson* case felt the punishment, disdain, and judgment in health-care settings, in jail, in the media, and in court.

The Interagency Policy included a list of things that could trigger a drug test: no prenatal care, late prenatal care, incomplete prenatal care, abruptio placentae (a condition where the placenta separates from the wall of the uterus before birth), intrauterine fetal death, preterm labor, intrauterine growth restriction, and unexplained congenital abnormalities. If patients tested positive for an illegal substance the interdisciplinary team thought could endanger the fetus, they would be pressured to complete a drug treatment program. If the patients failed to do so, they would be reported to the police, arrested, placed in jail, and prosecuted. Black feminist legal historian Dorothy Roberts asks, "Had Charleston officials really done everything they could to treat patients' addiction? Women caught using drugs were simply handed a piece of paper announcing their drug treatment appointment. No provision was made for transportation to the treatment center or for child care. In fact, there was not a single residential treatment center for pregnant addicts in the entire state at the time the interagency policy was instituted."[28]

All but one of the thirty patients arrested under the MUSC protocol was a Black woman. MUSC was one of the only local hospitals that accepted Medicaid insurance. As such, the population seeking care at the hospital was disproportionately impoverished and Black. Only one patient was white. It was noted on her medical record that she had conceived the baby with a "negro." It seems relevant that Shirley Brown, the nurse who helped law enforcement create the protocol, testified in deposition in preparation for a lawsuit against MUSC that she was raised to believe "race mixing is against god's way." Roberts writes that Brown "frequently expressed negative views about her black patients to drug counselors and social workers, including her belief that most black women should have their tubes tied and that birth control should be put in the water in Black communities."[29]

Thirty women were arrested and held in local jails. Some were released from jail with the requirement that they immediately enroll in drug treatment, which was not always available. Others were held in jail until they went into labor—arguably unconstitutional indefinite detentions. Lynn Paltrow, the attorney who later founded National Advocates for Pregnant Women, now called Pregnancy Justice, filed a class action lawsuit on Crystal Ferguson's behalf, against Charleston and the Medical University of South Carolina. One of Paltrow's arguments was that the urinalysis tests were illegal searches in violation of the Fourth Amendment. The Fourth Amendment states, "The right of the people to be secure in their persons, houses, papers, and effects, and against unreasonable searches and seizures, shall not be violated, and no warrants shall issue, but upon probable cause, supported by oath or affirmation, and particularly describing the place to be searched, and the persons or things to be seized."[30] This means that if the government wants to perform a search (of people, homes, papers, belongings), they need to have probable cause and a detailed warrant explaining exactly what is to be searched. It is unconstitutional to perform a search otherwise.

The defendants from MUSC had their blood or urine searched during the course of medical treatment, but exclusively for the purposes of evidence collection, not for treatment purposes. MUSC had no probable cause or warrant allowing them to perform these searches. MUSC argued that they were justified in performing these warrantless searches because there was a "special need" to protect the health and well-being of mothers and future children.[31] The case was heard before the US Supreme Court. The women included in the suit asserted that they had not consented to these warrantless drug tests. Moreover, in court testimony and in deposition interviews, they asserted that during their time receiving prenatal care, most of them were never offered drug treatment or counseling. Some of the patients explicitly requested help for substance use disorder but were told only about inflexible, inaccessible treatment programs: inpatient treatment for single moms with nobody to watch their children or outpatient treatment located an hour away, for patients with no transportation.

When patients gave urine and blood at their prenatal or labor visits, they assumed this was for routine medical testing, but the samples were not taken for medical purposes. They were taken to be tested and used as evidence against them in criminal cases. One of the patients described being misled and coerced into giving a urine sample. She was due to leave the hospital when a nurse told her she was dehydrated and needed to stay at the hospital to receive IV fluids. She was taken to a different room and strongly encouraged to drink cup after cup of water, never actually receiving the IV fluids she was told she needed. Finally, she was handed an empty cup and told that she needed to provide a urine sample.

The court agreed with the plaintiffs' Fourth Amendment argument, finding that "the interest in using the threat of criminal sanctions to deter pregnant women from using cocaine cannot justify a departure from the general rule that an official nonconsensual search is unconstitutional if not authorized by a valid warrant." The court went on to state that because MUSC was a state hospital, it is subject to the Fourth Amendment, and, as such, it required a warrant or "probable cause" to conduct searches without the patients' informed consent. The court wrote that the individual patients' privacy was being weighed against the test and report program's "special need" of protecting the health and well-being of mothers and potential children. They found that because the immediate result of the arrests was not assistance with substance use but simply detention or criminal charges, the "special need" present in the case was not enough to outweigh the need for probable cause or a warrant prior to the use of urinalysis as a form of evidence collection. In other words, the use of a warrantless urinalysis test as a form of evidence collection without the consent of the patients is unconstitutional.[32]

Ferguson v. City of Charleston did not address the central question of whether pregnant people could be held criminally responsible for crimes against their own pregnancies. So if a state policy required that *all* people receiving prenatal care or giving birth at medical facilities consent to such urinalysis tests as a requirement for receiving care, or if evidence was collected otherwise (via a blood, feces, or urinalysis test from the newborn, for example), it may be found to be constitutional, given the state's "special interest" in promoting morality, maternal health, and potential life. And so the tests, reports, arrests, and prosecutions have continued.

At the state level, by 2022 only three states had formally criminalized pregnant people's actions with regard to their own pregnancy since 1973: South Carolina, Alabama, and Tennessee. Each state had a different path toward criminalization, one using a slow build of case law, one with courts making dramatic departures from law, and one passing a criminal law with a two-year expiration date. These three paths to criminalization demonstrate the importance both of the courts and of the legislature in creating what are essentially status crimes for people with the capacity for pregnancy. They also demonstrate that, while some of these legal changes occur slowly and over time due to building case law or over the course of a battle in the legislature to pass a law, in other cases the change can happen more suddenly, with a single court ruling.

SOUTH CAROLINA

South Carolina was the first state to formally criminalize pregnant people's actions with regard to their own pregnancies in 1997. This was a gradual process that moved through the judicial system, beginning with tort law. Through this process "protective" law provided a foundation for punitive law and practice. In *Fowler v. Woodward* (1964) the state supreme court found in favor of allowing a civil action for damages in the "wrongful death of an unborn, viable infant."[33] In this case a woman was in a car accident "caused by the negligent and willful misconduct of the defendant," Freddie Woodward. The woman was in her eighth month of pregnancy and experienced a stillbirth as a result of her injuries. The administrator of the estate of "Baby Fowler," the deceased, sought damages from Woodward for causing this stillbirth. The court found in favor of Baby Fowler's estate, agreeing that "a viable child is a person before separation from the body of its mother," and, as such, its death is actionable. Woodard could be held financially responsible for the damages to Baby Fowler.[34]

Twenty years later the South Carolina Supreme Court gave its decision in *State v. Horne* (1984).[35] Terrance Horne attacked Deborah Horne, his wife. She sustained multiple stab wounds to the neck, arms, and abdomen. Deborah was about nine months pregnant when she was attacked. She experienced a stillbirth after losing a considerable amount of blood, which reduced blood flow to her uterus. Terrance Horne was convicted of assault and battery with intent to kill for attacking Deborah. He was also convicted of voluntary manslaughter for causing "the death of an unborn full-term viable female child." Terrance Horne appealed his conviction for voluntary manslaughter, asserting that there was no law explicitly criminalizing harm against a viable fetus in South Carolina. Citing *Fowler,* the court found, "It would be grossly inconsistent for us to construe a viable fetus as a person for the purposes of imposing civil liability while refusing to give it a similar classification in the criminal context." So the fetus is a person when it comes to civil damages *and* third-party harm.

After *Horne* South Carolina clarified the law's application to pregnant people's actions as they relate to their own pregnancy, in *Whitner v. State.*[36] Cornelia Whitner, a Black woman, was the mother of two children when she developed cocaine use disorder. She stole or had sex in exchange for cocaine when she couldn't afford it.[37] In December 1991 Whitner, who was pregnant, left her children in the custody of an elderly aunt, who called the police when Whitner didn't come by to pick them up.[38] Whitner was arrested and charged with child neglect, to which she pled guilty.[39] She was given a ten-year prison sentence that would be suspended if she successfully completed probation. Her two children were removed from her custody and placed with family members.[40] She was ordered to not use drugs as a condition of her probation—something Whitner specifically requested help with. She never received the help she needed. When Whitner gave birth at a local medical center in February 1992, her newborn's urine was screened for drugs and tested positive for cocaine. Three days after her baby was born, he was taken into protective custody, and Whitner was arrested for child neglect—this time in relation to her actions relating to her baby before he was born.[41] In April 1992 Cornelia Whitner pled guilty to criminal child neglect under section 20-7-50 of the state Children's Code, which reads, "Any person having legal custody of any child . . . who shall . . . refuse or neglect to provide . . . the proper care and attention for such child . . . so that the life, health or comfort of such child . . . is endangered or is likely to be endangered, shall be guilty of a misdemeanor." She was sentenced to eight years in prison.[42]

The South Carolina ACLU took Whitner's case on appeal and filed a petition for postconviction relief on the basis of fair notice and ineffective council. The principle of fair notice means that people have a right to know what sorts of actions are considered crimes. As such, the ACLU argued that Whitner's attorney should have challenged the interpretation of the child neglect statute to include prenatal drug use. If South Carolina wanted to use the child neglect statute to punish prenatal drug use, the statute needed to state it explicitly. The petition for postconviction relief was granted, and Whitner was released from prison in November 1993.[43] Then South Carolina appealed.

On July 15, 1996, the South Carolina Supreme Court voted three to two that Whitner had been granted postconviction relief erroneously and reinstated Whitner's sentence. The court drew from the precedent set in *Horne,* arguing, "It would be absurd to recognize the viable fetus as a person for purposes of homicide laws and wrongful death statutes but not for purposes of statutes proscribing child abuse."[44] The case was again appealed, this time to the US Supreme Court, but the court declined to hear the case—something the court does as a matter of course and is not obligated to explain.

In 2006, almost a decade after *Whitner v. State,* the South Carolina legislature adopted a bill that would go even further than the courts had. Case law had defined only *viable* fetuses as victims of crime, perhaps in an attempt to align with the precedent set by *Roe v. Wade,* which established that once the fetus was viable, the state's interest in potential life could outweigh the pregnant person's rights. Republican state senator Glenn McConnell introduced SB 1084, which defined fertilized eggs, embryos, and fetuses as potential victims of crime. This law explicitly *excluded* pregnant women from prosecution, stating intent "to prohibit the prosecution of a woman with respect to her unborn child."[45] However, because *Whitner* directly addressed substance use, and SB 1084 addressed violence, immunity for the pregnant person has not been interpreted as applicable to substance use cases.

ALABAMA

In 2006 Brody's Bill was signed into law, creating victim status for fetuses in Alabama. Like so much other protective legislation, the bill was passed in the wake of the murder of a white pregnant woman. In July 2005 twenty-three-year-old Brandy Parker, who lived in Albertville, about an hour and a half northwest of Birmingham, was driving home from work when she stopped at an intersection and was shot. She was found dead in her pickup truck. She was eight months pregnant at the time she was shot and killed, and her murder has never been solved. Angered that the shooter could be charged for killing Brandy but not for the loss of the pregnancy, Brandy's parents lobbied for a bill to extend victimhood status to the fetus.[46] Brody's Bill makes it a capital offense to harm an "unborn child" and includes an explicit exemption for the person who is carrying the pregnancy. Brandy's father explained, "Our family can't benefit from it, but it will help future children. . . . It speaks for them. It's like they didn't exist."[47]

However, the Marshae Jones case shows the extent to which protective laws can be used to punish the very people they are purported to protect. In 2018 a twenty-eight-year-old Black woman named Marshae Jones was about five months pregnant when she got into a fight with Ebony Jemison, who was dating the father of Marshae's baby. Ebony had a gun and used it to shoot Marshae in the abdomen, causing a stillbirth. Marshae was interrogated by law enforcement for about twenty minutes while she was receiving medical care.[48] Several months later Marshae was arrested, charged with, and indicted for manslaughter for her pregnancy loss. Ebony Jemison, then twenty-three, was not charged, as prosecutors argued that she had acted in self-defense.[49] How could this happen? After all, Marshae wasn't the one who fired the shot that ended her pregnancy, and the law stipulated that the pregnant person would be exempt from charges. Prosecutors used Brody's Bill, arguing that Marshae had instigated the fight, and, as such, she had failed to protect her pregnancy from harm.[50] Ultimately, about a month after her arrest, after much public outcry and attention drawn to the actual text of the statute, the charges against Jones were dropped.[51]

In 2006, the same year that Brody's Bill passed, Democratic state senator Lowell Barron was the lead sponsor of SB 133, a bill creating the crime of Chemical Endangerment of a Minor. SB 133 created specific penalties related to the presence of children in clandestine methamphetamine labs. It passed both the House and Senate unanimously and was signed into law on March 9, 2006. Alabama 26-15-3.2 states,

> (a) A responsible person commits the crime of chemical endangerment of exposing a child to an environment in which he or she does any of the following: (1) Knowingly recklessly, or intentionally causes or permits a child to be exposed to, to ingest or inhale, or to have contact with a controlled substance, chemical substance, or drug paraphernalia as defined in Section 13A-12-260. A violation under this subdivision is a Class C felony. (2) Violates subdivision 1 and a child suffers serious physical injury by exposure to, ingestion of, inhalation of, or contact with a controlled substance, chemical substance, or drug paraphernalia. A violation under this subdivision is a Class B felony. (3) Violates subdivision (1) and the exposure, ingestion, inhalation, or contact results in the death of the child. A violation under this subdivision is a Class A felony.[52]

Months after the new chemical endangerment law went into effect, law enforcement and prosecutors began using it to charge pregnant or postpartum people who tested positive for drugs. This was curious. The chemical endangerment law said nothing about pregnancy, fertilized eggs, embryos, or fetuses. Barron himself commented on this application of the law, saying he did not intend for it to be used against new mothers, and that "I hate to see a young mother put in prison away from her child.... Maybe we need to revisit the legislation."[53] Alabama Democratic representative Patricia Todd commented on the application of the law to "unborn children" in an amicus brief submitted to the state supreme court, explaining that she had been involved in the legislature's *refusal* to apply the chemical endangerment law to pregnant drug users.[54]

With law enforcement and prosecutors taking such a dramatic departure from the law as written, an appeal challenging this legal interpretation was inevitable. In January 2013 the Alabama Supreme Court gave its decision in *Ex parte Ankrom.* The case addressed the consolidated appeals of two women who had been charged with chemical endangerment against their "unborn children." The case considered the criminal prosecutions of two women who used drugs during their pregnancies: Hope Ankrom and Amanda Kimbrough.

Hope Ankrom gave birth to a baby boy on January 31, 2009.[55] Ankrom, a white woman, lived in Coffee County, Alabama, about eighty miles south of Montgomery. Unlike most of the people arrested for crimes against their own pregnancies, Ankrom wasn't impoverished. Her husband earned a six-figure salary working as an airplane mechanic, putting their income well above the Coffee County average.[56] According to her medical records, Ankrom tested positive for marijuana and cocaine while she was pregnant, and her child tested positive for the drugs at birth.[57] Ankrom denies having used cocaine but admits to using marijuana during her pregnancy, explaining that her morning sickness was "relentless." She told the *New York Times* that "marijuana kept her functional," so she continued in spite of her gynecologist's warning that she faced prosecution if she did not stop. Her plan was to stop a few weeks before her son was due, so she wouldn't test positive, but then she went into labor six weeks early.[58]

The Department of Human Resources was notified of the positive drug tests and initiated an investigation.[59] First, Ankrom's three children were removed from her care and placed in the custody of her parents, which was very distressing for Ankrom. She explained "the first night without my children, I thought I was just going to die."[60] About two weeks later, the police showed up at her door with a warrant for her arrest. She told reporters, "Since I was breast-feeding, they let me pump a few times before they took me to jail. . . . Boy, did I leak while I was in there. . . . I had toilet paper crammed in my bra. There is nothing more painful than needing to express [milk] and not being able to." She was released on $10,000 bond the same day and indicted by a grand jury in August of that year.[61] Ankrom pled guilty in April 2010 and was given a three-year prison sentence, suspended on successful completion of one year of probation.[62] Ankrom explained the impact that the stigma of criminal prosecution has had on her life. She had been studying to be a physical-therapy assistant and is now barred from many caretaking professions: "When you want to work with children or the elderly, they see that abuse charge and they're like: 'Woah, no, thank you, ma'am. You're not going to work here.'"[63]

Amanda Kimbrough, a white woman who lived in Colbert County in the northwestern corner of Alabama, is the second woman whose case was appealed in *Ankrom.* At twenty-eight years old, Kimbrough was pregnant with a male fetus she called Timmy.[64] She had been notified by her doctor that the fetus may have had Down syndrome. Both of Kimbrough's other children had been born prematurely, and babies with Down syndrome are at an increased risk for premature birth. On April 29, 2008, Kimbrough was twenty-five weeks and five days pregnant when she started experiencing labor pains. At the hospital her obstetrician diagnosed her with occult cord prolapse and premature labor. Occult cord prolapse is an uncommon condition in which the umbilical cord descends through the cervical opening ahead of the fetus. As the fetus descends through the cervical opening, the umbilical cord is compressed, cutting off blood flow and depriving the fetus of oxygen.[65] Kimbrough's obstetrician ordered a drug screen, which showed a positive result for methamphetamine.[66] Kimbrough consented to an emergency cesarean section to save her son's life, but he wasn't breathing when he was born and was revived only briefly.[67] The hospital had no NICU to support this very fragile newborn. Kimbrough's baby lived for nineteen minutes after his birth.[68]

Notably, Down syndrome could have been a cause of Kimbrough's miscarriage; 43 percent of pregnancies involving fetuses with Down syndrome end in stillbirth or miscarriage, and, postamniocentesis, 23 percent are miscarried or stillborn.[69] The pediatrician who treated Timmy asserted that he had died from respiratory arrest secondary to prematurity—he was too premature to breathe. The obstetrician argued the cause of death was occult cord prolapse. The medical examiner, Dr. Emily Ward, thought that Timmy had died from "acute methamphetamine intoxication." Kimbrough was charged with and pled guilty to felony chemical endangerment of a minor. She was sentenced to ten years in prison.[70]

Ankrom and Kimbrough appealed their convictions, individually, to the court of criminal appeals, which argued that the plain meaning of the word "child" included viable fetuses.[71] Ankrom and Kimbrough then appealed to the Alabama Supreme Court, who consolidated the cases. Ankrom and Kimbrough were supported by National Advocates for Pregnant Women (now Pregnancy Justice), the Drug Policy Alliance, and the Southern Poverty Law Center, who provided legal representation, and many other individuals and organizations who signed on to an amicus brief, or friend of the court brief.[72] First, they argued that these charges were a misapplication of the chemical endangerment law.[73] When the Alabama legislature passed the chemical endangerment law, they were explicit in that this law did not apply to pregnancy but rather to born children.[74] Second, they argued that the court of criminal appeals' decision was bad public policy. Third, they argued that the court's decision violated the US and Alabama Constitutions.[75]

The Alabama Supreme Court gave its opinion in January 2013. Rejecting Ankrom and Kimbrough's second and third arguments outright, the court argued that the plain meaning of the word "child" in the chemical endangerment statute includes an "unborn child or fetus," from the moment of conception. Further, the court asserted that the legality of the substance and the pregnant woman's knowledge of her own pregnancy were also of no consequence.[76] In the language of the law, according to this ruling, a uterus is an environment that a pregnant person contaminates when they drink alcohol, smoke cigarettes, or take drugs or medications. So, for example, in the eyes of the court, a person who is two weeks pregnant and takes her legally prescribed epilepsy medication has committed felony child abuse. If a person drinks a glass of wine the night they conceive, they are a felony child abuser. Penalties for chemical endangerment are dependent on the birth outcome. A healthy baby triggers a sentence of one to ten years. An "injured" baby triggers a sentence of ten to twenty years. A miscarriage or stillbirth would trigger a sentence of up to ninety-nine years in prison, comparable to the state's mandatory sentence for murder.

The following year the Alabama Supreme Court gave its opinion in another appeal of a chemical endangerment charge in *Ex parte Hicks*. Sara Hicks, a twenty-two-year-old Black woman, gave birth to a healthy baby in 2008. Her baby was screened for drugs after his birth and tested positive for cocaine.[77] Hicks was arrested and charged with chemical endangerment She appealed her arrest up to the state supreme court in

2012, raising the same arguments that Ankrom and Kimbrough raised. In April 2014 Hicks lost her appeal. The state supreme court affirmed its ruling in *Ex parte Ankrom,* applying the precedent it set in that case, asserting that fertilized eggs, embryos, and fetuses are "children" under Alabama law. The chief justice in this case, Roy Moore, an unabashedly political and vocally antiabortion judge, who doesn't believe in the separation of church and state, wrote a separate concurring opinion "to emphasize that the inalienable right to life is a gift of God," and, as such, *Roe v. Wade* should be overturned and women should be punished for abortion in addition to chemical endangerment.[78]

In 2016 a bill sponsored by Republican state senator Clyde Chambliss, SB 372, was signed into law, creating an explicit statement of legislative intent to prosecute pregnant women for crimes against their own pregnancies, making no specification about the gestational age at which a fetus is a person and no exemption for abortion. It did, however, include a general exception for medical treatment. Chambliss told reporters, "If a woman is taking a drug prescribed by a doctor, and it unintentionally causes harm to the fetus, she should not be prosecuted."[79]

Some prosecutors didn't seem to get the memo. Take, for example, the 2020 case of Kim Blalock, a thirty-five-year-old white woman in Lauderdale County, in the far northwest corner of Alabama. Kim had severe back pain caused by degenerating spinal disks and then complicated by a car crash and botched spinal surgery.[80] She regularly used prescription pain medication, but, when she became pregnant, she stopped using it out of concern for her pregnancy.[81] However, as her pregnancy progressed, the pain became worse—even debilitating.[82] Kim explained, "Pain doesn't just stop because you're pregnant. . . . If you're pregnant, I don't think you should lay up and hurt."[83] So about six weeks before her due date, Kim renewed her old hydrocodone prescription. She later explained to reporters, "I thought if a doctor wrote you a prescription, you can take it." Lauderdale County's district attorney, Chris Connolly, who would try to prosecute her after her baby tested positive for opioids, disagreed. He argued that Kim had failed in her obligation to notify the prescribing doctor of her pregnancy. Kim says that she told her doctor about the pain pills, and she ultimately gave birth to a healthy baby. The hospital notified social services of the positive drug test, but once Blalock showed them the prescription bottle, social services dropped their investigation.[84] She thought the trouble was over, but it was only just starting.

The police had been notified of Kim's positive drug screen and initiated their own investigation.[85] About two months after she gave birth, Blalock and her husband went out of town, leaving behind their two teenage sons.[86] The day Kim left home, seven armed police officers showed up at her home, demanding that Blalock's sons tell them of her whereabouts. The boys were panicked. They called their mom, asking, "Mom, what have you done?" Kim asked them to hand the phone to police officers, so they could explain what was going on, but they refused to speak to her.[87]

Kim woke up early the next day so that she could go to the police station. According to a news article, "She was floored when, after arriving at the Florence police department, the lead investigator on her case asked her how much heroin she had done." She explained that she hadn't used any heroin; she had just taken her legally prescribed medication. Realizing that, with the recent amendment to the chemical endangerment statute, Blalock hadn't technically committed a crime, the police let her go.[88]

The district attorney had other plans. Realizing he couldn't charge Kim with chemical endangerment, he explored other options, settling on prescription fraud.[89] Blalock was indicted on February 23, 2021, and wouldn't be cleared for over a year.[90] She explained with sadness that her kids had a pretty bleak Christmas that year; afraid that she may be arrested and need to post bond, she saved all the money she would have spent on gifts, for an emergency bail fund. She also noted that she developed postpartum depression, which made it challenging for her to bond with and breastfeed her newborn son.[91] She told reporters, "I suffered severe depression and withdrew from everyone I loved." Eventually, after pressure from health-care professionals and from the very legislator who had written the amendment to the chemical endangerment law, the district attorney relented.[92] He required Blalock to submit to a drug test and to be clinically assessed for substance use disorder. After she cleared both, he dropped the charges.[93]

Most of the people charged with chemical endangerment in relation to a pregnancy were not using legally prescribed medications. Though the harm and trauma enacted on people like Kim Blalock is undeniable, this law arguably had the effect of carving out the "respectable" from condemnation, while furthering the understanding that a fetus is a person. Those left behind have continued to face prosecution as a result of a single positive drug screen. Respectable mothers are awarded with understanding, while mothers deemed unrespectable, by virtue of their choice of drugs, their poverty, and their race, are punished.

TENNESSEE

Tennessee is unique among the three states in that formal criminalization came directly and explicitly from state law a year after Alabama's decision in *Ankrom*. In 1989 Tennessee adopted a law that criminalized third-party harm against viable fetuses.[94] Then, driven by antiabortion, "fetal personhood" ideology, in 2011 the legislature adopted a law defining victims of violent crimes and vehicular offenses to include "a fetus of a human being."[95] This was adjusted the following year, in a twenty-eight-to-two vote, to adopt language that more explicitly included embryos and fetuses "at any stage of gestation in utero."[96]

In 2013 HB 277 was introduced to address the "growing misuse of prescription drugs by pregnant women," citing negative infant health outcomes and the "heavy financial burden" of paying for these newborns. It passed the House and Senate unanimously, and in May 2013 the Safe Harbor Act was signed into law.[97] Before this law went into effect, if pregnant people tested positive for drugs, their parental rights may be terminated and the baby removed from their custody after birth. The Safe Harbor Act was meant to encourage pregnant people who tested positive for drugs to seek help by reducing the likelihood that they would automatically lose custody of their children. Under this law if pregnant people agree to comply with a drug treatment plan, their drug use during pregnancy would not trigger the termination of their parental rights. This may seem like a nonpunitive solution; however, drug treatment in Tennessee was scarce, especially for pregnant people. The Safe Harbor Act did not expand availability or accessibility of drug treatment.

Still concerned about pregnancy and drug use, district attorneys approached two state legislators, Republican representative Terri Weaver, a white woman, and Democratic senator Reginald "Reggie" Tate, a Black man, seeking to use the threat of criminal punishment to coerce pregnant drug users into treatment programs. Tate and Weaver sponsored bills in their respective chambers to do just that, creating the offense of "fetal assault." In 2014 Tennessee adopted Tate's bill, SB 1391. As chaptered, the law reads, "Criminal Offenses—As enacted, provides that a woman may be prosecuted for assault for the illegal use of a narcotic drug while pregnant, if her child is born addicted to or harmed by the narcotic drug; law expires July 1, 2016." It included an affirmative defense if the pregnant woman completed a drug rehabilitation program prior to giving birth. This time support for the bill was more mixed. SB 1391 passed the Senate in a twenty-six-to-seven vote, with every Senate Democrat voting in its favor, and it passed the House in a sixty-four-to-thirty-one vote, with ten Republicans voting against it. The bill was considered controversial at both the state and national level, drawing opposition from experts in obstetrics and substance use disorder, from feminist organizations who saw the "fetal personhood" ideology embedded in the law, and from some antiabortion advocates who feared the law would incentivize abortion.[98]

Over the course of twenty-five years, Tennessee gradually adopted laws that began to privilege the fetus—first, as victims of third-party harm, next as legal persons in the criminal code, and, finally, as victims of the people who gestate them. Weaver and Tate sought to make the fetal assault law permanent, but the proposed legislation, HB 1660, didn't make it out of committee. Two years of bad press, organizing against the law, and testimony from health-care providers and people arrested because of the law had turned the tides.

Laws introduced with the stated intention of *protecting* pregnant (white) women from violence seemed to facilitate the *punishment* of pregnant people, even in the absence of laws explicitly criminalizing pregnant people's actions. West Virginia offers an illustrative example. According to attorney Lynn Paltrow and sociologist Jeanne Flavin's study of arrests and detentions made throughout the United States from 1973 to 2005, no arrests or detentions of pregnant women had been documented in West Virginia.[99] In 2005 West Virginia's new fetal assault law, the Unborn Victims of Violence Act, went into effect This law asserted that, from the moment of conception, "a pregnant woman and the embryo or fetus she is carrying in the womb constitute separate and distinct victims." The West Virginia law also prohibited the application of this law to pregnant women and their own pregnancies.[100]

After this law went into effect on July 1, 2005, West Virginia made its first documented arrests of pregnant women for crimes against their own pregnancies. For example, a 2016 case, *West Virginia v. Stephanie Louk*, concerned a woman who was about a week shy of her due date when she overdosed on methamphetamine. She survived the overdose and underwent an emergency cesarean section to save her baby, but her baby daughter lived for only eleven days. Louk was indicted by a grand jury for causing her child's death, and she was eventually convicted of felony child neglect resulting in death. She was given a three-to-fifteen-year prison sentence. She appealed to the West Virginia Supreme Court and ultimately found relief on May 27, 2016, when the court wrote, "We have read the law and it is clear: when enacting our child neglect resulting in death statute, the Legislature did not criminalize a mother's prenatal act that results in harm to her subsequently born child."[101] Still, at least one pregnant person was charged between the introduction of the law and the state court intervention, and it took years to overturn her sentence.

Another example comes from Texas. The Texas feticide law was introduced in 2003. Like the West Virginia law, the Texas feticide law prohibits the application of the charge to pregnant women and their own pregnancies.[102] The following year a woman gave birth to healthy twins and admitted that she smoked marijuana when she was pregnant to treat a condition called hyperemesis gravidarum, or chronic nausea and vomiting during pregnancy. This can be incredibly debilitating and also dangerous for a pregnancy if the pregnant person is unable to consume and keep down enough water, calories, and nutrients to sustain her own body and the developing pregnancy. The woman was found guilty for "delivering a controlled substance to a minor," a second-degree felony. She was given a suspended sentence of five years in prison and confessed, "If I would have known that I'd get in trouble for telling my doctor the truth I would have either lied or not gone to the doctor."[103]

Pregnant and postpartum people have been arrested and detained in states under varied legal conditions, including in states with vague laws about crimes against fetuses, in states that explicitly bar the application of crimes against fetuses to maternal conduct, and in states that had no laws about crimes against fetuses, like Colorado, Connecticut, Hawaii, New Jersey, New Mexico, Oregon, and Wyoming.[104] This suggests that, rather than operating only in a condition of legal vagueness, law enforcement and prosecutors have the discretion to make vast departures from the law as written and to even pursue cases in explicit opposition to written law. As was the case in South Carolina and Alabama, the prosecutions themselves are driving changes to criminal law, not the other way around. This is not how the creation of new criminal law is supposed to work.

Typically, if a person is unable to look at a criminal law as written and determine what actions are prohibited, the problem isn't with the person but with the vague law.[105] It would typically be considered an unconstitutional violation of the right to due process to pursue those criminal charges on the basis of such a vague law.[106] If a criminal law is vague, the prosecutor and the courts are supposed to side with the defendant and drop the charges. The onus is on the legislature to clarify its vague laws, not on the individual to guess at how any prosecutor may decide to interpret any given law.[107]

These gaps between the stated purpose of a law and the actual exercise of the law and between codified law and law enforcement undermine the legitimacy of the law. They show that a person can be arrested and successfully prosecuted for actions that are not crimes. They show that even when legislative intent is explicit, possibly even written into the law with statements of exemption, that law enforcement, prosecutors, and judges may simply reinterpret those laws, essentially suspending the right to due process and right to fair notice of law. While it seems that having a written law (legislative or case law) does facilitate the criminal prosecution of pregnant people, it is not a necessary condition for arrests and prosecutions to occur. The will and ability to protect and punish pregnant people exists beyond the scope of the law.

Maternal protection is undergirded by the idea that the environment and lifestyle of pregnant women influence the quality of their offspring. As the Supreme Court stated in *Muller v. Oregon* (1908), a case that established the constitutionality of laws that set upper limits on work hours for women, "as healthy mothers are essential to vigorous offspring, the physical wellbeing of woman is an object of public interest."[108] Because pregnant people are, for any number of reasons, considered vulnerable, they need to be protected by others in a way that is unique among legally competent adults. Maternal protection in the law, with its focus on the protection of pregnant people, has largely, but not entirely, been replaced by a greater focus on the protection of fetuses. Legally, it was perhaps most visible in laws regulating workplace environments or excluding women from certain kinds of employment.

Fetal protection generally rests on the assumption that a third party needs to intervene to represent the best interests of the fetus, because pregnant people are incapable of doing so or are seen as actively threatening to their own pregnancies. Laws requiring the appointment of lawyers to represent the interests of fertilized eggs, embryos, and fetuses in child abuse trials or laws appointing attorneys to represent the interests of unborn children in judicial bypass hearings for minors seeking abortion are two contemporary examples of the state constructing policy based on fetal personhood and the need to protect the fetus. The idea that the pregnant person doing the gestating and the fertilized egg, embryo, or fetus being gestated are separate entities, perhaps with opposing interests, is central to this understanding.

Protection is a two-sided coin—on one side is the kind of freedom from fear, insecurity, violence, and other threats that compose the "state of nature," earned by giving up certain kinds of autonomy or rights.[109] The other side, however, is not benevolent. It is the punitive force that lashes out when people are not in order—not willing to surrender their own personhood when "good" mothers are supposed to be entirely self-sacrificial. Both sides rely on pregnancy exceptionalism to justify the benevolent or punitive treatment, and both sides demand a sacrifice of the legal personhood of the pregnant person.

2 Angels and Antimothers

Laura Pemberton was in labor when her legs were shackled together, and she was removed from her home for a cesarean section she didn't need and didn't want. Alicia Beltran was forced into an inpatient drug treatment program because she was pregnant and had previously struggled with substance use disorder. The police accused Christine Taylor of throwing herself down the stairs to cause a miscarriage after she told a nurse that this was an unplanned pregnancy. Mary Craig was sterilized after her employer set a policy barring fertile women from their jobs on a battery-production line. Rennie Gibbs was charged with "depraved heart murder" after she had a stillbirth.[1] Each of these cases is an example of cultural and legal treatment that define people with the capacity for pregnancy as distinct from and enjoying fewer rights than other similarly situated people without the capacity for pregnancy. I refer to this as *pregnancy exceptionalism,* where pregnant people are defined as a separate and lesser legal class of person.

Women, as a legal class, have been defined as distinct from others in the US legal system. This singular category, of course, obscures within-group differences that span other, "separate" legal classes; for example, socioeconomic class, race, sexuality, and ability. While voting rights, educational rights, and protections from workplace discrimination for women are currently in place, there is no constitutional prohibition on discrimination on the basis of sex or gender. People with the capacity for pregnancy continue to be defined as exceptional cases, justifying the suspension of otherwise fundamental rights in a variety of legal areas. The numerous exceptions applied to the rights of people with the capacity for pregnancy indicate that pregnant people have fewer rights than other similarly situated people.[2] Gestational ability has historically provided a legal basis for the suspension of equal protection, due process, liberty, privacy, and other rights. Even in areas where women's rights and legal personhood have been expanded in recent decades, these laws have been shaped and influenced by an ideology that defines pregnant people as a lesser class of person.

Typically, a positive drug test at a doctor's office cannot be shared with law enforcement, but pregnant and postpartum people have been arrested after their health-care providers reported a single positive drug test. They also may be prosecuted for doing things that are not crimes, like self-harm. Generally, adults who survive a suicide attempt are not criminally prosecuted, but pregnant and postpartum people have been charged with felonies when they survive but lose their pregnancies.[3] Accidental falls down the stairs turn into murder investigations.[4] Gunshot wounds inflicted by a third party may lead to criminal charges for the pregnant person who was shot.[5] Pregnant people occupy a lower space in the US system of criminal law.

In this chapter I explore two legal frameworks that have been used to establish people with the capacity for pregnancy as distinct and in need of protection or control. The first, maternal protection, relies on an understanding that women are vulnerable and, as mothers of the nation, must be protected to ensure quality offspring for the state. I analyze early twentieth-century labor law, showing that maternal protection was ultimately more powerful than the Supreme Court's refusal to regulate private businesses. Social, political, and technological shifts, including bans on pregnancy discrimination in employment, the formation of the religious Right as an anti-abortion political movement, the development of federal child abuse legislation, and ultrasound and photographic imaging of the fetus mark the shift from maternal protection to fetal protection. Fetal protection requires a construction of fertilized eggs, embryos, and fetuses as legal persons that must be protected from the people who gestate them. I discuss the maintenance of an explicit state interest in controlling reproduction and parenting, even as the rights of pregnant people to access contraceptives and abortion through the right to privacy were expanded. Tracing these court cases indicates that even as some rights were expanded, the state maintained an interest in regulating pregnancy. Though the protective frameworks have shifted over time, the foundational understanding that people with the capacity for pregnancy are exceptional has been used to justify the suspension of rights that, for other similarly situated people, remain intact.

MATERNAL PROTECTION

The Progressive Era (1896–1917) in the United States was a time of tremendous change. Increased industrialization brought people from rural areas to large cities, looking for employment in factories. Immigrants, mostly from eastern and southern Europe and China, poured into the cities, looking for work. The growing movement for women's suffrage and women's increasing participation in the wage labor force, especially among white women, challenged existing notions that women belonged in the private, domestic sphere. The white birth rate in the United States was falling, while immigrant populations grew. Political scientist James Morone writes, "These middle-class groups fretted about the rapidly breeding others. They knew that the immigrants threatened us with their low morals and vicious habits. The active loins of the Italians or the Germans or worse were threatening to populate those American plains—and fill the cities—with aliens."[6] The fear of "race suicide," of Anglo-Americans being outbred and replaced, was prevalent.[7]

In this context the image of the mother was promoted as an essential part of maintaining the white supremacist vision of the nation. Morone writes that "the politics of private lives—of purity and virtue—went decidedly public."[8] Anne McClintock, professor of women and gender studies, asserts, "Nationalism requires a specific construction of women as mothers to justify many of its political prescriptions." She continues, "Women are typically construed as the symbolic bearers of the nation, but are denied any direct relation to national agency."[9] Legal theorist Martha Fineman writes, "When one considers the relationship between motherhood and patriarchy, motherhood has always been, and continues to be, a colonized concept—an event physically practiced and experienced by women but occupied and defined, given content and value, by the core concepts of patriarchal ideology."[10]

The ideal women of *this* era were defined as "pure, spiritual beings, wafting above gross carnality." They weren't sexual, "never becom[ing] sexually awakened" and never feeling "physical pleasure" or "yearning." The proper women's sphere was in the home, doing her "high and sacred duty, . . . the duty of the mother."[11] The mother was expected to train her children, in particular the boys, who would one day enter the public spheres of politics and capitalism, in "important elements of American citizenship": industry, individualism, Christianity, and social hierarchy.[12] Men of this era were understood to be sexual brutes, and the mother, the "angel spirit of the house" was meant to tame them. Demonstrating self-control and reserving sex for reproduction and not for pleasure, they thought, "was one way [middle and upper-class Anglos] distinguished themselves from the 'dirty immigrants and the dangerous classes.'"[13]

LABOR REGULATION

It is within this context that the US Supreme Court gave its opinion in *Lochner v. New York* (1905).[14] In the decades that followed this case, the Supreme Court applied substantive due process to laws attempting to regulate newly industrialized labor, striking down regulatory and protective laws. This would come to be known as the *Lochner* era. The court argued, again and again, that employers and employees were equally situated, and that it was unconstitutional for the government to interfere in their ability to define the terms of employment.[15] Labor regulation was popular during this time, as people suffered in unregulated factories, slaughterhouses, and mills. States passed laws regulating foreign corporations, banning yellow-dog contracts (which barred employees from joining labor unions), regulating the coal industry, and regulating child labor, but the Supreme Court struck down all the laws, arguing that they were unconstitutional violations of the right of employers and employees to make labor contracts.[16]

Lochner v. New York concerned the constitutionality of the Bakeshop Act, a law that limited the maximum working hours for bakers. Lochner, the owner of multiple bakeries, argued that maximum-hours regulations were unconstitutional—he should be free to set his employees' work hours, and employees should be free to accept or reject those work hours. New York argued that the Bakeshop Act was passed in the interest of promoting public health, claiming that commercial baking, a predominantly male occupation, was in need of regulation. Long work shifts in poorly ventilated, hot, and dusty bakeries endangered the health not only of the bakers but of bread consumers as well. The court found, however, that this health risk was not significant enough to justify government regulation. It asserted that the Bakeshop Act wasn't actually a public health law at all—it was a labor law in disguise. The Bakeshop Act was struck down.

The *Lochner* era, in which the Supreme Court struck down labor regulations, would continue for several decades. However, when presented with laws regulating women's labor, the court found in favor of regulation.[17] Only three years after the *Lochner* opinion, the court upheld an Oregon law that set limits on the number of hours that women were allowed to work.[18] Like the Bakeshop Act, the Oregon law was passed with the stated purpose of promoting public health, one of the few instances in which states were constitutionally permitted to regulate private business.[19] In *Muller v. Oregon* (1908) the Supreme Court argued that the maximum-hours law for women was fundamentally different than the maximum-hours law for men. Treating these laws the same way wouldn't be appropriate. The court asserted that the difference between the sexes justified a different rule. Allowing women to work shifts longer than ten hours was a threat to public health, safety, morality, and general wellbeing. Due to their "physical structure" and "performance of maternal functions," women were at a disadvantage and required state intervention and protection from free-market capitalism. The court wrote, "As healthy mothers are essential to vigorous offspring, the physical wellbeing of woman is an object of *public interest*. . . . The right of a State to regulate the working hours of women rests on . . . the right to preserve the health of the women of the State."[20]

The court articulated several key arguments used to justify the regulation of women as a class of laborers. Women were generally found to be incapable of bargaining or otherwise making claims for themselves in job markets. This argument was made on both biological and sociopolitical grounds. The biological argument stated that women, much like children, occupied a secondary class and were incapable of self-dependence: "As minors, though not to the same extent, she has been looked upon in the courts as needing special care that her rights may be preserved." As such, the state had a responsibility to intervene and create protections for women in the interest of public health and general well-being. The court stated that the maximum-hours law was reasonably related to women's health and thus to the health of "the race" through her potential procreative abilities. The court wrote that even if women had full legal equality, "it would still be true that she is so constituted that she will rest upon and look to him for protection; that her physical structure and a proper discharge of her maternal functions—having in view not merely her own health, but the wellbeing of the race—justify legislation to protect her from the greed, as well as the passion, of man. The limitations which this statute places upon her contractual powers . . . are not imposed solely for her benefit, but also largely for the benefit of all."[21] The court makes clear that the protection of women, then, is less about the women themselves as people and more about nation, race, and the social good.

The court's second argument addressed the social status of women: the state needed to protect women who were vulnerable in part because of their unequal sociolegal status and the burden of child-rearing. In this way *Muller* can be read as the court affirming a piece of maternal protectionist legislation—one that the labor movement was seeking to apply to the entire workforce. The court was clear in its stance that the state had a duty to protect women in a way that would be inappropriate were it applied to men, in part because women give birth and parent children.

Nearly thirty years after its decision in *Muller*, the court heard another case on the regulation of women's labor. *West Coast Hotel Co. v. Parrish* (1937), a case testing the constitutionality of a Washington minimum-wage law for women, is said to have ended the *Lochner* era. The Supreme Court found that a Washington law establishing a minimum wage for women was constitutional, suggesting that labor regulations are reasonable if "adopted for the protection of the community against evils menacing the health, safety, morals and welfare of the people." The court wrote that the state has a "special interest" in protecting women from poor working conditions, long hours, and insufficient pay that might leave them inadequately supported and undermine their health on the following grounds: "1. The health of women is peculiarly related to the vigor of the race; 2. Women are especially liable to be overreached and exploited by unscrupulous employers; and 3. This exploitation and denial of a living wage is not only detrimental to the health and wellbeing of the women affected, but casts a direct burden for their support upon the community."[22] The court rearticulated its previous arguments about social and biological female inferiority and the state's special interest in reproduction, but it also argued a minimum wage for women was permitted because it promoted morality and protected public welfare. The court suggested that, without a minimum wage, the economic burden of maintaining women and their children would rest on the state and opted to let it rest instead on private business.

Though labor regulation was sorely needed for all workers, by granting these protections to women only, the court singled them out as exceptional and in need of protection. Even when they were members of the paid labor force, their presumed procreative functions were still centered as their primary social role. These mothers of "the race" needed to be cared for or else the nation would be threatened. One physician (who also favored eugenic sterilization) emphasized the importance of maternal protection for the nation, declaring that "there is no State womb, there are no State breasts, there is no real substitute for the beautiful reality of individual motherhood."[23] However, as Morone writes, "every angel comes with its demonic counter—in this case, the fallen woman. One slip and a woman lost every claim to virtue. She became an outcast, an untouchable."[24] Not every mother could be trusted. Legal historian Dorothy Roberts writes, "Society's construction of mother, its image of what constitutes a good mother and what constitutes a bad mother, facilitates its continuing control of women. Society considers women who fail to meet the ideal of motherhood deviant or criminal."[25] The image of the deviant mother would play a central role in future efforts to regulate pregnancy.

THE SHIFT FROM PROTECTING MOTHERS TO VILLAINIZING MOTHERS

Maternal protectionist law has morphed over time in response to expansions in civil rights law that limited pregnancy-based discrimination in employment, eventually moving away from protection of mothers and future mothers for the general social good and toward the protection of *individual* fertilized eggs, embryos, and fetuses. Title VII of the Civil Rights Act of 1964 prohibits discrimination against employees on the basis of, among other things, sex. A Supreme Court decision spurred further action by Congress.[26] In 1976 in *General Electric Co. v. Gilbert,* the Supreme Court rejected sex discrimination claims in response to an insurance policy that excluded pregnancy coverage.[27] The court found that because not all women are pregnant all the time, pregnancy discrimination was not a form of sex discrimination.[28] Labor unions, women's rights organizations, and civil rights activists urged Congress to respond.[29] In 1978 Congress passed the Pregnancy Discrimination Act, which amended Title VII to prohibit discrimination "on the basis of pregnancy, childbirth, or related medical conditions."[30] Political scientist Cynthia Daniels notes the impact of this legislation on protectionist law as it applies to pregnancy, writing, "Just as the spectre of gender difference appeared to breathe its last, taking with it the basis for state protectionism, it was infused with new life by the powerful ideology of fetal rights."[31]

Technological developments played a role in elevating the status of the fetus. Sociologist Elizabeth Armstrong writes, "As ultrasonography became widespread in the 1970s, doctors and the public could 'see' the fetus in ways that had not been possible. The relationship between the pregnant woman and the fetus was thus reconfigured, and the relationship between the pregnant woman and society was transformed as well."[32] The work of Swedish photographer Lennart Nilsson was also influential. His photo essay "The Drama of Life before Birth," which depicted high-quality images of fetuses, seemingly floating alone in empty space, was published in *Life* magazine in 1965. Some of these photographs depicted fetuses still inside the uterus. Others though, were actually photographs of aborted embryos that Nilsson posed and manipulated to make them appear more baby-like. For example, in one photograph, he placed the fetus's thumb into its mouth.[33] Now the once-hidden fetus was made visible and misleadingly personified. Armstrong writes, "Elevating the status of the fetus had the consequence of devaluing the pregnant woman."[34] The maternal-fetal conflict offered "a new social mythology [which] encouraged the view that some women were not just bad mothers but 'anti-mothers,' who violated their most fundamental natural instincts and who threatened to destroy the institution of motherhood altogether."[35]

The Child Abuse Prevention and Treatment Act of 1974, also known as CAPTA, requires that states enact laws mandating reports of known or suspected child abuse to Child Protective Services.[36] CAPTA issued funds for the investigation and prevention of child maltreatment. Mandatory reporting flooded the foster care system, along with children who had been removed from the custody of their families. Children often languished in foster care, drifting between multiple different placements and sometimes remaining in foster care until they aged out—never reunited with their families or placed in adoptive families.[37] The child welfare system, or, as Roberts calls it, the family-policing system, disproportionately targets Black and Indigenous families and, at lower rates, poor white families in impoverished areas.[38] A 1996 study conducted by pediatrician Daniel Neuspiel found that "among newborns testing positive for cocaine, those with black mothers are more likely to be discharged to non-maternal care."[39]

Another federal law, the Adoption and Child Welfare Act, was passed in 1980. Under this law states could receive federal grant monies only if they made "reasonable efforts" to prevent child removal and to encourage reunification in the event that children were removed from their family. This would ultimately be met with criticism, as reports of children being returned to their families and subsequently being tortured and murdered proliferated. In 1997 the Adoption and Safe Families Act was enacted. Now, instead of keeping children in foster care or prioritizing family reunification, the child's health and safety were favored. The Adoption and Safe Families Act requires states to begin to terminate parental rights if a child has spent fifteen of the last twenty-two months in foster care.[40]

In 2003 Congress amended CAPTA to address substance use and to specify when reports to Child Protective Services were required. States were left to develop their own policies under this new law. Roberts writes,

"Whether considered a crime, infliction of civil child maltreatment, or reason to question the ability to parent in the future, using drugs during pregnancy is often seen as warranting a call to child protection authorities."[41] In the context of the crack crisis, Black women were far more likely to be reported, to lose custody of their children, and to be arrested and charged with crimes.[42] Though many health-care providers interpret CAPTA to require reports to Child Protective Services of all substance use during pregnancy, that is incorrect. CAPTA requires only the notification of substance use for the purposes of providing services to the family and only under certain circumstances: if a baby is born "affected by illegal substance abuse," has "withdrawal symptoms resulting from prenatal drug exposure," or is diagnosed with fetal alcohol spectrum disorders. These notifications are specifically not for the purposes of reporting child abuse but for the provision of resources and services to the family. Today, though only three states have explicitly criminalized drug use during pregnancy, medical anthropologist Kelly Ray Knight writes that "every state in the United States has a surveillance system in place to identify prenatal substance use exposure."[43]

FETAL PROTECTION AND MATERNAL-FETAL CONFLICT

Different from maternal protection, fetal protection generally positions the pregnant person as a living vessel. The fetus and the pregnant person are conceptualized as separate entities in this formulation, and their interests are placed in opposition to each other. Legal sociologist Katherine Beckett writes, "To the extent that the fetus is defined as a separate patient, the mother is increasingly seen as a barrier to optimum medical care of the fetus. . . . The image of the fetus as separable from its mother-to-be . . . has its roots in patriarchal ideology, which views women as mere vessels of a more 'precious cargo.'" Fetal rights and the rights of pregnant people, in this construction, were at odds. Beckett continues, "Insofar as the fetal rights movement seeks to punish pregnant women who fail to act in a manner consistent with idealized concepts of motherhood, its spread can be seen as part of a larger reaction against the breakdown of traditional gender roles."[44]

Though fetal protection was elevated by the passage of regulatory legislation and technological development, it originated long before. Indeed, the concept of fetal protection and the separation of pregnant people from their pregnancy predate civil rights legislation by more than a century. Roberts describes an early instance of fetal protection within the institution of chattel slavery in the United States, where the fetus was conceptualized not as a person in need of protection but as property. Roberts shares the words of a formerly enslaved woman named Lizzie Williams: "Dey [the white folks] would dig a hole in de ground just big 'nuff fo' her stomach, make her lie face down an whip her on de back to keep from hurtin' de child." Roberts explains, "The beating of pregnant slaves reveals that slave masters created just such a conflict between Black women and their unborn children to support their own economic interests. The Black mother's act of bearing a child profited the system that subjugated her. . . . It is the most striking metaphor I know for the evils of policies that seek to protect the fetus while disregarding the humanity of the mother."[45]

Roberts compares this early moment of brutality to contemporary instances of fetal protection and maternal-fetal conflict. For example, courts have been known to construct a pregnant woman's opposition to certain birth interventions as stemming from an "adversarial relationship between the pregnant woman and her unborn child."[46] By inventing an adversarial relationship between the pregnant person and her own pregnancy, the government is given reason to restrict the pregnant person's autonomy in favor of protecting the "innocent" fetus. Fetal protectionism generally rests on the assumption that third-party intervention in a pregnancy is necessary to represent the best interests of the fetus, because the pregnant woman is incapable of doing so.

The construction of the pregnant drug user runs against the image of the good mother. Medical sociologist Sheigla Murphy and Marsha Rosenbaum, founder of the Safety First Project at the Drug Policy Alliance write, "No woman inhabits the all-giving mother role entirely, but drug-using mothers may miss by the most. Mother as fetal poisoner, or user of illegal drugs, is the antithesis of the prevailing myth of the mother as unflagging, unselfish caregiver."[47] Though the targeted drug and population of drug users shifts over time, the punitive approach to drug use during pregnancy remains intact. Roberts writes, "Choosing these particular mothers makes the prosecution of pregnant women more palatable to the public. Prosecutors have selected women whom society views as undeserving to be mothers in the first place.[48] Contemporary examples of fetal protection include Laura Pemberton's forced cesarean section, Alicia Beltran's institutionalization, the criminal investigations of Christine Taylor's fall down the stairs and Rennie Gibbs's miscarriage, and the policy banning fertile women from certain employment, which led Christine Taylor to be sterilized. Even as pregnant people gained the right to abortion through a right to privacy, the government maintained its interest in protecting the fetus.

Prosecutors who pursued charges against pregnant people for pregnancy-related crimes often invoked the ideology of fetal personhood as well. Solicitor Charles Condon frequently referred to a fetus in one case as a "fellow South Carolinian." Assistant solicitor Catherine Christophilis, from Greenville, South Carolina, referred to them as "special little citizens."[49] Alabama district attorney George Lester explained, "I thought it was a legitimate argument to say that a mother who is injecting, ingesting drugs and they're going, in utero, through the child. I don't think that's a, 'Wow, y'all are twisting the facts here to get the result you want.' I mean, I believe that's a correct analysis of what that is. That's chemically endangering what I believe is a child."[50] However, in one media interview he contended that he wasn't promoting fetal personhood but rather just following the law.[51]

Others who supported the prosecutions using existing laws shared these sentiments, perhaps in pursuit of fetal personhood being written into other areas of law as well. Of the Alabama Supreme Court's decision in *Ex parte Ankrom,* Alabama attorney general Luther Strange said, "It is a tremendous victory that the Alabama Supreme Court has affirmed the value of all life, including those of unborn children whose lives are among the most vulnerable of all."[52] Chief justice Tom Parker explained, "The decision of the court today is in keeping with the widespread legal recognition that unborn children are persons with rights that should be protected by law. . . . Today, the only major area in which unborn children are denied legal protection is abortion, and that denial is only because of the dictates of *[Roe v. Wade].*"[53] Of course, today this legal contradiction no longer exists.

PRIVACY

Medical privacy is one of the areas where pregnant people may be held as exceptional, justifying the suspension of their rights. The principle of medical privacy is ancient, dating back to the Greek Hippocratic oath.[54] The US legal understanding of medical privacy was initially drawn from English common law but was not defined as a constitutional right until 1965 in *Griswold v. Connecticut.*[55] The 1996 Health Insurance Portability and Accountability Act, or HIPAA, created federal standards for the regulation of patient health information. It states that medical information may be shared only for law enforcement purposes in six circumstances:

> (1) As required by law (including court orders, court-ordered warrants, subpoenas) and administrative requests; (2) to identify or locate a suspect, fugitive, material witness, or missing person; (3) in response to a law enforcement official's request for information about a victim or suspected victim of a crime; (4) to alert law enforcement of a person's death, if the covered entity suspects that criminal activity caused the death; (5) when a covered entity believes that protected health information is evidence of a crime that occurred on its premises; and (6) by a covered health care provider in a medical emergency not occurring on its premises, when necessary to inform law enforcement about the commission and nature of a crime, the location of the crime or crime victims, and the perpetrator of the crime.[56]

Pregnant people, however, seem to enjoy a lesser degree of medical privacy based on the interpretation that potential fetal endangerment fits under HIPAA's sixth circumstance—that a health-care provider believes this is a medical emergency and needs to inform law enforcement about the victim (fertilized egg, embryo, fetus, or newborn) or perpetrator (the pregnant person) of a crime.

Modern privacy rights find their start in *Griswold v. Connecticut.* In this case the US Supreme Court was asked to decide if a Connecticut law banning contraception was an unconstitutional infringement on the right of marital privacy. In the opinion the court acknowledged that, while privacy is never explicitly stated in the constitution, the *idea* of a right to privacy can be found in the First, Third, Fourth, and Ninth Amendments. As such, after *Griswold,* laws banning contraception could not be enforced for married couples.

Just as the right to privacy was being extended to married couples in the privacy of their home in *Griswold,* the federal government began to approach child abuse as a problem. Though child abuse has certainly occurred for thousands of years, it was not defined as deviant and criminal until the latter part of the twentieth century In the 1950s pediatric radiologists linked bone fractures in children to parental conduct or carelessness, narrowing in on "misconduct and deliberate injury" as the primary factors. In 1962 a report in the *Journal of the American Medical Association* labeled abuse as a "clinical condition" and child abuse as a product of "psychiatric factors" representing a deficient character.[57] It was in this report that Dr. K. H. Kempe presented the term "battered child syndrome."[58] Child abuse was labeled as a problem to be managed, either by medical intervention and treatment or criminalization. Between 1962 and 1966, every US state had passed child abuse statutes.[59] In 1963 the federal government issued a piece of model legislation requiring the reporting of child abuse, which went on to be adopted by every state over the next four years.[60]

In 1972 the Supreme Court expanded the right to privacy to include unmarried, straight couples, in *Eisenstadt v. Baird,* writing, "If the right of privacy means anything, it is the right of the individual, married or single, to be free from unwarranted governmental intrusion into matters so fundamentally affecting a person as the decision whether to bear or beget a child."[61] Only a year after *Eisenstadt,* the Supreme Court would use privacy again to undergird the right to abortion in *Roe v. Wade.*[62] The court stated its interest in both maternal health and fetal life (or the potentiality of life) in *Roe v. Wade.* While often regarded as a victory for those who desired expanded reproductive rights for women, *Roe* left room for the imposition of state regulation of gestating bodies. As law professor Reva Siegel writes, "*Roe* expressed the abortion right as a form of liberty protected by the Due Process Clause, never mentioning equal protection or reasons rooted in sex equality."[63] At the same time, the court contended that this liberty right was not absolute and that the *state could intervene* when the interest in maternal health or the potential life of the fetus becomes sufficiently compelling. This decision left room for further state intrusion, not only in the area of abortion but for reproductive life in general. Asserting the maternal-fetal conflict, the court wrote that once the fetus was viable, "the woman's privacy is no longer sole and any right of privacy she possesses must be measured accordingly." The decision, written by Justice Harry Blackmun, asserted that the right to bodily autonomy was limited and that the regulation of reproduction fit well within the state's interests. By establishing a legal basis for the right to abortion in privacy rather than equal protection, the rights of pregnant people were weakened from the start. In the coming years, states would begin to pass laws once again imposing on the rights of pregnant people. As medical sociologist Miranda Waggoner writes, "The rise of the conservative right in the 1980s . . . produced a political climate toward elevating the status of the fetus and being particularly hostile to women, women's rights and women's health."[64]

Many feminist theorists and legal scholars have critiqued the use of privacy for such foundational constitutional protections. For example, feminist philosopher Martha Nussbaum writes, "The pursuit of sex equality through constitutional law has sometimes taken a detour through the disputed and murky concept of privacy." She goes on, "Is privacy a useful concept, a concept that gives good guidance in law and public policy? And is it a concept that helps law advance the cause of sex equality? I shall answer 'no' to both of these questions."[65]

Law professor Khiara Bridges makes two claims about privacy doctrine in relation to socioeconomic status and motherhood: "One version, the moderate claim, takes the statement that poor mothers have been deprived of privacy rights to assert that poor mothers have been deprived of *effective* privacy rights. The other version, the strong claim (which I strongly encourage you to accept), takes the statement that poor mothers have been deprived of privacy rights to assert that poor mothers actually *do not* possess privacy rights; they are not bearers of the right to privacy."[66]

In 1973 white evangelical Christians were not mobilized against abortion. Abortion was generally considered a Catholic issue, and evangelical Christians couldn't come to a consensus. Instead, white evangelicals were organized against racial integration, shrouded in terms of religious rights. To avoid sending their children to racially integrated schools, many white Christians established private, religious academies, also known as "segregation academies," that were free to restrict admission to white children only. There was concern among some evangelical organizational leaders that racial segregation was no longer an issue that brought evangelicals to the polls. It wasn't until the late 1970s that the religious Right adopted abortion as a defining issue. Politically, it was a winning proposition. Evangelicals could now bring Catholics with them in votes for antiabortion Republican candidates.[67]

States began adopting laws that blatantly violated the court's finding in *Roe v. Wade:* state-mandated informed consent with corresponding waiting periods, spousal notification laws that required married women to notify their husbands before receiving abortion care, and parental consent laws that required minors to get permission from a parent. Other restrictions came from the federal government. For example, the 1977 Hyde Amendment banned federal spending on abortion except in cases of rape and incest and to save the life of the pregnant person. The right to choose an abortion may have been protected by the constitution, but exercising that right was a matter of personal responsibility. This had the effect of making legal abortion available only to those who could afford it.

When Pennsylvania adopted restrictive abortion laws, Planned Parenthood of Pennsylvania sued the state, and the case made its way to the Supreme Court in *Planned Parenthood v. Casey* (1992). The composition of the court had changed considerably since *Roe v. Wade* and was now much more conservative. Reproductive rights advocates feared that *Roe v. Wade* would be overturned entirely.[68] Instead, the Supreme Court rejected *Roe*'s trimester framework in favor of a new regulatory framework: the undue burden standard. In their rearticulation of the findings in *Roe,* the court held that, among other things, "the State has legitimate interests from the *outset* of the pregnancy in protecting the health of the woman and the life of the fetus that may become a child." Yes, the right to abortion was still protected by the Due Process Clause, "but States may regulate abortion procedures in ways rationally related to a legitimate state interest" as long as they don't pose an "undue burden" on the right to abortion.[69]

What counted as an undue burden? Of the restrictions mentioned here, only the spousal notification requirement was found to be an undue burden. *Casey* imposed a clear state interest in pregnancy from conception onward. The court was not only articulating an interest in whether a fetus is born or aborted but was also setting a legal precedent for state concern over the pregnant or potentially pregnant person's behaviors throughout pregnancy. By describing the fertilized egg, embryo, or fetus as a potential life, the *Casey* opinion gives the state more flexibility to pursue fetal protection. Whereas the potentially pregnant woman in *Muller* and *West Coast Hotel* was regarded as a sole entity, the pregnant woman in *Roe* and *Casey* is explicitly positioned as a dual entity, a woman *and* a fertilized egg, embryo, or fetus. As such, it could be found that the regulation of the pregnant person's behaviors and activities, beyond abortion, are within the state's interest in protecting the fetus.

In June 2022 the US Supreme Court gave its opinion in *Dobbs v. Jackson Women's Health Organization.* After almost fifty years of legal precedent defining abortion as a constitutional right, this is no longer the case today. States are free to regulate abortion in any and every way, including banning it outright. The *Dobbs* court argued that, as abortion is not part of the history and tradition of the United States (a patently false statement) and as privacy does not exist explicitly in the constitution and as *some* people believe that abortion is the taking of a human life, that the court got it wrong in *Roe.*

People with the capacity for pregnancy have consistently been defined as uniquely in need of regulation. Maternal protection that defined women as ignorant, incapable of self-advocacy, and biologically vulnerable eventually shifted in favor of fetal protection that defined people with the capacity for pregnancy as threatening—potential perpetrators of harm to their "unborn children." Even when framed as a form of state benevolence, by defining pregnant people as unique and exceptional, these laws, policies, and attitudes have opened the door for abuse of, and discrimination against, pregnant people.[70] Though protectionist law has shifted over time in response to expanded women's rights in some areas, like employment, the legal road for depriving pregnant people of rights in other areas was already paved. People with the capacity for pregnancy enjoyed forty-nine years of a limited right to bodily autonomy. However, the protectionist through line remained, and the growing image of the fertilized eggs embryos, and fetuses as living, sole entities would motivate new kinds of control over pregnant bodies.

3 Bad Breeders

Carrie Buck, a seventeen-year-old white girl from Charlottesville, Virginia, was the first candidate for forced sterilization under the 1924 Virginia Sterilization Law.[1] Raised by her mother, Emma, Carrie grew up poor. Emma was left to support her family alone after Carrie's father died. Emma had two other children, both by different men she was not married to. Emma may have turned to sex work to support herself and her family.[2] At around age forty-eight, in 1920, Emma was committed to the Virginia State Colony for Epileptics and Feeble Minded, near Lynchburg, for her supposed "imbecility," a euphemism for sexual immorality.[3] Eugenicists had decided that Emma's sexual immorality made her unfit to reproduce.

Carrie, still a child, was left without a guardian, and so she was placed in the care of the Dobbs family, who removed her from school in the sixth grade so she could do chores around the house.[4] When she was seventeen, the nephew of her foster parents, Clarence Garland, raped her, and she became pregnant. Her foster parents arranged for her involuntary commitment to the Virginia State Colony for Epileptics and Feeble Minded in late January 1924 to hide her pregnancy and to protect the family from the shame of having a rapist nephew and from the shame of their unmarried ward having become pregnant.[5]

Sexual deviance, including "homosexuality" and, in women, "carnality," was a major concern for eugenicists, who believed that these traits would be inherited by the next generation. "'Feebleminded" women were known to be "notoriously immoral." The diagnosis could be applied for things as overt as performing sex work, running a brothel, being pregnant but not married, or having a sexually transmitted infection. It could also be incredibly vague. Legal historian Paul Lombardo writes that evidence might have included demonstrating a "fondness for men," spending time in a "sporting house," or having a promiscuous reputation. Some sterilization victims were considered "over-sexed," "man crazy," or nymphomaniacs. One teenage girl was sterilized because, at the orphanage where she lived, she "stole opportunities of talking to the little boys" and sometimes passed notes to them. A married woman went under the knife because she was said to suffer from "wanderlust," told "coarse stories," and showed signs of "homosexuality."[6]

Anthropologist Francis Galton coined the term "eugenics" in 1883. Derived from the Greek *eugenes,* it literally means "well born."[7] An English scientist and a cousin of Charles Darwin, Galton believed that humans could be selectively bred to improve the species, asserting, "What Nature does blindly, slowly, and ruthlessly, man may do providently, quickly, and kindly."[8] Social traits like criminality, laziness, and promiscuity were considered to be inherited, and thus crime, unemployment, and sexual impropriety could be eliminated from the population through selective breeding. Galton also believed in a hierarchy of genetic racial types, which of course placed Anglo-Saxons at the top of "Mongolians, Jews, Negroes, Gipsies, and American Indians," each with its own physical features and ascribed social characteristics. Legal historian Dorothy Roberts notes, "Whites invented the hereditary trait of race and endowed it with the concept of racial superiority and inferiority to resolve the contradiction between slavery and liberty. . . . Because race was defined as an inheritable trait, preserving racial distinctions required policing reproduction. Reproductive politics in America inevitably involves racial politics."[9] Galton's positive eugenics sought to improve the race by facilitating increased reproduction of the "best stock," as opposed to negative eugenics, which sought to reduce or eliminate reproduction of the socially defined worst. Galton believed that charity was wasteful and counterproductive, arguing that it only perpetuated the spread of negative traits. He wrote, "the time may come when such persons [the poor] would be considered enemies to the state, and to have forfeited all claims to kindness." Better to let the natural order take over and, in the words of Charles Dickens's Ebenezer Scrooge, "decrease the surplus population."[10]

The U.S. eugenics movement began in the late 1800s.[11] Eugenic policies in the United States during this period were three-pronged: antimiscegenation (anti–race mixing), anti-immigration, and purposeful breeding to improve the gene pool.[12] Fear of the Anglo race being outbred by new populations of immigrants and "unfit" white people was a cause of deep concern at the time. The white birth rate had fallen to about 3.5 children per couple by 1900—not enough to compete with the "others."[13] In 1905 President Theodore Roosevelt, an ardent eugenicist, professed his belief in "race suicide" and called on Anglo-American women to give birth to at least four children: "enough so the race shall increase and not decrease." But encouraging the reproduction of the "most fit" wouldn't be enough. There were some degenerate elements at the fringes of whiteness that threatened the purity of the whole race—a *domestic* threat. Something needed to be done about them. In 1903 one Michigan legislator proposed that the state should kill off the unfit to prevent their spread.[14] Forced sterilization was supposed to provide a less extreme solution.

Eugenicists believed that once made incapable of reproducing, these "unfit" individuals would no longer pose a substantial threat to society, be more capable of self-dependence, and thus would not need to be institutionalized. The concept was thought by many to be progressive: future generations would remain unburdened by poverty, crime, and other social ills. A utopia could become a reality with careful breeding. Political scientist James Morone writes, "Eugenics offered a confident, scientific way to protect the nation from criminals, prostitutes, and low races" because "prostitutes, paupers, thieves, murderers, alcoholics and bootleggers could all be identified in advance—defective people sprang from defective parents."[15] Law professor Khiara Bridges notes that, in addition to people who were seen as criminal, early eugenic targets included people thought to have "mental illness, feebleminded-ness, physical disabilities, laziness, [and] promiscuity" all residing in their genes.[16]

Alcohol use was tied to eugenic thought in the United States, especially alcohol use by people with the capacity for pregnancy. For some time the tendency to drink had been seen as an inherited quality, though the causal mechanism of alcoholism in the genes wouldn't be specified until the late 1800s. Alcohol use, it was thought, would produce offspring who had "not just a tendency to drink but a package of constitutional weaknesses." In the late 1800s, alcohol was identified as a "germ poison" that damaged the genes of those who drank it. Soon after, alcohol use by white women became defined as "race poison." Drinking among white people with the capacity for pregnancy was thought to weaken their offspring—and this at a time when concern about the supposedly superior white race being outbred by emancipated Black people and immigrants was at a peak.[17] White women who drank represented the degradation of the white race.

This era also saw a shift in who was seen as primarily responsible for birth outcomes. In the mid-1800s, both men and women were thought to contribute to the quality of the offspring. But by the turn of the century, the focus was primarily on women. People with the capacity for pregnancy were seen as responsible for the quality of individual offspring and for the survival of the white race and nation. As sociologist Elizabeth Armstrong writes, "Female responsibility extended beyond children and family to the notion of race. Women were 'mothers of the land.'"[18] Though both men and women were sterilized, the majority of forced sterilization victims were women. From 1928 to 1932, 67 percent of sterilizations that took place in institutions were performed on women.[19] Bridges writes, "Eugenicists tended to believe that although both men and women could possess inheritable defective genes, women posed the bigger threat of disseminating those genes to the future generation."[20] A pregnant woman who drank was not only ruining her own genes. It was thought that she was soaking the fetus in alcohol. Long before fetal alcohol syndrome would first be diagnosed in 1973, there was some understanding that drinking during pregnancy may have contributed to infant death—white babies that the race couldn't afford to lose.[21]

The first compulsory sterilization law in the United States was passed in Indiana in 1907.[22] In 1910 Charles Davenport, a University of Chicago biology professor, founded the Eugenics Record Office in Cold Spring Harbor, New York.[23] This would become the "semiofficial arm and repository of data" for the eugenics movement in the United States.[24] Family studies, published as small books with names such as *The Jukes* and *The*

Kallikak Family, became a defining feature of eugenic pseudoscience. They included photographs, family pedigree charts, and narratives showing a white family's descent into genetic ruin.

The Kallikak Family, written by psychologist Henry H. Goddard, followed generations of one man's children with two different women—one, his wife, the other a "feebleminded tavern wench." All seven of the children Kallikak had with his wife were "normal." The other family turned out differently. Kallikak and the barmaid had a son, Martin Jr., and though he *passed* as "normal," he carried the "feebleminded gene." Martin Jr. married a "normal" woman named Rhoda, and they had ten children together. Five of their offspring were labeled "feebleminded." Two of the children died as infants and were not yet labeled, though infant death could also be interpreted as a sign of constitutional weakness. A son was noted to be an alcoholic, a daughter was labeled as sexually immoral, and another daughter, identified as "Old Moll," was labeled as both sexually immoral and an alcoholic. In three generations the introduction of feebleminded genes had poisoned the family. Lombardo writes, "that single alcohol drenched dalliance [with the "tavern wench"] led to "hundreds of the lowest types of human beings."[25]

Dr. Albert Priddy became the superintendent of the Virginia State Colony for Epileptics and Feeble Minded in 1910. Priddy was an enthusiastic eugenicist and considered the "'feebleminded' a 'blight on mankind.'" Lombardo writes, "Priddy warned that the rapid growth of the feebleminded would only continue 'unless some radical measures are adopted.'" As superintendent of the Virginia Colony, Priddy would go on to promote unofficial sterilization policies.[26]

The ideology of the eugenics movement led to unofficial sterilization policies. Consider the story of the Mallory family. Willie and George Mallory had nine children. The family was known to the local government in Richmond, Virginia. Willie had been held at a mental hospital for five months with postpartum depression. Her father had been married four times, and her mother and children were labeled "feeble minded." George was reported to the police when he was drunk at least once. The family fell on hard times after a devastating house fire in 1916. They became homeless and were forced to stay at other people's homes and beg on the streets. Willie had been known to "street walk" or do street-based survival sex work. Eventually, the family got back on their feet. George found a job in a neighboring town at a sawmill, and the family once again had a home to live in. Every other week George traveled back home to visit his family. One night in 1916, when George was away at work, a stranger came to the Mallory house seeking to rent a room. This stranger may have been working undercover, because after he came inside, so did the police. Willie was accused of running a brothel.[27]

She and two of her daughters, fifteen-year-old Jessie and thirteen-year-old Nannie, were arrested and placed at the State Colony for Epileptics and Feeble Minded. Willie and Jessie were sterilized, though there was no law providing for compulsory sterilization in Virginia at the time. It took weeks for George Mallory to find out where his family had gone, and once he did, he threatened to sue. Willie and Jessie were released, but they continued to hold Nannie at the State Colony. George followed up his threat of a lawsuit with a letter addressed to the superintendent of the State Colony, Albert Priddy. George wrote, "Just to think my wife is 43 years old and to be treated in that way, you ought to be a shamed of your selft of opreateding on her at that age Just stop and think of how she have been treated. . . . I am a humanbeen as well as you are I am tired of bein treated this way for nothing I want my child." George lost his lawsuit, but Priddy was shaken.[28] He didn't want any more lawsuits for his unofficial policy. He wanted a law.

By 1913 eleven more states adopted involuntary sterilization laws, and twenty-four states banned the marriage of people considered genetically defective. Harry Laughlin, the superintendent of the Eugenics Record Office, lobbied for eugenic policies and bans on southern and eastern European immigrants. In 1914 he compiled a report outlining his plan to sterilize fifteen million people over two generations.[29] To accomplish this goal, in 1922 Laughlin wrote a piece of model legislation calling for the sterilization of the "socially inadequate."[30]

For eugenic laws, 1924 was a big year. The federal government passed the Immigration Act of 1924, which imposed national-origin quotas for southern and eastern European immigrants to the United States and prevented immigration from Asia. In that same year, Virginia adopted the Racial Integrity Act, which banned marriage of white people to nonwhite people. Most eugenic laws passed in the United States, including the law eventually adopted in Virginia in 1924, were derived from Laughlin's legal model.[31] The text of the Virginia sterilization law is as follows:

> *Whereas* both the health of the individual patient and the welfare of society may be promoted in certain cases by the sterilization of mental defectives under careful safeguard and by competent and conscientious authority, and
>
> *Whereas* such sterilization may be effected in males by the operation of vasectomy and in females by the operation of salpingectomy, both of which said operations may be performed without serious pain or substantial danger to the life of the patient and
>
> *Whereas,* the Commonwealth has in custodial care and is supporting in various state institutions many defective persons who if now discharged or paroled would likely become by the propagation of their kind a menace to society but who if incapable of procreating might properly and safely be discharged or paroled and become self-supporting with benefit both to themselves and to society, and
>
> *Whereas,* human experience has demonstrated that heredity plays an important part in the transmission of sanity, idiocy, imbecility, epilepsy and crime.

The law permitted the superintendents at five Virginia hospitals to order the sterilization of patients if they thought doing so "shall be for the best interests of the patients and of society." The law lists "hereditary forms of insanity that are recurrent, idiocy, imbecility, feeble-mindedness or epilepsy" as conditions justifying sterilization. The law further states that the superintendent must meet with a board of directors to argue in favor of the sterilization. The "inmate" patient is required to be notified of this petition at least thirty days before the hearing with the board.[32]

Carrie gave birth to her daughter Vivian at the State Colony in March, 1924, just a few months after the law was passed.[33] Vivian was removed from her care and placed with the Dobbs family, where Carrie had grown up and where she had been raped.[34] Carrie never saw her daughter again.[35] When Vivian was six months old, a social worker determined that Vivian was "not quite a normal baby" but was unable to put her finger on anything specific and acknowledged that she could have been prejudiced by knowing about Vivian's mother, Carrie. Based on this vague determination, the social worker recommended that Carrie be sterilized. Vivian being "not quite normal" meant that the state now had constructed evidence of three generations of the socially, and thus biologically, unfit.[36] Carrie was eligible for sterilization. Procedures at this time typically involved the removal of the fallopian tubes (salpingectomy) or the vas deferens (vasectomy). Both were considered irreversible at the time.

Carrie did not pursue legal action to prevent her sterilization. Rather, she was used by the eugenics movement to bring a test case before the Supreme Court.[37] Carrie was assigned a lawyer, Irving Whitehead, for the legal proceedings, but Whitehead was not truly her advocate. A supporter of eugenic sterilization, Whitehead was friends both with Priddy, the superintendent of the colony, and with the author of the eugenic law itself, Harry Laughlin.[38] As Bridges writes, "These powerful men selected Carrie to be the plaintiff in this test case. They thought that she was ideal—with her alleged family history of feeblemindedness, her unwed motherhood, and her youth, which virtually guaranteed that she would give birth to several more illegitimate, feebleminded children."[39] Whitehead put forward no argument for Carrie—no facts, no witnesses, no evidence.[40]

In 1927 the "height of respectability [for the] campaign for forced eugenic sterilization," Carrie's case went to the US Supreme Court in *Buck v. Bell*.[41] The eight-to-one decision, written by Justice Oliver Wendell Holmes, argued that the right to freedom from bodily intrusion does not outweigh the state's compelling interest in who gives birth, under what conditions, and the quality of the offspring. The court found that the Virginia sterilization law was a constitutional exercise of state power. Biologist and historian Stephen Jay Gould asserts that Justice Holmes "gave eugenic theory the imprimatur of constitutional law in his famous declaration."[42]

The court argued that individuals thought to be socially, mentally, or physically inadequate posed a threat to the well-being and strength of the nation. The court also asserted that the unfettered reproduction of these undesirables would drain the state coffers, foreshadowing the language it would use ten years later to justify a minimum wage for women in the *West Coast Hotel Co. v. Parrish* case. Rather than allow these individuals to breed new generations of inadequate children and live out their lives in costly state-funded institutions, the court found in favor of proactively, and cost effectively, sterilizing those deemed unfit. Holmes wrote, "It would be strange if [the state] could not call upon those who already sap the strength of the State for these lesser sacrifices, not often felt to be such by those concerned, in order to prevent our being swamped with incompetence. It is better for all the world if, instead of waiting to execute degenerate offspring for crime or to let them starve for their imbecility, society can prevent those who are manifestly unfit from continuing their kind. . . . Three generations of imbeciles are enough." By invoking the constitutionality of the war draft and mandatory vaccination and warning of rising tide of "incompetence," Holmes described the existence of the genetically and socially unfit as a national security crisis. The court's opinion was influential. According to Roberts, in the years after *Buck v. Bell*, thirty states had compulsory sterilization laws. There was also a shift in the primary targets of the sterilization policies, from both men *and* women to women alone.[43]

Carrie was sterilized.[44] Her half sister, Doris, was also sterilized when she was hospitalized for appendicitis, though she was not informed of the sterilization at the time. She eventually got married, but she and her husband were never able to have children and understood why only when she was an old woman and researchers came knocking. In 1980 Dr. K. Ray Nelson, director of the Lynchburg Hospital, formerly the Virginia Colony, discovered that more than four thousand sterilizations had been performed at the institution, the last as late as 1972. He found Carrie living near Charlottesville, along with her half sister, Doris, who was devastated when she learned why she had never been able to have children.[45]

Certain populations of poor white people in the United States had long been a source of social, political, and economic anxiety.[46] Though whiteness is often viewed as a uniform racial category or even a raceless neutral category, in reality whiteness is a fluid racial construct. Carving out certain populations of "degenerate" whites as racially distinct allowed for even more racial hierarchy. Sociologist Matt Wray describes the evolution of deviant whiteness in the United States from the early colonial "cracker," a dangerous, wilderness-dwelling trickster, to the jaundiced, lazy, hookworm-ridden "clay-eater" to the bad breeders targeted for eugenic sterilization in the 1920s and 1930s.[47] Contemporary labels now include "hillbilly" and "white trash" for those primarily located in Appalachia. Anthropologist John Hartigan writes about the white trash identity, which relies on the production and maintenance of class and gender boundaries and is typically defined by backwardness, perversion, and polluted, malformed bodies.

Hartigan asserts that "white trash" invokes biological contamination of the body and mind, conjuring images of backwardness, monstrousness, violence, laziness, infestation, decay, deformity, incest, and ignorance.[48] The supposed sexual immorality of degenerate whites figures into their demonization. They are said to "violat[e] every sexual norm, from fathers cohabitating with daughters, to husbands selling wives, to mothers conniving illicit liaisons for daughters."[49] Hartigan's analysis of Lothrop Stoddard, an influential twentieth-century eugenicist, shows the connection between the sterilization of poor whites and of other racial groups. Initially concerned with the reproduction of nonwhites, Stoddard eventually came to focus on degeneracy within the white race: white trash.[50]

When taken into consideration alongside social and political hostility to nonwhites—Indigenous people, specific populations of immigrants, and emancipated Black people—the construction of white trash serves to distance the supposedly supreme race from *degenerate* whites. White trash is a distinct kind of subwhiteness that imperils any notion of white supremacy. What's more, it was said that white trash socialize with Black and Native American people, producing mixed-race children. Eugenics had transformed degenerate whites from "simply freaks of nature on the fringe of society" to "congenitally delinquent, a withered branch on the American family tree, . . . a 'fungal growth.'" One eugenicist described them as "of the 'homo genus without the sapien.'"[51] This is what Harry Laughlin meant at Carrie Buck's trial when he testified (though he had never actually met Carrie) that she and her family members were part of the "shiftless, ignorant, and worthless class of anti-social whites of the South."[52] As I explore in chapter 6, the image of degenerate whites and their threatening reproduction would be invoked again in the 2000s, when methamphetamine use during pregnancy was described as an "epidemic."

This image of white degeneracy and moral failure continues to influence culture, law, and politics. For example, consider J. D. Vance's memoir, *Hillbilly Elegy*, a *New York Times* bestseller that was also made into a film. The story relies on white trash stereotypes and "bootstraps" ideology to position Vance himself as different from and better than his dysfunctional Appalachian family. He focuses on and decontextualizes promiscuity and child sexual abuse, substance use disorder, and criminal behavior. As filmmaker and critic Richard Knox Robinson writes, "In place of feeblemindedness there is a lack of 'personal responsibility.'"[53] Instead of bad genes, there are "cultural deficiencies."[54] The film opens with a message that "Vance's memoir 'reflects on three generations of family history and his own future,'" echoing the language about three generations from the *Buck v. Bell* decision.[55] Now a Republican senator, Vance espouses Far Right views that bury the structural causes of Appalachian poverty—exploitation by coal corporations, deindustrialization, and neglect that has led some scholars to refer to Appalachia as an internal colony.[56]

I grew up in Virginia, on the fringes of Appalachia, but didn't think critically about the scapegoating of the southern rural poor as white trash until I was attending graduate school in New Jersey. I immediately felt the socioeconomic disparities between my fellow students and myself—my family had struggled financially since I was a small child. Being surrounded by people who had seemingly always had what they needed made me feel like an impostor. I noticed a tendency, especially among white upper-middle-class liberals, to locate every instance of white immorality in white trash and *only* in white trash—people who lived far away and were nothing like them. Apparently racism didn't exist in New York or New Jersey. This was an effort to distance themselves from the reality of their own white privilege and internalized racism and to recuse themselves from the responsibility of fighting the racism where *they* lived. It made me feel defensive about the place where I grew up and the people who lived there. It made me wonder what my PhD cohort thought about me, and it made me think about the ways I had been taught, as a white woman from that region but whose parents were from Washington, DC, to distance myself from white trash images. We may have been poor and white, but we weren't poor white trash.

. . . . .

The US Supreme Court would address the constitutionality of forced sterilization again in 1942, in *Skinner v. Oklahoma*. In this case the court was asked to determine the constitutionality of an Oklahoma law allowing for the sterilization of incarcerated people. Oklahoma's Criminal Sterilization Act of 1935 was essentially a "three strikes and you're out" legal scheme for fertility, applying only to crimes "amounting to felonies involving moral turpitude." Jack Skinner had been convicted three times—once for stealing chickens and twice for armed robbery. Upon a fourth conviction, Skinner was sentenced to be sterilized. The court found that the Oklahoma sterilization law violated the Fourteenth Amendment's Equal Protection Clause. Because the law focused only on certain *kinds* of criminal violations, it was unconstitutional. One might interpret the *Skinner* case as a reversal of *Buck v. Bell,* but this is incorrect. Under the court's ruling in *Skinner,* the sterilization law would have been constitutional if it had ordered sterilization for triple offenders of *all* felonies. The sterilizations continued. Through the 1950s, around twenty thousand people were sterilized in California institutions alone.[57]

The eugenics movement in the United States was celebrated and adopted by political leaders in Nazi Germany and vice versa. Alexandra Minna Stern, a professor of English and history, writes, "Laughlin was fond of extolling Nazi Germany and corresponded with leading German eugenicists until his death in 1943.[58] One eugenic institution superintendent commented, with admiration and envy, that "the Germans are beating us at our own game."[59] The German eugenics program included many of the same laws and regulations of the US eugenics program and eventually culminated in the systematic murder of millions politically determined social undesirables, predominantly Jewish people but also Slavic peoples, communists, socialists, Jehovah's Witnesses, and queer people.

While eugenics largely fell out of favor after World War II, the idea that some people were better suited for reproduction than others continued to be expressed and practiced in law and policy throughout the United States through at *least* the 1970s. Stern writes, "From the 1920s to the 1970s the rationale for sterilization had gradually but never entirely shifted from one based on the transmission of faulty genes down to the family line to one centered more and more on the purported negative consequences of unfit parenthood, dysfunctional families, and overpopulation.... [Sterilization] would save the state money, impede irresponsible parents from having more children, and boost the well-being of society."[60] By the 1960s the targeted population shifted away from degenerate whites and focused on poor Black women in the South and Northeast and Chicanas in the West. Most sterilizations took place at public institutions, which had admitted only white people prior to the civil rights movement. Roberts writes, “The demise of Jim Crow had ironically opened the doors of state institutions to Blacks, who took the place of poor whites as the main target of the eugenicist’s scalpel.” The forced sterilization of Black women in the South was so common that hysterectomies were known as “Mississippi appendectomies.” Sterilizations could be done under existing eugenic laws but more frequently were done at the discretion of individual obstetricians who thought Black women weren’t intelligent enough to use birth control. Some obstetricians thought that Black women on public assistance didn’t deserve to have children and resented that their tax money was being “wasted” on supporting these families.[61]

The mythical figure of the “welfare queen” shaped public support for cutting welfare benefits and cutting fallopian tubes. The welfare queen is understood to be a Black single mother in the inner city. She abuses the welfare system, giving birth to more and more children so that the government will give her more money, which she inevitably does not spend on the children. Instead, she uses this financial support to buy drugs, jewelry, and luxury cars. People of color had been largely excluded from New Deal programs of support for mothers and children. After Black mothers were made eligible to receive welfare benefits, these benefits became stigmatized, and public opinion shifted away from welfare benefits for poor mothers and children.[62] Political theorist Ange-Marie Hancock demonstrates that the image of the welfare queen as irresponsible, lazy, and promiscuous was invoked politically in efforts to cut welfare support.[63]

The sterilization of the Relf sisters may be the most well-known example of sterilization abuse of Black women and girls in the United States. Nurses from the Montgomery Community Action Agency gave Minnie and Mary Relf, fourteen and twelve years old, respectively, injections of Depo-Provera, at that time an experimental, long-acting contraceptive. Their mother had signed a consent form for the injections, but she was unable to read and didn’t understand the form. Then, after the government stopped the use of Depo-Provera because of links with cancer in lab animals, Minnie and Mary were sterilized. In 1973 the Relfs sued, with the help of the Southern Poverty Law Center. Their lawsuit revealed that between 100,000 and 150,000 poor women and girls had been sterilized under federally funded programs. Almost half of them were Black.[64]

As Stern notes, the sterilization of Mexican-origin women was used to solve the so-called Mexican problem of irresponsible immigrant breeding. Stern cites notable eugenic scientist Charles M. Goethe: "It is this high birthrate that makes the Mexican peon immigration such a menace. Peons multiply like rabbits."[65] Hundreds of working-class migrant women were sterilized at Los Angeles County General Hospital in the 1960s and 1970s.[66]

Between 20 and 50 percent of women of childbearing age in some Native American communities were sterilized without their consent—a genocidal attempt to eradicate entire nations and cultures.[67] In New York City, the majority of women sterilized in the late 1960s and early 1970s were Puerto Rican.[68] In total almost seventy thousand people were sterilized under the eugenic laws.[69] Though the last eugenic sterilization law was repealed in 2003 in South Carolina, forced sterilization still happens in the United States. Writer and reproductive justice advocate Rachel Roth and attorney Sara Ainsworth discuss sterilizations of more than one hundred women incarcerated in California between 2006 and 2010.[70] In 2020 a whistleblower nurse alerted the public to the unusually high rates of hysterectomies, or nonconsensual sterilizations, being performed on women in immigrant detention centers.[71]

For some learning that Carrie was never actually the "feebleminded," sexually immoral girl that the eugenicists claimed may feel like a twist of the knife. Carrie was taken from her mother, raped, and institutionalized. She had her daughter taken from her and was sterilized against her will—and all on the basis of lies about her morality and intellect.[72] It is, indeed, deeply disturbing that these baseless claims were used by doctors, social workers, lawyers, and judges to justify the eugenic sterilization of Carrie and many thousands of others. However, this perspective also reveals lingering eugenic thoughts about sex and about disabled people, implying that her sterilization would have been less bad if Carrie had been pregnant from consensual sex or if she had been disabled. Many of the people targeted for eugenic sterilization were targeted because they were considered sexually deviant or because they were disabled. Harry Laughlin's model sterilization law called for the sterilization of the "feebleminded" (including intellectually disabled people), the "insane" (which at the time included queer people), the "epileptic," "the diseased" (including people with sexually transmitted infections), "the blind," "the deaf," and "the deformed."[73]

The forced sterilization of disabled people is still permitted in certain circumstances.[74] Today, thirty-one states and Washington, DC, have laws explicitly permitting forced sterilization for disabled people, and forced sterilization laws were most recently passed in 2019 in Iowa and Nevada. In states without explicit laws, guardians and conservators are regularly allowed to make all health-care decisions decision for the people under guardianship, including sterilization. Disabled people of color with the capacity for pregnancy, in particular, are targeted for sterilization.[75]

Notions of sexual immorality and disability were invoked again in efforts to criminalize substance use during pregnancy: hordes of broken, expensive children with irresponsible, promiscuous mothers. In some cases defendants were ordered to use birth control or be sterilized as a condition of their plea bargain or bond or after threats by health-care personnel.[76] For example, one woman who gave birth at the Medical University of South Carolina Hospital explained, "Previously I had signed papers saying that I would have my tubes tied ... because [MUSC] wanted me to." A nurse midwife explained to her that, though she had signed the papers, she could change her mind and not go through with the sterilization. The woman continued, "This all happened so quickly. It was the very next morning after I had the baby was the first time I heard about [Norplant]." Norplant, an implanted birth control device, was supposed to be a compromise, but the woman had hepatitis, which was contraindicated for Norplant. She told the hospital that she couldn't have the Norplant, and they responded that she couldn't leave the hospital until she had it done. She would later experience health problems from the device and had to make her own arrangements to have it removed.[77]

Another woman, Sandra Simon, described in a deposition how she came to have a tubal ligation:

ATTORNEY. You described in your testimony that—that you had a tubal ligation?

SIMON. Yes.

ATTORNEY. What was that for?

SIMON. Okay. After I was—when I was using and stuff they wanted me to have a tubal ligation and I like, you know, they gave me the

> consent form and it was put to me like, you know, whether I signed or not, you know, it was going to be done.... Okay, they—since I used drugs and stuff they felt that I should have my tubes tied so I won't have any more children. And—and, you know, I—I was sort of like undecided but since it was like I didn't have any rights, you know, I went on and signed, you know, because I was told whether I agreed or signed or not it was going to be done anyway.[78]

Some prosecutors involved in these cases expressed the idea that their pregnant or postpartum defendants shouldn't have been pregnant to begin with. The Alabama district attorney for Houston and Henry Counties, Doug Velaska, said, "It's a real preventable crime in that when these individuals are hooked on drugs there's ways to prevent themselves from getting pregnant.... The bottom line is if they have a drug problem they should get treatment before they get pregnant."[79] The Alabama district attorney for Mobile County, Ashley Rich, shared this sentiment, telling reporters, "What the public needs to understand and what young women who are thinking about becoming pregnant need to understand, is that when you make the decision to conceive, you are responsible for that child from the minute it's born." These statements imply that people are choosing both to get hooked on drugs and to get pregnant, as though they are able to manifest pregnancies on their own, at their will. Trey Gowdy, the then solicitor for Spartanburg and Cherokee Counties in South Carolina, proposed "streamlining the process for drug-dependent mothers to get birth control."[80]

People with the capacity for pregnancy who use drugs face a multitude of challenges in preventing pregnancy. Sociologists Sheigla Murphy and Marsha Rosenbaum's study of pregnant women who use drugs explored contraceptive practices and unintended pregnancy among drug users. Their study of pregnancy and drugs began in 1991, when the most politically salient drugs were heroin and crack cocaine. The participants in their study struggled to manage contraception. They write, "For the majority of the women in this study, successful family planning was not a feasible option." Condom use is an especially important harm-reduction strategy for people who inject drugs and for people who do sex work, as condoms can prevent both pregnancy and sexually transmitted infections.

Additionally, as condoms can be acquired at the store for a relatively low cost without doctor visits, prescriptions, or health-care provider interventions and maintenance, like the insertion and removal of contraceptive implants, they are a more accessible, less coercive contraceptive option. However, women who financed their substance use with sex work "feared that insisting on a condom might cause them to lose a customer."[81]

Even in committed relationships, negotiating condom use could be problematic. They write, "Asking for condom use could be interpreted by the partner as evidence of her infidelity or evidence that she suspected her male partner of infidelity. In volatile relationships, women worried that even discussing condom use would trigger violent responses." They also found that, because of the impact of extended substance use, many of the study participants had stopped menstruating. As such, many study participants thought that they were unable to get pregnant. In the event that a pregnancy did occur, they couldn't rely on a missed period to alert them. Many of the women "attributed morning sickness to withdrawal." By the time they realized they were pregnant, "many women felt they were too far along to obtain an abortion." Most of the women in their study decided to give birth.[82] Though Murphy and Rosenbaum's study was published over three decades ago, many of the issues that they identified are still pertinent today.

Expanding access to birth control is important and needed. A recent study charted so-called contraceptive deserts, which they defined as counties that lack reasonable access to the full range of contraceptive methods. As of November 2022, in Alabama 311,530 low-income women lived in contraceptive deserts, and 14,140 women lived in counties that had no health center providing the full range of contraceptive methods. Over 400,000 low-income women in Tennessee lived in contraceptive deserts. In South Carolina 310,000 low-income women lived in contraceptive deserts, and 15.8 percent of women of contraceptive age lacked health insurance coverage, compared to 11.7 percent nationwide.[83]

Despite this need, when targeting the reproduction of specific marginalized and demonized populations, the contraceptive push is also troublingly similar to earlier eugenic efforts. "High risk" populations are more likely to be encouraged or pressured to use long-acting reversable contraceptives (LARCs) like IUDs and hormone rod implants, based on the belief that they are unable to manage other contraceptive methods like the pill. LARCs require a health-care provider's prescription and insertion. They also require removal by a health-care provider. LARCs may be the preferred contraceptive method for some people, but this should be something they are able to choose freely. Anu Manchikanti Gomez, Liza Fuentes, and Amy Allina write, "The notion that membership in high-risk populations may lead the least privileged women to receive contraceptive counseling that steers them toward a particular method is worrisome given the long-standing devaluation of the fertility and childbearing of young women, low-income women and women of color in the United States, and the perception that these women have too many children."[84]

Notably, the three states in my study have rates of unintended pregnancy that are higher than the national average. Tennessee currently has the highest rate of unintended pregnancy in the United States, at 41 percent.[85] Neither Alabama or Tennessee have mandated statewide sex education in public schools, and South Carolina's state curriculum emphasizes abstinence.[86] Comprehensive sex education reduces rates of teen pregnancy, which I mention not to single out pregnant teenagers but because in the United States teen pregnancy is usually unintended.[87] In the United States, sex education is politically contentious. In her interview-based research, Kristin Luker found that political debates over sex education were "about how men and women relate to each other in all the realms of their lives," essentially in a battle between sexual conservatism and sexual liberalism.[88] In the 2023 legislative session, in addition to dramatic bans on the education of nonheterosexual orientation and noncisgender identities, the State of Florida passed a law that restricts instruction on sexual health to students in sixth through twelfth grade.[89] This includes a ban on instruction about menstruation—especially troubling given that the average age of menarche (or first menstrual period) is around eleven years old.[90] Because of this law, some children will start their first period and will not understand what is happening. Beyond offering students an education in harm-reduction strategies like sexually transmitted infection and pregnancy prevention, quality sex education gives people tools for cultivating healthy relationships and understanding their own bodies, sexualities, sexual orientations, and genders. Children in states that ban comprehensive sex education are being robbed of those tools in an effort to promote heterosexual "family values," personal responsibility, and sexual abstinence until marriage. This leaves them incredibly vulnerable.

Perhaps images of irresponsible, uncaring, and even villainous drug-using pregnant women have been so enduring because they tap into US myths about appropriate femininity, self-control, nation, and the threatening racialized "other." As Morone writes, "Eugenicists wrapped those old original sins [bigotry and oppression of a scapegoated other] in the cloak of science. But they did not tinker with the story line. The defective other—the American sinner—could be identified and controlled."[91] Eugenics promised to solve complex social issues like poverty with individualized solutions while maintaining the hierarchical social order. Once again imposing on the bodies of people with the capacity for pregnancy, this time with institutionalization and forced sterilization, US eugenics lays out the boundaries of citizenship and propriety. Those who fail to align themselves within those boundaries are defined as a threat and demand state intervention. Networks of professionals in social work, medicine, and law enforcement establish a program of surveillance and control to enforce these boundaries, sometimes with sterilization, but also by imposing family caps for welfare recipients (which limit the provision of additional state financial support despite the birth of additional children); by encouraging certain populations, like poor people and Black women, to use long-acting reversable contraceptives over other forms of contraception; and by arresting and incarcerating many millions of people who are disproportionately nonwhite and impoverished, as part of the so-called war on drugs.

4 "The Dead Babies May Be the Lucky Ones"

In 1971 President Richard Nixon declared a war on drugs. Historian Donna Murch explains, "The declaration of war mandated increased resources to fight the 'drug crisis' while also initiating a conflict without end."[1] Though he made some limited federal-level policy changes, this "war" wouldn't get started in earnest until the 1980s, during the Reagan administration. Jamie Fellner, senior counsel for the US Program of Human Rights Watch, writes, "Spearheaded by drug policy initiatives that significantly increased federal penalties for drug offenses and markedly increased federal funds for state anti-drug efforts, the drug war reflected the popularity of 'tough on crime' policies emphasizing harsh punishments as the key to curbing drugs and restoring law and order in America."[2]

Violence was increasing in the United States. The murder rate more than doubled from 1957 to 1980, from 4.0 homicides per 100,000 people to 9.9 per 100,000.[3] The violence was concentrated in large cities and dramatically disproportionately impacted the Black community.[4] Political science professor Lisa Miller calculated the risk of homicide over a lifespan based on annual homicide rates, in a study of the relationship between crime, crime policy, and mass incarceration. In the United States, the individual risk of homicide increased from the 1960 rate of 1 in 261 to 1 in

131 in 1980. The risk becomes even more dramatic when broken down demographically by race and sex. In 1960 the Black male lifetime risk of homicide was 1 in 36. This rose to 1 in 20 in 1980, dramatically higher than any other demographic group (for example, in 1980 the risk for white females was 1 in 417). Miller suggests that these concentrations of alarmingly high homicide rates can be interpreted as a failure of the state to remedy poverty and racial oppression.[5]

Drug use rates in the United States had actually been declining since the early 1980s.[6] However, Black urban communities were being devastated by crack cocaine. The CIA played a part in the emergence of the crack crisis. As Michelle Alexander writes, "The CIA admitted in 1998 that guerilla armies it actively supported in Nicaragua were smuggling illegal drugs into the United States—drugs that were making their way onto the streets of inner-city black neighborhoods in the form of crack cocaine. The CIA also admitted that, in the midst of the War on Drugs, it blocked law enforcement efforts to investigate illegal drug networks that were helping to fund its covert war in Nicaragua."[7]

Made by dissolving powder cocaine in water, adding baking soda, and then boiling the water away, crack cocaine is not only much less expensive than powder cocaine and more easily purchased in small quantities, but it is also more intoxicating. Crack cocaine is smokable, and smoking the drug produces a more immediate euphoric effect than the intranasal use (snorting) that is typical with powder cocaine. Processing cocaine into crack meant that a consumer could buy a small quantity of the drug for a few dollars, and it would be sufficient to produce a high.[8] People who had once been priced out of using cocaine could now purchase and consume the drug. Selling crack could be very profitable, and, with widespread unemployment and urban divestment, it could also be an appealing way to make money. Illicit informal markets of buyers and sellers developed around the drug as the synthesis of crack expanded the market.[9]

Historian David Kennedy describes the problem: "'Crack blew through America's poor black neighborhoods like the Four Horsemen of the Apocalypse,' leaving behind unspeakable devastation and suffering."[10] In 1989 California representative Maxine Waters emphasized the urgency of this crisis: "The most urgent problem facing ghettoized African Americans today is the lethal infestation of drugs in our communities."[11] Though the crises of crack cocaine and violence were concentrated in large cities in Black neighborhoods, the panicked response was widespread and sensationalized. As Murch notes, scholar and activist Clarence Lusane used the term "drug crisis" to refer to the reality of the devastation of crack cocaine, to distinguish it from the sensationalized, state-sponsored "crack epidemic."[12]

Economists Jeff Grogger and Michael Willis found that the emergence and legal prohibition of crack cocaine played a major role in increasing rates of violent crime, especially among young Black men. They write, "Because the cocaine trade is illegal, crack dealers lack the property rights enjoyed by participants in legal markets." Under prohibition those involved in the cocaine market are unable to use legal institutions and mechanisms to make or enforce contracts or to settle disputes. They continue, "Violence—or even the threat of violence—may be an effective if costly means of enforcing agreements, expanding one's operations, and protecting one's profits in an environment in which legal protections are unavailable."[13] The people who lived in these communities experienced multiple crises simultaneously—poverty, the sale and use of crack cocaine, and the gang violence associated with this informal economy.[14]

The increase in crime rates did not go unnoticed by the media—and neither did the emergence of crack cocaine. Dale D. Chitwood, Sheigla Murphy, and Marsha Rosenbaum assert that the national media first mentioned crack cocaine by name on November 17, 1985. In about ten months, national media had produced more than one thousand stories about crack.[15] Murch writes, "In contrast to sensationalized portrayals, the themes of social-service retrenchment, deindustrialization, intensification of poverty, and structural isolation are as foundational to the period as drug consumption, illicit economies, and the restructuring of the traditional nuclear family." The state appropriated these genuine concerns, obscuring structural inequalities and instead demonizing the people who bought and sold crack. Murch continues, "The state effectively co-opted much of the anger and disorientation created by the Reagan-era urban crisis into an anticrime framework that blamed the pathological culture of black and brown youth for the problems of poverty and urban divestment."[16]

The logic of the war on drugs allowed politicians to address multiple discourses at once, including family values and welfare reform, accompanied by some now familiar cultural images. Political scientist Julia Jordan-Zachery writes, "Reagan would invoke the image of the 'good' American society," contrasting this image with this era's villains: "those who sell drugs and those who buy drugs." In 1988 Reagan declared, "All Americans of good will are determined to stamp out those parasites who survive and even prosper by feeding off the energy and vitality and humanity of others."[17] The chief of the Los Angeles Police Department told the Senate Judiciary Committee that "the casual drug user ought to be taken out and shot."[18]

The "tough on crime" policies of the war on drugs were largely punitive. Prison sentences were lengthened and mandatory minimum sentences were imposed to eliminate judicial discretion. The focus on crack cocaine and police policies that concentrated on street-based drug crime in inner cities (instead of, say, in college dorms or in the suburbs) resulted in a tremendous expansion of carceral institutions and huge disparities in arrests and sentencing for Black people. In 1986 the Anti-Drug Abuse Act set mandatory minimum sentences for crack cocaine.[19] James Morone writes, "The legislation responded to [media outcry] and made crack the only drug to carry a mandatory sentence for a first offense of simple possession."[20] Legal historian Dorothy Roberts states, "While powdered cocaine was glamorized as a thrilling amusement for the rich and famous, crack was reviled for stripping its underclass users of every shred of human dignity."[21] As such, the penalties for powder cocaine were dramatically lower than the penalties for crack cocaine. The penalty for possession of five hundred grams of powder was the same as the penalty for five grams of crack.[22]

The constructed villains of this era were definitively Black. Crack distribution and gang membership were so associated with young Black men that in Los Angeles "by 1992 city sheriffs listed nearly half of the African American men under age twenty-five . . . as gang members."[23] Attorney, writer, and civil rights advocate Michelle Alexander writes, "The war on drugs proved popular among key white voters, particularly whites who remained resentful of Black progress, civil rights enforcement, and affirmative action." Alexander proposes that the war on drugs was a direct response to the end of Jim Crow: "more African American adults are under correctional control today—in prison or jail, on probation or parole—than were enslaved in 1850." Alexander writes, "In less than thirty years, the U.S. penal population exploded from around 300,000 to more than 2 million," mostly because of drug convictions, and 30–40 percent of those incarcerations were of Black people.[24] Jordan-Zachery asserts that the war on drugs created a new political image: "the crack addict." She writes, "consequently, the War on Drugs was refined as a war on the 'crack' house in the 'ghetto' and 'inner-city' neighborhoods."[25] Like the drug panics that came before it, crack cocaine was associated with a demonized racial group; crack was "imbued . . . with phenomenal qualities," leading to violent mania, intensified sex drives, and instant addiction.[26] And the crack scare involved anxiety over female sexuality. However, this time maternal protection had been replaced by fetal protection. The crack crisis didn't call for the patriarchal protection of Black women—it called for their punishment.

In 1985 Dr. Ira Chasnoff and his colleagues' study of cocaine use during pregnancy was published in the *New England Journal of Medicine*. They found that babies exposed to cocaine in utero "had significant depression of interactive behavior and a poor organizational response to environmental stimuli."[27] Though the study was limited in its scope, preliminary, not generalizable, *and* not demonstrating causality, it was picked up by the media. Chasnoff recalled, "Soon after our paper was published, within days, we were getting calls from media all over the country, and started hearing the term crack babies."[28]

Fetal personhood had crashed into the war on drugs. Concern about maternal deviance and the quality of offspring since *Roe v. Wade* in 1973 has been intimately tied to fears about drug use. Likewise, the policy response to pre- and postpartum drug use has been highly punitive—a part of the war on drugs. Legal sociologist Katherine Beckett writes that the punitive response to substance use during pregnancy "reflects the coincidence of the punitive orientation of the 'war on drugs' and the fetal rights discourse: the construction of drug use as an immoral choice reinforces the emerging image of the negligent mother whose willingness to support her fetus must be reinforced by medical and legal professionals."[29] Echoing earlier eugenic thought about threatening "others," irresponsible breeding, and damaged children that threatened the social and financial well-being of the nation, this response targeted mothers who exposed their children to drugs recklessly and carelessly created hordes who were said to grow into erratic, violent, irresponsible adults, while good, honest Americans were stuck with the social and economic costs.[30]

After fetal personhood had become a powerful political ideology, women's use of crack was a major element of the crack scare in the 1980s and 1990s.[31] Crack cocaine was popular among women. Roberts writes, "The concern about women's crack use was no doubt exaggerated by gender stereotypes that make female drug addicts more disturbing than male addicts." To the extent that women are seen as mothers, pregnant drug users violate cultural definitions of appropriate, respectable, disciplined motherhood. Instead of being viewed as moral, pure, and self-sacrificial, pregnant drug users are seen as immoral, polluted, and selfish. Consider the use of the terms "clean" and "dirty" for tests of both sexually transmitted infections and substance use. People with STIs or who test positive for drugs are "dirty." Pregnant drug users, defined as dirty for their substance use and lack of sexual responsibility, conflict with images of pure, clean, (white) motherhood. What's more, the description of the supposed pharmacology of crack seemed to attack mothers directly. The drug was "said to destroy the natural impulse to mother."[32]

The "crack mom" was discursively joined with existing cultural frames for bad Black mothers and pathological Black children. Though invoked by name less frequently than the "crack baby," the crack mom's irresponsibility and selfishness was invoked in the political discourse. She embodied the promiscuity and dysfunction of the Jezebel and the stubbornness of the Sapphire. She was aggressive like Mammy and abusive of social services like the welfare queen.[33] As Roberts explains, this discursive drama had two leading characters: "the pregnant addict and the crack baby, both irredeemable, both Black. The pregnant crack addict was portrayed as an irresponsible and selfish woman who put her love for crack above her love for her children."[34] This discourse would have a tremendous impact on the welfare reform of the mid-1990s. Family caps, where people would receive no additional welfare support even if they had more children, drug testing of welfare recipients, and forced sterilization of welfare recipients were all discursively linked to the image of the pregnant crack user.[35] The image of the pregnant Black crack user justified punitive policies in the criminal and civil legal systems. Ira Chasnoff, Harvey Landress, and Mark Barrett conducted a study of drug testing and reporting at five public health clinics and twelve private obstetrical offices in Pinellas County, Florida. They found that, despite similar rates of substance use, Black women were ten times more likely to be reported than white women.[36]

Law professor Michele Goodwin writes, "During the Reagan Administration, criminal surveillance of and policing pregnancy served to expand the 'War on Drugs' and inflamed narratives about 'bad mothering,' crystalizing in the harmful 'crack mom' and 'crack baby' nomenclature."[37] Professor of African American studies Naomi Murakawa asserts, "The crack baby diagnosis persisted in popular and political discourse because the diagnosis matched racial common sense, including notions that Black children burden the welfare state, Black women reproduce irresponsibly, and Black families self-replicate a permanent underclass."[38] In the US tradition of puritanical bootstraps liberalism, the problem was once again defined in terms of individual failure and not systemic oppression and deprivation. Roberts writes, "In addition to legitimizing fetal rights enforcement, prosecuting crack-addicted mothers shifts public attention from poverty, racism, and a deficient health care system, implying instead that poor infant health results from the depraved behavior of individual mothers."[39]

Crack exposure in utero was supposed to cause devastating, irreparable harm. Like prior drug scares, the supposed impact of crack was folded into existing stereotypes about Black moms and children.[40] These claims were taken up and exaggerated by news media. In 1986 *Newsweek* declared crack to be "The Plague among Us."[41] The *Washington Post* published a column by Charles Krauthammer, a Pulitzer Prize–winning columnist and political pundit, that warned, "The inner-city crack epidemic is now giving birth to the newest horror: a bio-underclass, a generation of physically damaged cocaine babies whose biological inferiority is stamped at birth." Krauthammer asserted that these babies constituted a "race of (sub) human drones, [whose] future is closed to them from day one. Theirs will be a life of certain suffering, of probable deviance, of permanent inferiority. At best, a menial life of severe deprivation. And all of this is biologically determined from birth. The dead babies may be the lucky ones."[42]

Mariah Blake, of the *Columbia Journalism Review,* describes a CBS story featuring a social worker who said the toddler she was treating "would grow up to be a 21-year-old with an IQ of perhaps 50, barely able to dress herself."[43] The Democratic US representative from California, George Miller, told ABC news, "These children, who are the most expensive babies ever born in America, are going to overwhelm every social service delivery system that they come in contact with throughout the rest of their lives."[44] Roberts notes, "Even the most careful reporters felt free to make wildly exaggerated claims about the effects of prenatal drug use.... Some articles attributed all 375,000 cases to crack, although experts estimate that 50,000 to 100,000 newborns at most are exposed specifically to cocaine (both powdered and crack) each year."[45]

The impact of so-called crack baby syndrome went beyond the symptoms described in Chasnoff and his colleagues' 1985 study. In utero exposure to crack was said to have a permanent, lifelong impact on overall development. So crack cocaine did not just destroy families and increase rates of violent crime. The use of crack cocaine during pregnancy was thought to be creating hordes of permanently damaged children—a lost generation. Chasnoff himself challenged the media's representation of his research: "I was at first stunned, and then angry that they would distort the information. That's when I started realizing how a lot of this can be taken out of context and used to bolster any kind of argument."[46]

Media outlets weren't the only ones spreading misleading information. Health-care providers and researchers joined in the fray. In 1989 a National Institute on Drug Abuse psychologist argued that prenatal substance use "was interfering with the central core of what it is to be human."[47] Nurses reported that these babies stiffened when cuddled and displayed "emotional detachment" and "impaired human interaction."[48] Of the mothers another nurse said, "The most remarkable and hideous aspect of crack cocaine seems to be the undermining of the maternal instinct"[49]

However, the voice of the scientific community was not united in support of the narrative about the impact of crack cocaine on a developing pregnancy. Some medical researchers were more skeptical. Dr. Claire Coles asserted, "The effects didn't seem consistent with the action of the drug itself.... You could have taken any premature baby and gotten the same image. I think that people got very focused on cocaine is the cause of this rather than thinking, substance abuse is a cause of this, maternal lifestyle is the cause of this, social issues are the cause of this."[50] There were significant flaws in much of the research on prenatal cocaine exposure. John Morgan, a drug policy expert and professor of pharmacology, and Lynn Zimmer, a professor of sociology, report three major problems with much of the research on prenatal cocaine use, including the lack of control groups, the lack of research on long-term effects of the drug, and an inability to distinguish between the impact of powder and crack cocaine.[51] Even as researchers found that exposure to crack cocaine in utero was inconsistent with popular narratives, they struggled to publish their findings. Journal articles demonstrating that crack had devastating impacts were five times more likely to be published than articles that showed more subtle effects or no effects at all.[52] This combination of flawed research and exaggerated media reporting created an image so lasting that decades of research disproving the crack baby myth have been unable to dispel it.

More recently, psychologist Laura Betancourt and her colleagues, in their study of adolescents who had been exposed to cocaine in utero, found "no evidence of latent effects of gestational cocaine exposure on inhibitory control, working memory, or receptive language."[53] Neonatologist Hallam Hurt and her colleagues found that either in utero exposure had no effect on neurocognitive function at middle-school age "or that effect is less pronounced than the effect of age or childhood environment."[54] In a twenty-five-year longitudinal study, Hurt and her colleagues found "no significant differences between . . . cocaine-exposed children and the controls." They argued, "Poverty is a more powerful influence on the outcome of inner-city children than gestational exposure to cocaine."[55] The idea that uterine exposure to crack cocaine causes "crack baby syndrome" is a zombie fact: despite all the evidence against it, it keeps coming back to life. Sociologists Murphy and Rosenbaum write, "There are ideological explanations for why these infants continued to be labeled 'crack babies' rather than, in light of scientific findings, 'poverty babies.' In an era of fiscal retrenchment, the notion of poverty babies might engender public sympathy and interfere with the conservative drive to demolish social welfare programs."[56]

South Carolina's targeted arrests of pregnant and postpartum people for drug use grew out of the "crack crisis." In 1989 Julia Graham, who was working as a prosecutor and a child legal advocate in South Carolina, developed what would become the first policy to use the threat of prosecution to try to compel pregnant people into drug treatment. She revealed what drove her to develop the new policy. One day, while she was working in family court, she encountered three babies who had been taken into protective custody by the police. Apparently, they had all been exposed to drugs in utero. She explained, "So, it just struck me, as we had two babies born, um, drug impaired, with crack cocaine and one with heroin, and so in these three hearings in one day, and it just came to me. . . . that this was a serious issue and nothing was really being done about it."[57] All the South Carolina attorneys I interviewed, along with an Alabama attorney who worked in a city with a large African American population, agreed that when they started their prosecution policies in the 1980s and 1990s, prenatal crack cocaine use was their primary concern.

Media interviews showed a similar pattern. Ninth Circuit solicitor of South Carolina, David Schwacke, said, "It is always our desire that no woman use cocaine during pregnancy because of the danger to herself and to her fetus." Fifth Circuit solicitor of South Carolina, Barney Giese, related a story about a woman who gave birth to a stillborn baby, asserting that it was her use of crack cocaine during her pregnancy that caused the stillbirth.[58] Matthew Payne, a solicitor in South Carolina, shared a story about a friend who fostered children exposed to crack in utero: "So, [my friend] would take in drug-addicted babies. And he would tell me stories about . . . a baby's crying, you pick him up, just holding them, whatever, console them. But these babies were inconsolable. 'Cause basically they were going through withdrawal. The babies would rub themselves raw in the cribs 'cause they were so agitated. Most babies gain a little weight when they're born; these babies would lose weight."[59]

Robert "Bobby" Hood, who represented the Medical University of South Carolina (MUSC) in the *Ferguson* case, explained, "I have seen these children die or become teen criminals and commit crazy crimes because their brains have been messed up by drugs in the womb."[60] Sometimes dramatic physical abnormalities were also attributed to prenatal exposure to crack cocaine. The primary sponsor of the fetal assault bill in Tennessee, Representative Terri Weaver, invited the adoptive father of allegedly cocaine-exposed children to testify before the Tennessee House Criminal Justice Subcommittee. He reported that his first cocaine-exposed child was born without an esophagus, that "half his brain was dead," and he had almost died twice while in the neonatal intensive care unit. This child's younger brother, also exposed to cocaine in utero, did not live past his first birthday.[61]

Although it is heartbreaking to hear about children suffering, these stories are troubling for three reasons. First, the use of a government platform to insist that extreme and dramatic harms are exclusively attributable to cocaine exposure is at best misleading and at worst dishonest. It is virtually impossible to determine single causes of birth outcomes, but exposure to stimulants in utero has not been linked to birth defects.[62] Second, they are using the image of child disability, in some cases using identifiable children, in a way that is deeply ableist and exploitative of vulnerable children who were removed from their families and placed in foster care. Third, they are using these exaggerated images to justify the adoption of a discriminatory criminal law with no evidence that it will actually help reduce substance use during pregnancy.

The first arrest case documented in South Carolina occurred in Greenville County in 1989, after a white woman gave birth to a baby that tested positive for opioids.[63] After this almost everyone arrested in South Carolina through the early 1990s was a Black pregnant or postpartum woman. The highest number of documented arrests was made in 2019. Arrests were made in thirty of forty-six counties, demonstrating a lack of uniform application of the test, report, and arrest policies. Horry County made the highest number of documented arrests, with 41 total. Though Horry County makes up only 7 percent of the total state population, it made 15 percent of documented arrests. Out of the 261 cases for which the race of the defendant could be determined, defendants in South Carolina were predominantly white (n = 156, or 59.7 percent), while Black defendants numbered 103 (39.4 percent). One defendant was identified as "Asian" and another as "Hispanic."

The vast majority of arrests occurred after a positive drug test of either the birth parent or the newborn. In South Carolina most arrest cases involved a positive test for cocaine (154 cases). Marijuana was the next most prevalent, with 67 arrest cases, followed by opiates (49). Amphetamines were involved in 23 arrests, and alcohol was cited in 8. Other cases involved benzodiazepine (14), and 7 involved medications

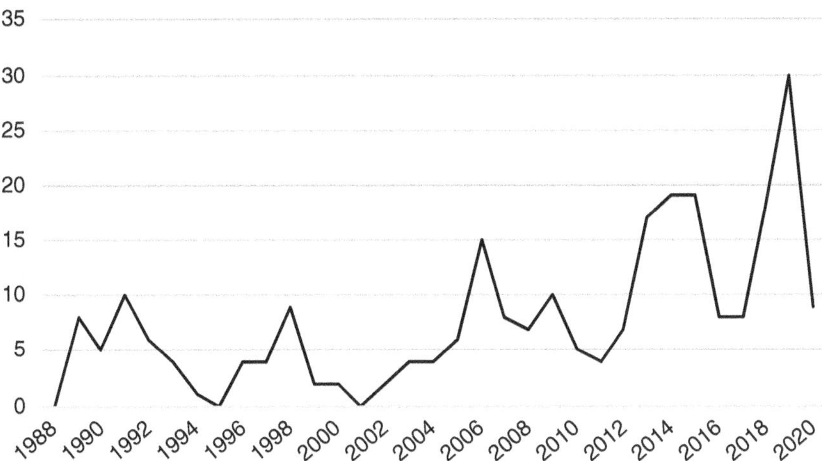

Figure 1. South Carolina pregnancy arrests by year.

used to manage withdrawal symptoms like methadone. South Carolina made 1 arrest each for cases involving cigarettes and antidepressants.

South Carolina arrest numbers briefly rose after the 1997 *Whitner v. State* case, in which the court found that pregnant people could be prosecuted for a crime against their own pregnancy, after which time the numbers declined until after the US Supreme Court's 2001 decision in *Ferguson v. City of Charleston.* Post-*Ferguson* South Carolina arrests followed a general upward trend. Charleston, the city facing a lawsuit in the *Ferguson* case, pursued prosecution more vigorously than other counties in the state. As such, it seems likely that the city, and perhaps other counties as well, paused prosecutorial activity while waiting for the Supreme Court's ruling on the lawsuit and reformulated the practice after the Supreme Court gave its decision. This suggests that prosecutors are attuned to, if not constrained by, the law.

The racial demographics of the people arrested in South Carolina are out of proportion with the state population. Census data indicate that, as of 2022, the South Carolina population is 26.3 percent Black and 68.9 percent white, while those arrested for crimes against their own pregnancies were 39.4 percent Black and 59.8 percent white. These racial demographics shifted over time. Annually, Black defendants were more

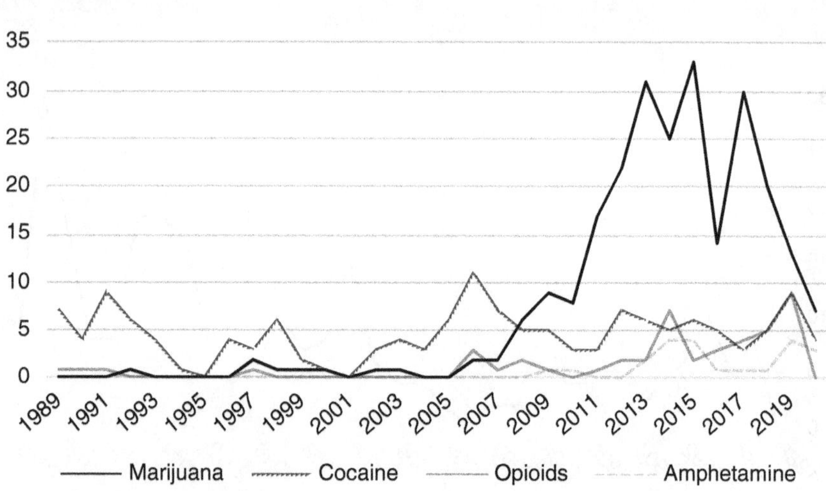

Figure 2. South Carolina pregnancy arrests by drug and year.

numerous than white defendants in South Carolina through 1999. After 1999 the demographic composition started to shift toward a greater proportion of white defendants, and by 2010 white defendants outnumbered Black defendants every year. In 2014 the ratio of white to Black defendants was seventeen to one.[64]

In South Carolina the percentage of cases involving cocaine declined over time, while cases involving amphetamine started to increase in 2008, potentially as a result of shifting political salience of various drug types. Notably, arrests involving marijuana skyrocketed in South Carolina, an upward trend starting in 2006 and then declining after 2017, though it is possible that this is due to an undercount of cases and not due to actual test, report, and arrest practice.

Drug types implicated in South Carolina pregnancy-related arrests are out of line with other state-level drug measures. The mean percentage of total drug seizure arrests in South Carolina from 1992 to 2020 involved mostly marijuana (61.80 percent), followed by cocaine (23.10 percent).[65] Meanwhile, the pregnancy-related arrests in South Carolina were weighted heavily toward cocaine, making up 45.53 percent of drug-related arrests. The next most commonly cited drug was marijuana, in 20.67 percent of cases. Marijuana was underrepresented by 41.13 percent, even with the

Table 1 South Carolina drug-related arrests

Drug type	*South Carolina drug-seizure arrests, 1992–2020 (%)*	*South Carolina pregnancy-related arrests, 1989–2022 (%)*
Marijuana	61.80	20.67
Cocaine	23.10	45.53
Amphetamine	6.66	9.24
Opiates	3.68	15.12
Others[i]	4.69	7.09

SOURCE: "South Carolina Crime Statistics" (n.d.).

[i] "Others" includes depressants, hallucinogens, nonamphetamine stimulants, and other unknown drugs.

dramatic uptick in marijuana arrests that occurred after 2000, and cocaine was overrepresented by 24.43 percent. These dramatic disparities indicate that pregnancy-related arrests were even more heavily focused on cocaine than nonpregnancy related drug arrests.

The second wave of pregnancy-related arrests revolved around methamphetamine use and aligns with Alabama's criminalization period. Heightened attention to the use of methamphetamine emerged in the late 1990s and grew through the mid-2000s. State senator Jeff Sessions, who would later become the US attorney general during the Trump administration, explained at a Judiciary Committee Hearing in 1999, "I believe in Alabama we are now seeing a major increase [in methamphetamine]. . . . It is an extraordinary increase in an illegal drug, comparable I would think only to the spread of crack cocaine that happened so rapidly, and I think it deserves great attention."[66] Use of methamphetamine had increased, but only slightly, from "just under 2% of the adult population in 1994 to approximately 5% in 2004."[67]

With methamphetamine, images of bad Black mothers and damaged Black children in poor urban areas were replaced by poor, rural white women in trailer parks and their damaged white children. Cheaper and more accessible to the poor than other prescription stimulants, like pharmaceutical grade methamphetamine or amphetamines like Ritalin and

Adderall, methamphetamine could be manufactured or "cooked" at home, using items that could be found at the grocery store. Methamphetamine was also supposed to be uniquely addictive. Law enforcement experts attested that "only 1% of meth users can overcome their addiction."[68]

News stories of the sudden saturation of communities with the drug and its uniquely harmful effects were plentiful. One sheriff told reporters, "Meth is the overwhelming drug of choice among . . . murderers." Asa Hutchinson, the then director of the Drug Enforcement Administration, said, "States are literally drowning in meth activity." Representative Brian Baird, a Democrat from Washington State, claimed that methamphetamine was the number one cause of crime.[69] In 1998 President Bill Clinton's drug czar Barry McCaffrey announced, "Meth is the worst drug ever to hit America, and officials need to work to eradicate the 'poor man's cocaine.'"[70] A 2003 *Rolling Stone* headline cautioned, "Crystal Meth: Plague in the Heartland."[71]

Reports about the harmful medical impact of the drug painted a similarly apocalyptic picture. A National Institute on Drug Abuse report stated that methamphetamine was associated with brain damage, memory loss, psychotic behavior, heart damage, hepatitis, and HIV transmission. A DEA official said, "It's the most insidious drug. . . . It eats up [users'] brain cells." Methamphetamine users were described as suffering from chronic wasting disease, and methamphetamine was said to turn people into monsters.[72] Methamphetamine addicts were described as almost zombies—the new, fast kind. Medical anthropologist Kelly Ray Knight suggests, "These new forms of fetal victimhood reflect emergent national anxieties about rising rates of methamphetamine use among women of childbearing age, particularly poor white women in rural areas."[73]

The discourse about methamphetamine users echoed earlier language from the eugenics movement of the 1920s and 1930s. One popular antimethamphetamine campaign, called "The Faces of Meth" (now called "Mug Shot Match-Up") shows time-ordered sequences of methamphetamine users' mugshots—series of deteriorating faces that seemed to age too quickly.[74] Cultural criminologist Travis Linneman and sociologist Tyler Wall assert that this campaign can be seen as an outgrowth of cultural anxieties, with its use of misleading and inaccurate depictions of the "meth face" as a pedagogical antimethamphetamine strategy of the threat of white-trashness to discourage drug use.[75] Murakawa explores the racialized character of the methamphetamine crisis and its associated pathologies, or phenotypes, as specifically "white trash" ailments and deformities. She focuses specifically on "meth mouth," a condition of advanced tooth decay said to be caused by methamphetamine use, challenging the evidence for the diagnosis and drawing parallels between white trash stereotypes of toothlessness and the characterization of methamphetamine users as having bad teeth. She asserts that "the meth epidemic is constructed as symptom and cause of White status decline, with dental decay the vehicle for anxieties about descent into 'White trash' status."[76]

Punitive policies were developed to try to cope. Senator Jeff Sessions arranged for all of Alabama's Drug Task Force members to train at Quantico on clandestine methamphetamine labs. Walmart employees were trained to flag customers who purchased large quantities of the household ingredients that can be used to make methamphetamine, such as pseudoephedrine and cases of matches. Pharmacies established networks to identify patients making smaller purchases of pseudoephedrine at lots of different pharmacies, a strategy called "smurfing."

Methamphetamine was not a new drug. Chemically synthesized in 1887, it was not used medicinally until 1927, and it began to be sold commercially in 1932.[77] Prescription methamphetamine is typically sold under the name Desoxyn and is approved for weight loss, attention-deficit disorder, and sleep disorders like narcolepsy. Methamphetamine was identified as a "drug of abuse" in the 1960s, and its nonprescription use was primarily associated with motorcycle gangs and gay men.[78] Methamphetamine is chemically and pharmacologically similar to amphetamine and even "appear[s] to produce a similar dose-related profile of effects in humans."[79] Another study went so far as to say that "there are no known neurobiological differences in action between [methamphetamine and amphetamine]."[80] Methamphetamine was also associated with people who worked long hours, like night- and swing-shift workers and truck drivers.[81] The stimulating effect of the drug helped them stay awake for work.

Despite popular claims about the instant destruction caused by methamphetamine, neuroscientist Carl Hart and his colleagues found that short-term, acute methamphetamine use can improve cognitive performance in some ways, including visuospatial perception, focus, and response speed.[82] US Air Force pilots have been authorized to use amphetamines "to sustain the performance of sleep-deprived pilots" since 1961.[83] Another study indicated that "amphetamines bring the performance of fatigued individuals 'back up to the baseline.'"[84] Amphetamine use is not uncommon among college students in the United States. Professor of epidemiology Sean McCabe and his colleagues found that 6.9 percent of US college students had used prescription stimulants for nonmedical purposes.[85] This reality was *not* in line with widespread tales of manic, psychotic, brain-damaged hillbillies.

The nationwide concern about methamphetamine seemed out of proportion with the data on methamphetamine use. Compared to annual deaths related to other substances, with tobacco causing more than 480,000 deaths annually and 88,000 annual deaths attributed to alcohol consumption, deaths involving methamphetamine were low, at fewer than 5,000 annually.[86] Beyond its relatively low risk of associated deaths, methamphetamine is just less popular than other illicit drugs. In 2008 only heroin was used by fewer people. Crack cocaine and ecstasy are marginally more commonly used, with 359,000 and 555,000 annual users. Nonmedical psychotherapeutic drugs and marijuana are far more popular, with 6.1 million users and 15.2 million users, respectively.[87] Indeed, most statistics I could find on substance use and drug-related crime didn't present data for methamphetamine on its own, instead lumping it in with other less commonly used drugs in groups called "other stimulants," "amphetamines," or "synthetic drugs." The "National Survey on Drug Use and Health" didn't start counting methamphetamine in its own category until 2015.[88]

In some instances, especially among prosecutors and law enforcement in Alabama, methamphetamine seemed to take crack cocaine's place as the chemical enemy number one—sometimes while even acknowledging that they had been wrong about crack. But methamphetamine was something new, terrifying, and certain. Other times they merely compared the two substances. South Carolina solicitor, Peter Hermann, explained that methamphetamine and crack cocaine are similar in some ways. "Obviously, meth is like crack was twenty years ago or twenty-five years ago. It's the cheap drug that's out there, that everybody can get a hold of and people can make."[89] While wealthier drug users may reach for powder cocaine or a prescription amphetamine, crack and methamphetamine were cheaper, and they could be manufactured at home. This had the effect of making the drugs more accessible. As Alabama district attorney David Campbell described it, internet instructions on how to make methamphetamine at home, together with the availability of pseudoephedrine and other ingredients used to cook methamphetamine, are part of why the use of the drug seemed to explode overnight.[90]

Campbell dramatically described the emergence of methamphetamine as a popular drug by invoking the public health language of epidemics: "This was something where everybody was screaming, 'Good Lord, what's going on!' . . . When the meth epidemic hit—and I call it an epidemic because it spread like wildfire throughout our county—it felt like it was almost overnight that, all of a sudden, we weren't just facing meth cases, we were facing huge meth busts, with, just, very large quantities of methamphetamine." Emphasizing the scale of the problem, he continued, "It became very easy to make the meth cases. And so, our numbers just, just get blown out of the water. I mean, you couldn't spit on somebody without hittin' a meth lab. . . . It was unbelievable. And it was obnoxious. And, our court system was overwhelmed. I mean, our case load went up over 200 percent. And it was virtually . . . in a period of months that this happened."[91]

One Alabama news article explained, "Meth, in fact, has replaced moonshine alcohol stills in the rural south. The highly addictive potion is brewed in kitchen sinks all through the back roads, and it's destroying a generation of young men and women, and threatens to destroy a succeeding generation." District attorney Jimmy Harp of Etowah County told Nina Martin, "Etowah avoided the worst of the crack epidemic. . . . Then we woke up one day and crystal meth came to town. And crystal meth was unlike anything I'd ever seen."[92]

According to prosecutors and law enforcement, methamphetamine seemed to take a uniquely devastating toll on the people who used it. South Carolina child legal advocate Julia Graham explained, "If they're really heavy [methamphetamine users]—you can really tell. I mean it's a little different than cocaine or, um . . . other drugs."[93] District attorney Campbell said methamphetamine users "are up for days without sleep. . . . They act very erratically. They don't think very rationally."[94] The police chief of Hackleburg, Alabama, Kenny Hallmark, said that drug addicts get "lost in the drug": "A person who is on meth forgets and forsakes everything. . . . Nothing else matters to them, and they will tell you they'll give up everything for the chance at that high."[95]

The image of out-of-control drug-using pregnant women and damaged newborn babies plays a notable role in the methamphetamine scare narrative, just as it did with crack cocaine. The district attorney of Franklin County, Alabama, Joey Rushing, said, "You [have] mamas . . . smoking meth on the way to the hospital."[96] District attorney Campbell recalled the increase of children born in the local hospital who tested positive for methamphetamine. He explained, "Another thing that was fairly alarming about it is that many of those children were being born very premature. And the statistics on premature children and the challenges that they face are pretty strong. And so, at that point, we did not have a lot of scientific literature out there that would tell us the long-range effect. The thing that concerned me the most was, was that premature part of it."[97] Covington County's district attorney, Greg Gambril, told reporters, "We've got a small community that has a very bad drug problem. When a child is born and lives a few minutes because the mother was addicted to methamphetamine, that's a very, very serious crime here."[98] Hallmark explained, "On more than one occasion, we've gone into a house and found pregnant women on their hands and knees smoking methamphetamine or shooting it up."[99]

Dr. Melvin Thornbury of Marshall County, Alabama, a supporter of the prosecutions, shared a story that a colleague told him: "A pediatrician told me that five or six years ago he had an 8 or 9 year old child that was born to a meth-addicted mother. The child was psychotic. You generally don't see that in a person that young." He continued, "There is definitely damage done to the baby's neurological systems. You see a lot of problems that can be traced back to being exposed to drugs like this in the womb." Like Thornbury's story, many of the narratives shared about the horror of methamphetamine exposure seem to be hearsay evidence—something a family member, a friend, or even a friend of a friend told them. Detective Robert Smith of the Columbia Police Department explained, "I have a family member who works in a neonatal intensive care unit and because of that, I constantly hear about these children who go through withdrawal symptoms. When you see that, you realize somebody has got to do something about it."[100] While methamphetamine use during pregnancy *has* been linked to decreased blood flow to the placenta and increased blood pressure, the catastrophic images of psychotic children are not substantiated by the medical literature.[101]

Another part of the emphasis on methamphetamine as a public health crisis involved the production of the drug—not simply its use. Michael Miller, a former Alabama district attorney who was among the first to press pregnancy-related charges in Alabama, recounted, "I can remember a lieutenant in the sheriff's department giving us a lecture about how dangerous these meth facilities were, for everybody. . . . There could be explosions and chemical burns and all these other things . . . even the, I guess just noxious fumes." It was concern about the hazards of amateur methamphetamine production that inspired the creation of the chemical endangerment law used to prosecute pregnant people in Alabama. Campbell explained, "We were going into these meth labs, and there was just heavy, toxic air in these labs. And we were going in, and we were finding babies, and . . . it was horrible."[102]

Arrests of pregnant people made under the chemical endangerment charge began about ten months after the law was implemented, in October 2006: two women in Coffee County, one in Covington County, and another in Houston County. The highest number of annual arrests occurred in 2017. Arrest rates differed by county, showing independent behavior in terms of using the chemical endangerment law to prosecute pregnant people. Over time a county began to use the law in this way, often followed by a peak in arrest numbers and then a decline. Etowah County showed a dramatic increase. In the pre-*Ankrom* period, only 1 arrest was made in Etowah County, but in the post-*Ankrom* period, 149 arrests were made there. Etowah accounts for only 2 percent of the Alabama population but made up 20 percent of total arrests for the state. Arrests were made in forty-six of Alabama's sixty-seven counties, with the highest concentration of arrests in the far north of the state.

Alabama arrest numbers trended upward after the first documented arrest in 2006. There is a slight dip in 2012, potentially in anticipation of the state supreme court opinion that came in January 2013. Another dip occurred in 2016, perhaps in response to the introduction of a bill amending

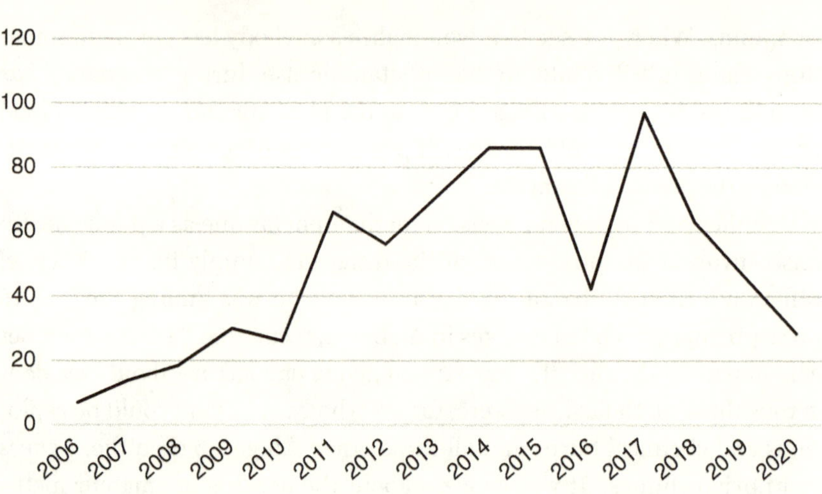

Figure 3. Alabama pregnancy arrests by year.

the chemical endangerment statute. The *Ankrom* and *Hicks* decisions themselves don't seem to have influenced arrest numbers, which were already increasing. Documented arrests declined after 2018, but it is likely that this is the result of an undercount of cases and may also be due to reduced incarceration during COVID.

In Alabama most arrests were related to a positive drug test. Of these the majority involved marijuana, with 241 cases, followed closely by amphetamine arrests (234) and then cocaine (172). Opiates were implicated in 159 cases, followed by 66 arrests involving benzodiazepine. Other drugs listed in arrest cases include medications for opioid use disorder (53), barbiturates (8), alcohol (4), cigarettes (1), MDMA (1), salvia (1), and tricyclic antidepressants (1). There is a difference between drugs implicated in arrests made prior to formal criminalization and arrests made afterward, though it is not clear that formal criminalization *caused* the change. In Alabama the percentage of cases involving cocaine peaked in 2011 and then declined dramatically, while cases involving opiates and amphetamines increased.

Drug types implicated in Alabama pregnancy-related arrests were out of line with other drug use and drug arrest measures, as was the case in South Carolina. Arrests made for drug possession in Alabama overwhelmingly involved marijuana (49.20 percent), while 27.42 percent involved opioids

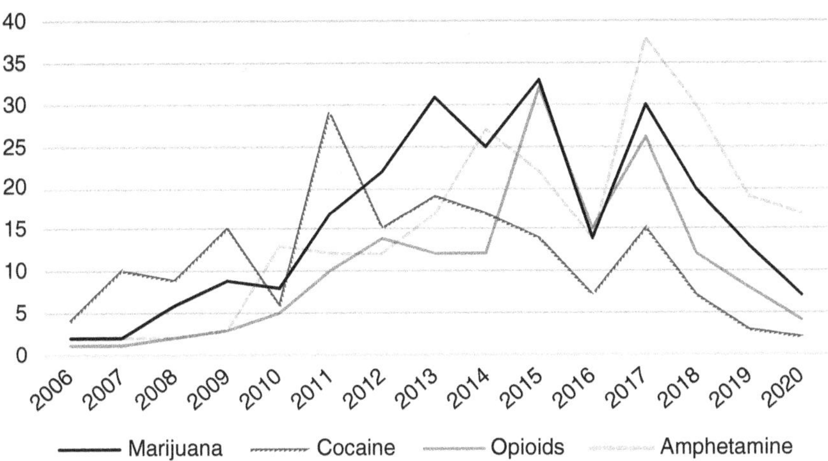

Figure 4. Alabama pregnancy arrests by drug and year.

and/or cocaine, and 23.38 percent involved other drugs like barbiturates, amphetamines, and methamphetamine.[103] Meanwhile, among pregnancy-related arrests, 241 (32.26 percent) involved marijuana, 308 cases (41.23 percent) involved cocaine and/or opioids, and 295 cases (39.49 percent) involved barbiturates, amphetamines, and methamphetamine. In pregnancy cases marijuana is underrepresented by 16.94 percent, opioids and cocaine are overrepresented by 16.46 percent, and barbiturates, amphetamines, and methamphetamine are overrepresented by 16.11 percent.

A comparison of drug *use* estimates with pregnancy-related arrests also shows disparities, with cocaine involved in approximately 23 percent of pregnancy cases, compared to the estimate of use at 10 percent.[104] A comparison of drug treatment admissions and pregnancy-related arrests shows disparities as well, with cocaine and amphetamines overrepresented in pregnancy-related arrests, almost double the percentage of cases involving those drugs for treatment admissions.[105] Marijuana and opiates are underrepresented in pregnancy-related arrest cases, each roughly half the percentage reported in drug treatment admissions.

Alabama arrests predominantly involved white women, making up 591 cases (about 80.0 percent). The defendant was identified as Black in 144 cases (19.5 percent), as Hispanic in one case, and as both white and

Table 2 Alabama drug-related arrests, 2006–2020

Drug type	*Alabama drug-possession arrests (%)*	*Alabama pregnancy-related arrests (%)*
Marijuana	49.20	32.26
Opioids and/or cocaine	27.42	41.23
"Dangerous non-narcotic drugs which include barbiturates, amphetamines, and methamphetamine"	23.38	39.49

SOURCES: "Drug Crimes" (n.d.); "Statewide Drug Crimes" (n.d.).

Latina in another. Black defendants are underrepresented in Alabama's pregnancy-related arrests, a shift from nationwide trends in pregnancy-related policing that disproportionately impacts women of color. According to the 2020 US census, 64.1 percent of the Alabama population is white, and 25.8 percent is Black.[106] In 2017 the ratio of white to Black defendants was nineteen to five.

At the time of this writing, opioids are the most politically salient "problem" drug. Opioids are narcotics, including prescription painkillers such as oxycodone and morphine, and illicit drugs, such as heroin, sometimes derived from poppies, sometimes artificially synthesized. According to the Centers for Disease Control and Prevention, in 2020 "75% of the nearly 92,000 drug overdose deaths in 2020 involved an opioid."[107] From 1999 to 2015, prescription opioid overdose deaths were more common than overdose deaths from nonprescription synthetic opioids, but this changed. Synthetic opioid overdose deaths began to rise dramatically in 2014 and have continued this meteoric rise through 2021, moving from fewer than five thousand deaths in 2013 to more than seventy thousand deaths in 2021.[108] A National Institutes of Health study found that incarcerated people, people without health insurance, and those who are living in poverty are especially vulnerable to fatal opioid overdoses.[109] The CDC describes "three waves of opioid overdose deaths." The first started in 1999, with a rise in prescription opioid overdose deaths, attributed to an increase in prescribing opioids in the 1990s Next, in 2010, the second wave of overdose deaths started with an increase in heroin-related overdose deaths. Finally, the third began in 2013, when synthetic opioid overdose deaths began to rise, which the CDC attributes to "illicitly manufactured fentanyl."[110] Excessive prescriptions of opioid painkillers, the inability to access medications for opioid use disorder, and pervasive chronic pain have been identified by the Department of Health and Human Services as contributing factors.[111]

Purdue Pharma, the company that manufactures OxyContin, also played a role in exacerbating the national opioid problem that must also be addressed. Chair Carolyn B. Maloney explained at a hearing before the House Committee on Oversight and Reform, "Since 1999, nearly half a million lives have been cut short by opioid overdoses in the United States alone. . . . And right there in the middle of all this suffering was Purdue Pharma, the manufacturer of a highly addictive prescription painkiller." Purdue Pharma started selling OxyContin in 1996, using false advertising that claimed their time-release pill was "less addictive than other immediate release alternatives." The company intentionally targeted doctors that prescribed a lot of opioids to switch to OxyContin, claiming it was safer. In 2007 Purdue Pharma pled guilty to felony misbranding and was ordered to pay a penalty of more than $600 million. This didn't stop Purdue Pharma's misleading advertising. "Purdue spent the next decade misleading the DEA, defrauding the United States, paying kickbacks to companies that would steer patients to OxyContin, and exacerbating the opioid epidemic."[112]

Some efforts to remedy opioid use disorder have sparked new problems. For example, efforts to reduce so-called doctor shopping (using a series of physicians to access multiple opioid prescriptions simultaneously and ensuring a steady supply in case a physician does not renew the prescription) have pushed people with substance use disorder to use heroin as an alternative.[113] This is particularly alarming, given that heroin has been increasingly laced with Fentanyl—an opioid that is fifty to one hundred times more potent than morphine.[114] What would typically be a nonlethal dose of heroin can become lethal in a heroin-fentanyl mixture.[115]

The third wave of prosecutions included in this study, and the one that lines up with Tennessee's adoption of a fetal assault law, involved opiates. Unlike methamphetamine and even crack cocaine, the use of opioid drugs is widespread. Policy responses to and depictions of this epidemic adopt a different tone than those related to methamphetamine and crack cocaine. Attorney Hernandez D. Stroud describes these differences: "Now, instead of harsh mandatory minimum sentencing laws and 'just say no' campaigns, there are diversion programs and drug treatment." In 2014 professor of psychiatry Theodore Cicero and his colleagues found that "nearly 90% of [survey] respondents who began use in the last decade were white."[116] An analysis of media coverage on white people who use opioids by Jules Netherland, managing director of research and academic engagement for the Drug Policy Alliance, and professor of psychiatry Helena Hansen similarly find that white drug users are typically described in more sympathetic terms than Black and Latino drug users. However, they also describe differences in the depictions of middle- and upper-middle class white drug users and low-income whites. For example, one news article from rural Virginia, written by a former member of the House of Delegates, stated, "I'm not talking about homeless, bum-looking street people—I'm talking about relatively affluent, well-dressed, high-achieving Volvo-driving kids, kids who belong to the honor societies, who play soccer and lacrosse, kids headed to the good schools." While methamphetamine users tended to be described as "white trash," white opioid users were not generally seen that way. They were usually described as young people who started using their parents' prescriptions, "fell in with a bad crowd," or became addicted to painkillers after they were given a prescription for an illness or injury.[117] However, the depiction of pregnant opioid users is much less compassionate.

The impact of opioid drugs on a developing pregnancy has, like with methamphetamine and crack cocaine, been a major cause of concern. Opioid exposure in utero is associated with a specific set of symptoms postpartum. Once known as NAS, or neonatal abstinence syndrome, it has more recently been referred to as neonatal opioid withdrawal syndrome, or NOWS.[118] Professor of public health Darla Bishop writes, "NAS, which typically develops within twenty-four to seventy-two hours after birth, includes uncontrollable shaking and seizures, constant crying, vomiting and diarrhea, and a rapid respiratory rate."[119] NOWS symptoms are eased or sometimes eliminated by allowing newborns to have skin-to-skin contact with their birth parent and to breastfeed.[120] Not every child exposed to opioids in utero will develop NOWS. After the withdrawal symptoms cease, a child born with NOWS is much like any other child.[121] Opioid use during pregnancy has not been found to cause birth defects, though some studies have shown slightly lower birth weights.[122] Research has shown that long-term outcomes of children exposed to opioids in utero are comparable to other children in their peer group.[123] Opioids are commonly given by physicians to ease the pain of childbirth.[124]

Media descriptions of so-called oxy-tots report "infants born into excruciating misery," who "shake, struggle to eat and often sputter and choke during feedings" and have "fits of sneezing and severe diarrhea." These babies are supposedly "rattled by even the slightest visual or audio stimuli, 'including a mother's smile.'" A nurse described the cry of a baby with NOWS as "a panicked, high-pitched wail, almost desperate, a sound you don't forget."[125] The language used to describe these children is strikingly similar to that used to describe the children exposed to crack and methamphetamine in utero, despite its different chemical structure. The imagined devastating lifelong negative impact of prenatal exposure to opioids was expected to create a tremendous financial burden to the State of Tennessee, because the children would need long-term treatment and care and would likely spend time in foster care. Weaver told the House Criminal Justice Subcommittee, "These babies are being born in our state being a huge liability to us, because there's nobody who will take them."[126]

Barry Staubus, the district attorney of Sullivan County, Tennessee, echoed this concern: "30% of children with 15 to 30-day stays, at thousands of dollars, ranging from 35 to 50 thousand dollars, and then the cost of children that are born this way with these cognitive . . . you think, what future do they have?"[127] Parallels were drawn between heroin and crack. Heroin is far less expensive than its FDA-regulated counterparts and can be more accessible, especially for individuals who lack insurance coverage. Prescription opioids might cost about one dollar per milligram, so a single sixty milligram pill could cost sixty dollars.[128] An equivalent amount of heroin can be purchased for a tenth of the price.

In Tennessee the first drug-related arrest occurred in 1992, after an impoverished Black woman tested positive for cocaine after giving birth. She pled guilty to aggravated child abuse and was given an eight-year prison sentence that would be suspended upon completing eight years of probation. She violated her probation and her prison sentence was reinstated.[129]

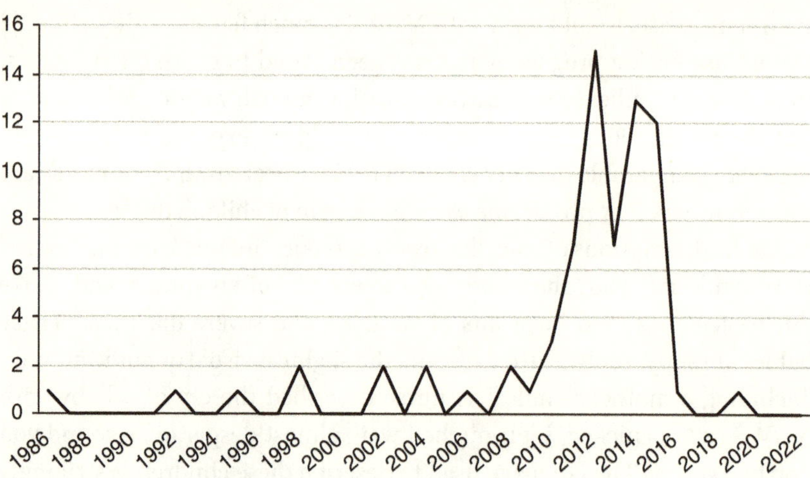

Figure 5. Tennessee pregnancy arrests by year.

The first person to be arrested under the 2014 fetal assault law was a white twenty-six-year-old who tested positive for methamphetamine and marijuana when she gave birth. She was arrested at the hospital two days later.[130] Drug-related arrests in Tennessee trickled in after 1992, with one or two recorded arrests made every few years until after 2010, at which time arrests increased. Tennessee's documented arrests peaked in 2012, followed by a sharp decline in 2013 and then rising again from 2014 to 2016, the years the fetal assault law was in effect.

Tennessee arrests were recorded in fifty-six of the state's ninety-five counties, suggesting that some jurisdictions were not participating in making pregnancy-related arrests. Shelby County, in the far southwest of the state, made sixteen arrests, more than any other county in the state, followed by Hawkins County in the northeast, with eight documented arrests. Of the sixty-nine cases for which the race of the defendant was reported, fifty-two were white (75.0 percent), one was Hispanic (1.4 percent), and sixteen were Black (23.0 percent). Law professor Wendy Bach's study of Tennessee's fetal assault law showed a dramatic difference between arrests made in the western part of the state around Memphis and the eastern part of the state, which sits in Appalachia. In Shelby County, to the west, where most of the state's Black population lives, most of the people arrested for fetal assault were Black. In northeast Tennessee, in Appalachia, most of the defendants were white.[131]

Of those charged with drug-related crimes in Tennessee, the majority involved opiates, with thirty-three arrests. The next most prevalent drug was cocaine, with twenty-six arrests, and then twenty-one arrests for methamphetamine or amphetamine. Other substances included marijuana (fourteen), opioid use disorder medications like methadone (six), benzodiazepine (seven), and cigarettes (two). One case cited gabapentin, a medication used to treat seizures. Three cases involved alcohol. In one case a sixteen-weeks-pregnant Hispanic woman was pulled over by police while she was driving and was asked to take a breathalyzer test.[132] Her blood alcohol content was well under the legal limit for driving, but she was arrested and charged for endangering her own pregnancy. She was four months pregnant at the time.[133] A total of 52 percent of pregnancy-related arrests involved opiates or cocaine, followed by amphetamine (19 percent).

An examination of these modern drug scares indicates that the old narratives about threatening racialized others and bad breeding are still alive and well. The stated motivation for prosecuting women in South Carolina was the use of crack cocaine—a drug overwhelmingly associated with poor Black women. South Carolina's early arrest period primarily involved Black women who tested positive for cocaine. The *Whitner* case occurred only one year after the *New York Times'* mentions of crack cocaine reached their peak.[134] Alabama's drug testing was primarily motivated by concern about methamphetamine—a drug overwhelmingly associated with poor whites. Alabama's pregnancy arrests disproportionately involved white women who tested positive for amphetamines. Tennessee's arrests were primarily motivated by concern about opioids, a drug associated with poor whites, and the majority of Tennessee's drug-related pregnancy arrests involved opioids.

It is possible that, as certain racialized drugs are identified as being newly and suddenly pervasive and dangerous, health-care providers then selectively test patients who fit the profile of a typical user of that drug. They then interpret pregnant or postpartum people who test positive for that drug as uniquely harmful and are more likely to view these substances as especially threatening for the "unborn child," justifying a breach of medical privacy and a report to social services or law enforcement.

A practice initially developed and fine-tuned to gain acceptance using the bodies and lives of pregnant Black people shifted over time, as newer drug scares replaced crack. Bridges writes, "We have a racist precedent, crafted just a couple of decades ago, for dealing with substance use during pregnancy. This racist precedent has presently led the nation to be punitive toward a population—white women—that, due to its racial privilege, might otherwise have escaped our nation's punitive inclinations."[135] While much of the early research on the supposed harm caused by prenatal exposure to crack cocaine has now been discredited, the image of the crack baby still looms over prenatal substance use and is used to explain negative birth outcomes of all kinds, whether or not they were actually related to drug use. The influence of the crack baby and crack mom images is seen in both the subsequent methamphetamine scare and the opioid crisis. Even as new drug scares took the place of the crack cocaine scare, among pregnant women Black women are more likely to be reported after a positive drug test.[136]

If pregnant people violate the norms associated with virtuous motherhood, either by way of their identity, reputation, or actions, they become fair game for disdain and punishment. Crack cocaine, methamphetamine, and opioid drugs are all described as creating mothers devoid of maternal feeling and warmth. Pregnant drug users may violate not only drug laws but also the social expectation that mothers be self-sacrificial and morally pure. If the impact of recreational substances on fertilized eggs, embryos, or fetuses is as bad as it seems, these people are seen as not only irresponsible and selfish but also cruel, deliberately harming their babies and unleashing their damaged children on the world. As such, they are understood to threaten not only their individual children but the rest of society as well. Children were being harmed, and some would go on to become violent criminals or expensive care cases, or both. Something *had* to be done. But not just *any* something. The long-standing and inaccurate understanding that substance use disorder is a matter of individual choice and morality led to policy responses that focused on the drug use itself and not the underlying factors that contribute to drug use. Additionally, the long-standing demonization of certain populations of people who use certain kinds of drugs drove punitive responses instead of public health approaches. Professor of criminal law and policy Michael Tonry sees this in the "persistent refusal to accept a 'treatment on demand' approach to drug treatment even when it was known that tens of thousands of drug users in cities wanted but could not gain admission to treatment programs."[137]

From crack cocaine to methamphetamine and opioids, drug use during pregnancy may be seen as an urgent issue, but the lack of quality treatment options and expanded state support position punitive responses as the only solution. In each of the three periods of racialized drug scares, the drug was described as uniquely and especially harmful. Even as the sensationalized rumored harms were debunked, this hadn't stopped the pattern from repeating in the subsequent drug scare. Preexisting attitudes about good and bad mothers and racialized threats make a reliable foundation for punitive policy—even when these policies are unable to accomplish their stated goals of protecting infants. These punitive attitudes have led to frequently devastating and traumatizing experiences for the pregnant drug users who have been punished. At least 1,116 arrests of pregnant and postpartum people for pregnancy-related offenses have been made in South Carolina, Alabama, and Tennessee alone.

5 "I Felt Like Nobody"

Regina McKnight was the first person to be convicted by a jury of a crime against her own pregnancy in South Carolina. McKnight was a twenty-one-year-old Black woman who worked as a seasonal tobacco farm laborer. She had a tenth-grade education and attended special education classes in high school. Until her mother was tragically killed in a hit and run, McKnight had lived with her.[1] After her mother died, McKnight became homeless and, perhaps due to this compounded trauma and stress, she started using cocaine. Then she became pregnant.[2] In May 1999 McKnight went into labor and was transported to a hospital, where she gave birth to a five-pound stillborn baby girl, whom she named Mercedes.[3] McKnight, who suffered from hyperthyroidism and syphilis, had lost the baby due to placental and umbilical inflammation. She was devastated over the loss of her little girl, requested to hold her stillborn baby, and asked to keep photographs, footprints, and the baby's hospital bracelet.[4]

McKnight was drug tested after giving birth and was arrested in the hospital for "homicide by child abuse," a felony, for causing "the death of a child under the age of 11 while committing extreme indifference to human life."[5] Forensic evidence in the case was scant—two forensic pathologists explained that cocaine was not conclusively the cause of the stillbirth and that chorioamnionitis (a bacterial infection of the membranes surrounding the fetus and the amniotic fluid), funisitis (inflammation of the umbilical cord), hyperthyroidism, syphilis, a lack of nutrition, and tobacco use could have also contributed to the stillbirth.[6] The jury deliberated for only fifteen minutes and returned a guilty verdict.[7] McKnight was sentenced to twenty years in prison.[8] After eight years McKnight was released on appeal, her attorneys demonstrating that her counsel at trial had been ineffective in not showing that the cocaine couldn't be found to have caused the stillbirth.[9]

This is just 1 of the 1,116 arrest cases included in this study. Each case is so much more than a number. The cases represent real people with histories, families, and sometimes complicated lives. It is evident that many of the people arrested for crimes against their pregnancies experienced trauma before their pregnancies and during their pregnancies, births, and incarceration. They have one thing in common: they were arrested for crimes against their own pregnancies between 1973 and 2022.

The earliest arrest was made in 1986 in Tennessee, twenty-eight years before the state had adopted its fetal assault law. A twenty-seven-year-old white woman was charged with criminal abortion after she attempted suicide and had a stillbirth. Though she hadn't attempted to end her pregnancy, but rather to end her own life, prosecutors wanted to charge her with a crime for causing the pregnancy loss and used the state's existing "criminal abortion" statute. She was arrested and was held on a $5,000 bond. She pled not guilty by reason of insanity.[10]

Almost all the defendants, about 85 percent, qualified for indigent defense, with appointed public defenders or contract attorneys. I suggest that the disproportionate representation of low-income defendants is indicative not of their greater likelihood of using substances during pregnancy but rather of the greater likelihood that they would be tested and reported for substance use and the greater contact that impoverished people have with government agencies that surveil them. People of all socioeconomic statuses use substances, though the types of substances they use may vary. Law professor Michele Goodwin states that "studies suggest white women and women with higher levels of education are more likely than others to seek and acquire prescription medications, including Xanax, Oxycontin, Demerol, . . . and Tylenol with codeine during their pregnancies."[11] A 2012 study of socioeconomic status and substance use found that in young adults (the age group most likely to use drugs), lower family socioeconomic status was associated with smoking cigarettes, while higher family socioeconomic status was associated with alcohol and marijuana use.[12]

Though a more robust study of hospital testing policies is necessary to confirm this, I suspect that income level and race play a major role in decisions to test and report patients for substance use. Journalist Nina Martin writes that reports and investigations can "be highly subjective, influenced by small-town politics, family squabbles, class and gender biases, and personal beliefs about drug use and how children ought to be raised."[13] Studies have consistently found disparities in testing and reporting. For example, a 1990 study in Pinellas County, Florida, indicated that, although people at public and private doctors' offices use substances at similar rates, poor women were more likely than others to be reported to the authorities.[14]

Hospital test and report policies remain, largely, a mystery. Some hospitals, such as Gadsden Regional Medical Center in Alabama, "do not publicly disclose such data."[15] Other hospitals do not have official testing policies, instead testing and reporting at their own discretion, as was the case at Eliza Coffee Memorial Hospital in Alabama. The testing policy at the Medical University of South Carolina that was ultimately found to be unconstitutional called for testing if a person met any of the following criteria: no prenatal care, late prenatal care (after twenty-four weeks gestation), incomplete prenatal care, abruptio placentae (when the placenta separates from the uterus), intrauterine fetal death, preterm labor of "no obvious cause," intrauterine growth restriction of "no obvious cause," a prior history of drug or alcohol use, and unexplained congenital anomalies.[16]

CRIMINALIZED ACTIONS AND CHARGES

Defendants were arrested under a variety of charges. In South Carolina charges included great bodily injury to a child, unlawful performance of abortion, homicide by child abuse, distribution of drugs to a minor, unlawful exposure of drugs to a child, and involuntary manslaughter. The most common charges were for unlawful neglect of a minor and unlawful conduct toward a minor. The majority of the documented arrest cases in Alabama involved an initial chemical endangerment charge, but some defendants were ultimately offered lesser charges as part of a plea bargain. Still others were *initially* charged under a different law, with the charge later changed to chemical endangerment. Some of these initial charges included willful abuse of a child, distribution of drugs to a minor, contribution to the delinquency of a minor, reckless endangerment, manslaughter, assault, domestic violence, and possession of a controlled substance. Most Alabama arrests involved a positive drug test either during pregnancy or immediately after birth. Charges were also brought for "abuse of a corpse" and the failure to protect a fetus from violence. In Tennessee people with the capacity for pregnancy were charged with crimes including unlawful abortion, assault, reckless endangerment, vehicular homicide, murder, and child abuse.

Independent of the charges ultimately brought against them, people in South Carolina were arrested for a suicide attempt, an illegal abortion, the burial of an early-second-trimester fetus in the backyard, and positive drug tests during pregnancy or immediately after birth. In Alabama people were charged for the failure to protect a fetus from violence, abuse of a corpse, and inadequate prenatal care. Tennessee defendants faced charges for obtaining an unlawful abortion, being at fault in a car accident, denying a course of recommended medical treatment, attempting suicide, and fleeing police in a car and then on foot. In all three states, the pregnant person or a newborn testing positive for drugs accounted for the majority of law enforcement contact.

In four cases charges were brought for illegal abortion. In a case from 2006, a nineteen-year-old Black woman attempted to end her pregnancy by drinking bleach. The man who impregnated her no longer wanted the baby, and she was devastated. She drank four sips of bleach and sought medical treatment when she started having a hard time breathing. She survived and failed to terminate the pregnancy but was charged with attempting an illegal abortion.[17] A twenty-one-year-old Tennessee woman was arrested in 2018 when she attempted to induce a miscarriage by punching herself in the abdomen and allowing a young relative to sit on her belly.[18] She gave birth prematurely to a baby that lived for two hours.

She was arrested, held on $50,000 bond, and ultimately pled guilty. She was ordered to serve a year in prison.[19]

In December 2015 a thirty-one-year-old white woman named Anna Yocca was charged with attempted first-degree murder after she tried to end her twenty-four-week pregnancy using a wire coat hanger.[20] That September Anna tried to insert the coat hanger into her uterus as she sat in a bathtub, but then she started bleeding.[21] Her boyfriend drove her to the hospital, where Anna had an emergency cesarean section to save the twenty-four-week fetus. The very premature baby survived and would ultimately be adopted by another family. Anna was held in jail for over a year on a $200,000 bond. Eventually, the first-degree murder charge was dropped, and Anna pled guilty to three new charges—attempted criminal abortion, aggravated assault, and attempted procurement of a miscarriage. She was sentenced to prison, with credit for time served.[22]

In 2004 Gabriela Flores was a twenty-two-year-old mother of three, who had migrated from Mexico to the United States to earn money for her family.[23] Flores had a fifth-grade education and didn't speak English.[24] She found a job picking lettuce in South Carolina for $1.50 per hour. Then she learned she was pregnant.[25] She later explained, in a handwritten note to police, "I knew that I was not going to be able to support four kids—two here and two in Mexico."[26] About sixteen weeks pregnant, Flores was too far along to have a legal abortion in South Carolina. She could have traveled to Charlotte, North Carolina, for a legal abortion, but, with such low wages, she wouldn't have been able to save the $700 needed for a second-trimester abortion. Instead, her sister mailed her some misoprostol tablets from Mexico.[27]

Misoprostol, used to treat gastric ulcers, can be purchased over the counter in Mexico but requires a prescription in the United States.[28] Misoprostol can also be used to terminate a pregnancy and is one of two medications used for medication abortion. According to the World Health Organization, misoprostol or Cytotec alone can also be used to safely self-manage an abortion.[29] Flores took the tablets and ended her pregnancy, expelling the fetus on her bed.[30] Her housemate helped her bury it in their backyard, maybe to hide the fetal remains or maybe in recognition of the pregnancy loss.[31] The housemate told a neighbor what happened, and that neighbor contacted law enforcement.

Six days after she ended her pregnancy, Gabriela Flores was arrested and charged for the self-management of her abortion and "failure to notify a coroner" about the fetal remains; she was held on a $10,000 bond.[32] The roommate who helped her was charged with obstruction of justice.[33] Apparently, the county solicitor had initially sought homicide charges against Flores and had wanted to seek the death penalty in her case.[34] Flores wrote, "Please understand me. [My kids] need me a lot. They are little. Please forgive me."[35] Flores spent four months in county jail before she was even granted a public defense attorney, a violation of her Sixth Amendment right to appointed council. Angela Hooten of the National Latina Institute for Reproductive Health said, "I don't know how anyone could be forgotten like that."[36] Flores ultimately pled guilty to the illegal abortion charge and was sentenced to serve an additional three months in jail.[37]

In a case from 2006 in South Carolina, a thirty-three-year-old white woman who was going through a divorce and grieving the death of her mother after a battle with cancer was arrested when her newborn tested positive for cocaine. With so many stressful things happening in her life, she didn't realize that she was pregnant until it was too late to have a legal abortion in South Carolina. She did not want to give birth and intended to have an illegal abortion, but she went into labor first and had a stillbirth. Her arrest warrant states that she hadn't had any prenatal care, suggests that she "did intentionally deny appropriate care and nourishment of the infant," and states that this, in addition to the drug use, caused the stillbirth.[38]

An "abuse of a corpse" charge was brought against a thirty-year-old white woman in Alabama who had a miscarriage in 2015 and buried the fetus in the backyard in a bag. Apparently she had been hiding her pregnancy from friends and family members, and her abusive husband "didn't want children." He had forced her to have an abortion several years earlier. She went into labor at least four weeks prematurely and gave birth to a baby who lived for only six minutes. A family friend who heard about the pregnancy loss reported it to law enforcement. The woman was arrested and held on a $3,000 bond. She was convicted and sentenced to ten years in prison, suspended on the completion of an eighteen-month drug treatment program. At her sentencing she told the judge, "Every day I look in the mirror I see shame and guilt. . . . I feel awful. The baby didn't deserve that."[39]

Three arrests were made after people survived attempts to end their lives. Suicide is not a crime, but attempting suicide during pregnancy has been determined to be criminal in these cases. In a case from South Carolina in 2009, a twenty-two-year-old white woman was arrested after she survived a jump from her apartment window. She was eight months pregnant and struggling with bipolar disorder. She and her boyfriend, whom she lived with, had an argument earlier in the day. He woke up in the night to smoke a cigarette and went outside. When the woman woke up and didn't see her boyfriend, she assumed he had left her. She leaped from her fifth-floor window in an effort to end her life and landed on an awning four stories down. She sustained life-threatening injuries and lost her pregnancy but ultimately survived. Around six months later, her medical condition stabilized, and she was arrested for involuntary manslaughter. She pled guilty to the charges and was given a sentence of eighteen months in prison, suspended upon serving two months in prison and eighteen months on probation.[40]

One arrest was made in 2013, when a twenty-one-year-old white woman in Tennessee rejected medical advice. Rejecting medical advice is not considered a crime, but in this case a pregnant person was found criminally responsible for it. She went to the hospital when she started experiencing labor pains. The doctor treating her thought she should be transferred by ambulance to a different hospital, fearing for her condition (the reasons why aren't clear). Instead, she left the hospital and ended up giving birth in the hospital parking lot. Her newborn died soon after.[41] She was charged with second-degree murder and was arrested and held on a $50,000 bond. The charges were eventually reduced from second-degree murder to aggravated child abuse and neglect.[42]

A woman in Alabama was the victim of a car accident with a driver who was under the influence of alcohol. The woman, who was eight months pregnant at the time of the accident, had a stillbirth caused by her injuries. While receiving medical treatment, she tested positive for illegal substances. As the district attorney prosecuting the case explained, "The issue is, whether the death was caused by the trauma versus the chemicals. So . . . we charged [the driver] with manslaughter for the child. And we charged her with chemical endangerment of the child." The prosecutor explained that this was the woman's second time facing criminal charges for losing a pregnancy in his jurisdiction.[43] Another car-related case comes from Tennessee. This time the woman was found to be at fault in a car accident. She sustained injuries in the accident that caused her to miscarry. She was charged in 2002 with vehicular homicide.[44]

In one 2014 case from Tennessee, police attempted to pull over a twenty-two-year-old white woman who was not wearing a seatbelt. She was also driving with a suspended license, and, to avoid criminal penalties, she tried to flee the scene. After a vehicle chase, she ran on foot from the police officer, but she was eventually caught. She was charged with felony evading arrest and driving on a suspended license—standard charges for her actions. However, because she was nine months pregnant at the time, she was also charged with felony reckless endangerment of the fetus she carried.[45]

The vast majority of arrests of pregnant people were related to substance use. Of the 1,116 arrests included in the study, 1,100 (98.5 percent) involved substance use. In one case from Alabama, a woman named Casey Shehi was arrested after a positive test for benzodiazepine. She had been advised to use over-the-counter sleep medication to help with her insomnia, but it was ineffective.[46] One night, after getting in a bad argument with her ex-husband, Shehi took half of one of her boyfriend's Valium pills to calm herself down. The following night, unable to sleep, she took the other half. She went into labor about four weeks early, giving birth to a healthy though premature baby boy. Shehi tested positive for the benzodiazepine, but her newborn's urine tested negative, and her doctor assured her that "everything's cool." Law enforcement didn't think everything was cool. Almost two months later, police officers showed up at the nursing home where Shehi worked and arrested her for chemically endangering her baby. She was in the middle of a custody battle with her ex-husband at the time, and, based on her chemical endangerment arrest, her ex-husband was awarded sole custody of her preschool-age son.[47] Her charges were dismissed around nine months after her arrest.[48]

Katie Darovitz, a twenty-four-year-old white woman in Alabama, had severe epilepsy that she managed with the medications Keppra and Zarontin. She'd had a miscarriage and worried that her prescription medications could have caused it. She was pregnant again, and her seizures became even more severe—her neurologist recommended that she increase the dosage of her medication, and her obstetrician agreed, explaining that she could become seriously injured or even die from her seizures. However, her doctors acknowledged that the seizure treatment could also be harmful for her pregnancy. Katie was conflicted about what she should do. Surely the seizures weren't good for her or for the fetus, but the medication she had to treat the seizures could also be harmful. She read that marijuana might be a safer option and started to use marijuana instead of her prescriptions. It was effective. She said her seizures were under control. In December 2014 Darovitz gave birth to a healthy baby boy.[49] He was drug tested and was positive for marijuana. Darovitz was charged with chemically endangering her baby and, about two weeks after giving birth, was brought to the county jail.[50] I can't help but wonder if Katie would have also faced charges if she had instead continued taking her prescription medications. People who rely on medications to manage chronic illnesses are put in an impossible position, where the only way to comply with the law is to never become pregnant to begin with.

A few of the people in this study faced charges because they were found to have overdosed, which could have been purposeful or accidental. In 2013 a thirty-six-year-old white woman arrived at the hospital when she was overdosing. She was given an emergency cesarean section at only twenty-two weeks of pregnancy. She was then arrested and held on a $20,000 bond.[51] A twenty-eight-year-old white woman in Alabama was found to have overdosed at thirty-two weeks pregnant. She was in a car with a man who was using drugs. When police tried to pull the car over, the man sped off and ran a stop sign. Eventually, the police caught up. Initially, when they looked into the car, police thought the woman was dead. After receiving medical treatment, she was charged with possession and public intoxication in addition to chemical endangerment. In another case a twenty-six-year-old white woman in Alabama arrived at the hospital in 2013, after she overdosed on her deceased grandmother's prescription of Klonopin. She was about five and a half weeks pregnant at the time. She was arrested two days later, charged with chemical endangerment for testing positive for using clonazepam while pregnant.[52]

BIRTH OUTCOMES

A total of 682 cases from all three states involved the birth of a healthy baby. In 89 cases the health of the infant was recorded as being compromised in some way—typically babies born prematurely, babies who were lower than typical weight, and babies reported to exhibit symptoms of withdrawal. Even when attempts are made to standardize the assessment and diagnosis of withdrawal symptoms in newborns, these tools aren't immune to racial bias in the person doing the assessment. Pediatrics expert Dr. Matthew Grossman and his colleagues asserted that the scoring tools for infant withdrawal symptoms are vulnerable to racial bias.[53] For example, the Modified Finnegan Neonatal Abstinence Score tool asks whether a newborn's crying is "normal" or "excessive" and whether tremors are "mild" or "moderate-severe."[54] A health-care provider using that scale may interpret the normality of the crying or the severity of tremors through a racist or classist lens. As such, it is possible that some of these "complicated" birth cases are more an indication of bias among health-care providers than they are an indication of an actual medical condition. Pregnancy ended with a miscarriage or stillbirth in 77 cases. It is likely that cases involving a complicated birth outcome or a miscarriage or stillbirth are overrepresented, as pregnancy complications can trigger additional testing and investigation: drug tests, autopsies, and toxicology reports.

People were criminally charged for causing deaths and injuries with their substance use, which were usually associated with heightened penalties. However, it can be difficult to prove that substance use was the cause of the injury or death. For example, a thirty-four-year-old white woman in Alabama was arrested in 2015 on chemical endangerment charges when she tested positive for opioids and amphetamines after having a stillbirth. The state's doctor argued that her use of oxycodone had contributed to the birth outcome, but the case was eventually dismissed when a panel of physicians argued not only that the oxycodone did not contribute to the pregnancy loss but that her continued use of it was actually medically appropriate at the time.[55]

The eleven twin pregnancies and one triplet pregnancy in the study triggered multiple charges—at least one charge for each fetus. In some cases of multiple births, the condition of the newborns was different for each baby—one "healthy" and one "complicated" or one surviving and one stillborn. Multiple pregnancies are likely overrepresented in arrest cases because they are medically riskier than singleton births. Multiple pregnancies are more likely to result in premature birth, low birth weight, and pregnancy loss.[56]

Although it sounds outlandish, two of the women charged with crimes against their pregnancies in Alabama were not pregnant. In one case, from Etowah County, a woman was being investigated by a family services agency, and her daughter wrongly told investigators that she was pregnant. A warrant was issued for the woman's arrest, saying that the woman had chemically endangered her (nonexistent) fetus with amphetamines. After testing negative for pregnancy at the jail and after she was "admonished" by a member of the sheriff's department, she was released from jail, having been warned that if she became pregnant within the next few months, she would be charged.[57] This shows that, indeed, even if people only *appear* to have the capacity for pregnancy, they can be subject to state surveillance and even attempts at punishment, because of assumed procreative abilities. It also shows the depths of the sexism, racism, classism, and ableism at play in the criminal prosecution of pregnant people.[58]

While most arrest cases involved a postpartum defendant, each state made arrests of people who were still pregnant—208 cases in all, or about 19 percent of arrests. People who were still pregnant when they were arrested often gave birth while in custody—shackled in the hospital or unattended in a jail cell. South Carolina arrested 26 pregnant people, Alabama 166 pregnant people, and Tennessee arrested 17. Cases involving pregnant people typically involved investigations for other crimes (80) or probationary drug testing related to a prior offense (29), especially for those in the earliest stages of pregnancy. Some of these cases involved reports made to law enforcement by prenatal health-care providers (24) or by social workers (7). Notably, some of the defendants who were pregnant at the time of their arrest could have legally procured an abortion, either within their home state or in another state. A total of 17 were in their first trimester at the time of their arrest, and 4 were as early as six weeks gestation, or two weeks after a missed period. At the time of their arrest, 57 defendants were in their second trimester, and 43 were in their third trimester.

One woman who was still pregnant when she was arrested and jailed wrote a letter to her judge, begging to be released before she went into labor, writing, "I don't want to have my new baby here in prison." In another letter she explained that she was four months pregnant when she was first arrested and was still in custody when she gave birth and had her newborn taken away.[59] Several people gave birth while shackled or handcuffed to the hospital bed. The use of shackles on pregnant or postpartum people is especially problematic, as it presents unique health risks, including the "potential for injury or placental abruption caused by falls, delayed progress of labor caused by impaired mobility, and delayed receipt of emergency care when corrections officers must remove shackles to allow for assessment or intervention."[60] Shackling during birth has been found to be a violation of the Eighth Amendment's prohibition on cruel and unusual punishment and a violation of international human rights law, being described as a form of torture.[61] In testimony from the *Ferguson v. City of Charleston* Supreme Court case, Diamond Jones described giving birth while shackled in custody.

ATTORNEY. When you went into the Medical University of South Carolina in the handcuffs and shackles, were those things taken off so they could give you medical treatment, the handcuffs and the shackles?

JONES. No, sir.

ATTORNEY. The doctors who examined you at the university, did it with the leg shackles on?

JONES. Yes, sir. They would a—they would lift—let one leg be free and the next leg they would attach to the bed.

ATTORNEY. When you say attach? Is that with the handcuff devices?

JONES. Yes, sir.

ATTORNEY. Is that also true with your hands and arms?

JONES. One arm was attached as well.[62]

The threat of harm posed by shackling, both for pregnant people and their newborns, undermines the claim that pregnant people should remain in police custody during their pregnancies. The shackling of pregnant people with the use of a chain or belt around the belly or chaining them to the bed during labor are both potent images of the criminalization of pregnancy and the intrusion of policing in health-care settings.

People gave birth in a variety of locations, including more than one hundred different healthcare facilities. Nonhospital birth locations included a motel bathroom, on the side of the highway, and in an abandoned house. Nonhospital births were overrepresented in this study. In the United States, 1.64 percent of births take place outside of a hospital, while 7 percent of the births in this study occurred outside of the hospital.[63] It is possible that this overrepresentation of out-of-hospital births exists because the knowledge of punitive policies drove people away from care, disincentivizing hospital births.

SOURCES OF INFORMATION

People were detected and reported for pregnancy-related offenses by friends, family members, neighbors, health-care providers, social workers, and police officers. A total of 96 arrest cases (8.6 percent of arrests) were initiated by law enforcement investigations. For example, in one case a woman was charged with chemical endangerment when the car she was riding in was pulled over, and the driver of that car was found to be in possession of methamphetamine.[64] Her crime was sharing space with another person who happened to be carrying drugs. Health-care providers reported their patients to social services or directly to law enforcement in 853, or 75 percent, of pregnancy-related arrest cases. Of the 1,100 arrest cases involving substance use, 848 arrests (about 77 percent) occurred after a drug test administered in a health-care setting. I identified more than one hundred hospitals, doctors' offices, or medical clinics involved in arrests of pregnant people. Hospitals with the most arrests, in descending order, were Eliza Coffee Memorial (thirty-three), Decatur Morgan General (thirty-two), Medical University of South Carolina, or MUSC (thirty-one), Decatur Morgan Parkway (twenty-one), Shelby Baptist (fifteen), and Athens Limestone (fifteen). Hospitals involved in arrest cases were public and private; some were associated with universities, and some were religious hospitals: Baptist, Methodist, and Catholic. This indicates that strategic avoidance of certain health-care settings would be difficult, as the practice was already widespread. A total of 30 cases originated from positive drug tests issued while defendants were on probation for prior offenses, and 9 cases resulted from drug tests conducted by social services.

In at least one case, law enforcement used social media to gather information about a defendant. After she gave birth, one woman's newborn was drug tested using the meconium, or the newborn's first bowel movement. Law enforcement was notified of the positive drug test, and they began an investigation. They searched her publicly available Facebook profile and found a post announcing her pregnancy. They used this information to argue that she was aware of her pregnancy when she used drugs.[65] This is the only documented case in this study where social media was used as supporting criminal evidence. Electronic information, like search histories or text messages, has been used in pregnancy criminalization cases in other states. However, in every documented pregnancy-related case in the United States, the initial point of contact was a person making a report to law enforcement, not electronic monitoring.[66]

In another case an Alabama "crisis pregnancy center," or CPC, gave information over to law enforcement. CPCs are antiabortion centers that frequently pose as actual health-care providers to lure, gather information on, and provide misinformation to prospective abortion patients, advertising free ultrasounds to bring people through their doors In this case a woman was arrested after her newborn tested positive for cocaine. In 2016 she had sought a free ultrasound at the Sav-A-Life center. After her arrest the center gave law enforcement information about the date of her last menstrual period, the regularity of her menstrual cycle, and her birth-control practices.[67] Like in the aforementioned case, this information was used to argue that she was aware of her pregnancy at the time she had used drugs. This is the first documented case of a crisis pregnancy center giving information about a client to law enforcement.

There is evidence that people with the capacity for pregnancy made conscious efforts to avoid being reported to authorities and arrested. Indeed, when health-care providers have essentially become an arm of local law enforcement, patients in need of care might make other plans. Numerous studies have found that punitive test and report policies deter people from medical care, for fear that they will be reported and incarcerated and lose custody of their children.[68] Pregnant people who use drugs have strategies to avoid detection, including isolating themselves, skipping prenatal appointments, and avoiding treatment.[69] There is also evidence that the stigma associated with pregnant drug users has the effect of driving them away from care, because care providers also treat them with disdain and hostility.[70]

Sociologists Sheigla Murphy and Marsha Rosenbaum's study of pregnant drug users found that they often had negative experiences at the hospital: "When hospital staff were aware of the women's drug use, they became less than supportive and often abusive." Even women in treatment "reported that when they went to the hospital to give birth, they were faced with the stigma of being 'just a junkie.'"[71] Dorothy Roberts writes that patients at a hospital in Greenville, South Carolina, felt the hospital nurses intentionally neglected them and withheld pain medication when they were in labor, seemingly as a punishment for using drugs.[72]

Evasive efforts identified in my study included giving false identification or a fake name at the hospital, fleeing the hospital without their newborns, withholding the fact of their pregnancies from jail staff (when pregnant people were arrested for other kinds of crimes), avoiding prenatal care, and giving birth outside of health-care settings. One woman was arrested in relation to an unlawful possession charge and never told jail staff she was pregnant. She eventually developed medical complications and miscarried her pregnancy. Several people indicated that they avoided prenatal care throughout their pregnancies because they were afraid of arrest. One woman finally went to the hospital only when she was on the brink of sepsis from an infection in her foot. Another woman received prenatal care at the hospital and never returned once she was told she was under investigation. At least two women fled the hospital only three hours after giving birth. Still another woman attempted to leave the state of Tennessee when she went into labor, hoping she would make it to a hospital where she wouldn't face prosecution or risk losing her children. She ended up giving birth on the side of the highway.[73] One defense attorney said she knows a woman who drove to Georgia to avoid detection and another who gave birth to a baby in her bathtub at home.[74] These examples illustrate that, as other research has shown, this punitive effort to help pregnant drug users and their fetuses drove people away from care and into situations that were harmful or potentially harmful.[75] The threat of arrest created harm.

In one case a woman who had already been charged and who was diverted to drug court stopped showing up for court-mandated care out of fear for her safety. As she explained in a letter, the drug court judge was pressuring her to disclose the names of people who had sold drugs. She didn't want to participate in this, fearing that she and her family would be in danger if she started snitching on people.[76] So she stopped going to drug court and was ultimately sentenced to prison for six years, suspended upon eighteen months of prison and two years of probation.[77] This case is a striking example of the danger of combining health care and criminal justice.

Some of the prosecutors expressed concern about avoidance as well. District attorney David Campbell wondered, "If we start arresting women right after they've given birth, is this going to cause somebody to not seek prenatal care? To not go to the hospital to deliver their child? . . . So we tried our best to . . . every time there was something in the paper about a case like that . . . always we would just, you know, put out there, 'Look, if you're, if you're drug addicted and you're pregnant, you know, contact our office. . . . [You] will not be prosecuted.'" Solicitor Peter Hermann shared the same concern. He said, "Threat of prosecution can either do one of two things. For some of us it may bring us to where we need to be to have a healthy child. For others, it may drive them away from neonatal care."[78] Alabama district attorney James Palmer noticed that, after the prosecutions started, the populations getting care at the local hospital shifted, suggesting that they had been deterred from receiving care. "Other than the anecdotal, DHR saying, . . . 'We don't think we're seeing as many hospital cases from Tennessee and Mississippi and other counties that we were seeing since we started doing this. We think they may not be, necessarily, coming to our hospital, 'cause they might get charged.'"[79]

While more systematic research is needed to understand the scope of the avoidance problem, the leaders of health-care advocacy groups and health-care providers provide anecdotal evidence that fewer pregnant people were seeking treatment or prenatal care after these punitive policies went into effect. Drug treatment providers specializing in the treatment of pregnant women in northern South Carolina indicated that the *Whitner v. State* decision had a negative impact on their patients. One of these drug treatment specialists, Della Bricker, disclosed in a research interview that news vans were following pregnant women home from her treatment facility. "Then the women, uh, because they were being incarcerated, stopped coming to treatment. Or . . . they would go over the South Carolina line into North Carolina and give birth."[80] When asked what percentage of women she thinks are crossing state lines, Bricker replied, "If ten women were pregnant in [our city], I would say—and using drugs—three went across the line."[81]

Allison Glass, state director of Healthy and Free Tennessee, a health advocacy organization, reported, "We are getting lots of anecdotal information about women not seeking critical prenatal care, and avoiding going to the hospital to give birth, because they are scared of being arrested and having their baby taken away." Mary Linden Salter, the executive director of the Tennessee Association of Alcohol, Drug, and Addiction Services, asserted that fewer pregnant women were seeking treatment after the introduction of the Tennessee law as well. As arrests made headlines and stories spread about the arrests, "there was definitely a drop-off after that point." A Tennessee obstetrician specializing in opioid use disorder and pregnancy reported that patients were planning on delivering out of state and that others stopped showing up for their appointments. She stated, "We often don't know why, but we would not be surprised if the law was part of that reason."[82] A 2021 study on the impact of Tennessee's fetal assault law confirmed those suspicions, indicating that, after the law was implemented, there was a "sharp decline in the receipt of prenatal care." Even after the law expired, those numbers did not recover.[83]

In addition to driving pregnant people away from pre- and postnatal care and drug treatment, there is evidence that punitive policies implemented with the stated purpose of reducing or eliminating harm do not reduce harm and actually create harms for the birth parent and for babies. One study found that overdose increased 45 percent in states with policies criminalizing substance use during pregnancy.[84] Another study found that rates of neonatal opioid withdrawal syndrome increased after the implementation of punitive policies.[85] An additional study found that states that define substance use during pregnancy as child abuse or neglect have an increased risk of low birth weight, premature birth, and a lower Apgar score (a scoring tool used to assess the health of newborns), and that states requiring reporting of pregnant substance users have an increased rate of premature birth.[86]

ARREST, CASE OUTCOMES, AND SENTENCES

Mugshots of arrestees were commonly published in police blotters, daily, weekly, or monthly records of local arrests that can be found online or for sale next to newspapers at convenience stores or gas stations. For some people police blotters are a form of entertainment, giving the public the opportunity to look at the faces of newly arrested people in their community next to a brief description of the charges. The mugshots from these pregnancy-related cases are illuminating and heartbreaking, commonly showing tired, exhausted-looking faces, eyes puffy and red from tears.

Some of the defendants described their arrests. In particular, many of the women who received care at MUSC and would later be involved in the *Ferguson* case discussed details of their arrests in the deposition. Most of them were arrested at the hospital—something they found humiliating, as they were visible to others in this public space. They were commonly shackled, with wrists and ankles joined to a belt worn around the belly. They were also typically arrested while wearing hospital issue gowns that are open in the back, leaving their buttocks exposed.

In the deposition one woman explained how she felt when she was arrested and shackled: "I was devastated. I was, was in total shock. I didn't understand what was going on. I never broken the law before and for them to just come and arrest me I couldn't understand." She continued, "I was numb. I felt like nobody. I felt like there was a hole that I could just crawl in and die. I couldn't respond to anything. It was horrible."[87] Another woman, Angela Waters, expressed her embarrassment:

ATTORNEY. They took you down the hall. How did you feel being wheeled down the hall, having just given birth, with handcuffs, shackles and the sheet over you?

WATERS. Embarrassed.

ATTORNEY. Was the back of your hospital gown open?

WATERS. Yes, sir.

ATTORNEY. When you went into the holding cell, were you covered with anything other than the hospital gown?

WATERS. No, sir.

ATTORNEY. And when you went into that jail section, were you covered with anything other than the hospital gown?

WATERS. No, sir.

ATTORNEY. Was it still open in the back?

WATERS. Yes, sir.[88]

Another woman described being arrested and shackled at the hospital and then being put in the back of a police car to be transferred to jail. Her arresting officer made a stop at Burger King, ordering a cheeseburger and fries—for herself.[89] Though it is not unusual for on-duty police officers to purchase and eat fast food, it felt like salt in the wound for this defendant, who was facing a life-changing crisis right after giving birth. To purchase and eat food in front of an arrestee, especially one who had just given birth, emphasizes the lack of care and regard for pregnant people.

Like all criminal cases in the United States, the majority of the cases involving pregnant people ended with guilty pleas instead of criminal trials.[90] If every criminal case went to trial, the criminal court system would be completely overwhelmed. In 595 of 837 cases (about 71 percent) that had concluded and for which the outcome could be determined, the defendant pled guilty to the charges. In at least 4 cases, the case went to trial and the defendant was convicted.

Brooke Shoemaker, a thirty-six-year-old white woman, pled not guilty, and her case went to trial. In Alabama, in March 2017, Shoemaker was just on the cusp of her third trimester of pregnancy when she noticed a clear, odorless fluid leaking from her vagina. She wrote it off, but the next day started to experience abdominal pain. She took a bath, hoping that the warm water would ease her pain, but she ended up miscarrying her pregnancy in the tub. She wrapped the fetus in a towel, drained and rinsed the bathtub, and called 911.[91] She admitted that she had smoked methamphetamine during her pregnancy and that she hadn't received any prenatal care—but not because she didn't try.[92] She had sought care with the obstetrician who delivered her older child, but was turned away because she still had an outstanding $700 medical bill.[93] Shoemaker was arrested over two months later.[94] Though the medical examiner couldn't prove that Shoemaker's methamphetamine use had caused the pregnancy loss, Shoemaker was charged with Chemical Endangerment of a Minor and held on a $20,000 bond.[95] The jury took only one hour to find her guilty of a class A felony, punishable by ten to ninety-nine years in prison.[96] She was sentenced to eighteen years in prison.[97] District attorney Brandon Hughes said the case was a victory, telling reporters, "The result is real justice for this baby and a drug-addled baby killer off the streets."[98] Shoemaker is serving her sentence at the notoriously dangerous and overcrowded Julia Tutwiler Prison for Women.[99]

Sentences varied considerably and included deferred sentences like drug court (113); split sentences, where good behavior in a shorter prison or probation sentence could eliminate a heavier prison sentence (310); and straight sentences, where every part of the sentence, including incarceration and probation, must be served (167). Outcomes were still pending in at least 203 cases as of October 2022. Ultimately, people sentenced for crimes against their own pregnancies were sentenced to serve time in prisons, jails, and on probation; ordered to drug court or court-mandated drug treatment; and in a few cases ordered to be sterilized or to use contraceptives as a condition of probation or bond. The variation in sentencing is difficult to statistically analyze in a meaningful way, as most defendants had some kind of split or deferred sentence. In these cases if the terms of probation or drug court are violated, or cannot be complied with in practice (a not-unusual occurrence), these deferred sentences are frequently terminated and replaced with straight sentences of prison or jail time. In any case the extreme variation in sentences is, in part, due to the prevalence of plea bargains established through negotiation between the prosecution and defense.

Some people died before they were able to complete the terms of their sentence. Still others met an early end after completing their sentences, illuminating the many challenges they were facing beyond the pregnancy-related criminal charges. One woman died only a year after her arrest and was discovered dead when she failed to show up for a court hearing. At least two of the defendants were murdered.[100] In another case, about a month after giving birth, testing positive for drugs, being arrested, and relinquishing her baby for adoption, a woman hanged herself. Her boyfriend found her hanging from a clothesline pole in her grandma's backyard. Her cousin told a journalist, "That's kind of the way the troubles of life choked her."[101]

Table 3 Sentence type and duration range

Sentence type	*Duration range*
Straight sentence: incarceration	1 month to 20 years
Straight sentence: probation	1 year to 20 years
Suspended sentence: probation	5 months to 12 years
Suspended sentence: part 1. incarceration	1 month to 8.5 years
Suspended sentence: part 2. probation	1 year to 18 years
Incarceration if probation revoked	6 months to 20 years

Many cases resulted in prison or jail time. For the sake of comparison, in the three study states, penalties for homicide range from fifteen years to life—and also include the death penalty in some cases. Straight sentences for incarceration and probation range from one month to twenty years, and one year to twenty years, respectively. Suspended sentences are a little more complex. Most suspended sentences started with probation, ranging from five months to twelve years. Other suspended sentences start with a shorter period of incarceration, followed by probation. Split prison sentences range from one month to eight and a half years, to be followed by one year to eighteen years in probation. Failure to comply with prison, jail, or probation requirements in these split sentences results in the full prison sentence being applied, which ranges from six months to twenty years in prison. Among those who receive straight prison sentences, the mean sentence length is sixty-six months.

After controlling for birth outcome (healthy) and specific charge (chemical endangerment in Alabama, unlawful neglect in South Carolina), some racial disparities were apparent. In Alabama, among people who were given straight prison sentences, the mean sentence for white people was 64 months, and the mean sentence for Black people was 72.3 months. Among people who were given split sentences, starting with incarceration and ending with probation, Black people were sentenced to 3.6 more months incarceration than white people and 4.4 more months of probation. However, if probation was revoked, white people were sentenced to serve 6.25 more months of incarceration than Black people. In

South Carolina, for people who received suspended sentences, white people were sentenced to 50 months of incarceration, suspended upon the completion of 25 months of probation, while Black people were sentenced to 58 months of incarceration, suspended upon 38 months of probation. In the four cases that went to trial, all involving stillbirths, defendants received sentences that were much longer than the average: 144 months, 132 months, 216 months, and a split suspended sentence of 102 months in prison followed by 36 months on probation. If the person with a split sentence violated the terms of her probation, she would be required to serve an additional 18 months in prison. People with suspended sentences starting with prison were given a mean sentence of about 22.26 months, with a mean of about 62 months (or about five years in prison) suspended.

Some of the people sentenced to prison were sent to Julia Tutwiler Prison for Women, a facility about a thirty-minute drive from Montgomery, in central Alabama. Julia Tutwiler Prison is the state's only maximum-security facility, with the only death row for women. It's also the oldest prison in the state. It was designed to hold around 550 people but typically holds several hundred more than that. The prison has earned a bad reputation from years of human rights violations and abuses.[102] Originally built in 1942 and made to hold 364 people, by 2002 it held over 1000 people. In 2002 the US District Court found that Julia Tutwiler Prison violated inmates' right to be free from cruel and unusual punishment due to the "combination of substantial overcrowding and significantly inadequate supervision in open dorms that deprives inmates of their 'right to be protected from the constant threat of violence.' . . . In addition, other circumstances, such as improper classification, access to weapons, and the lack of adequate segregation units exacerbate the problem, as do the problems with the prison's ventilation and heat." The judge who wrote the opinion emphasized the "alarmingly high rate of assault" at Tutwiler—then the highest of any prison in Alabama.[103]

Tutwiler was the subject of a 2013 Department of Justice investigation after the Equal Justice Initiative submitted a complaint based on reports of systemic sexual abuse of the people being incarcerated at the prison.[104] In 2014 the department released its report, finding "a history of unabated staff-on-prisoner sexual abuses and harassment." Verbal abuse, voyeurism, and sexual assault and rape were common at Tutwiler. The report found that more than a third of the prison's ninety-nine employees had sex with inmates. Due to the nature of prison confinement and the level of power and authority that corrections employees have over incarcerated people, this sex is not legally consensual. One employee had thirty-eight documented incidents of sexual abuse.[105] At least one inmate was impregnated by a corrections officer. People held at Tutwiler were "forced to use sex as currency to 'barter' for necessities such as uniforms and hygiene products, but also illicit items like drugs and alcohol."[106] Bryan Stevenson, the executive director of the Equal Justice Initiative, explained that the women at Tutwiler were forced to live in a constant state of fear: "This fear that you're always at risk, that it's not safe to take a shower, that it's not safe to go to sleep when certain officers are in the dorm, that you can be extorted, that you can be manipulated into sexual favors, it's really horrific."[107]

In the years after the Department of Justice finding, there have been some changes. Now 65 percent of the Tutwiler staff is female, who, while less likely to engage in sexual abuse of incarcerated people, are nonetheless still capable of sexual violence and other forms of exploitation and abuse.[108] They also installed a video surveillance system of more than three hundred cameras. Male officers are required to announce themselves when they enter the restroom, and they no longer are involved in searching the women held there. The Department of Justice sends an appointed monitor to visit the prison every six months, but the prison remains overcrowded—one of the conditions that the Department of Justice identified as contributing to unsafe conditions there.[109] While the scale of what happened at Tutwiler may be exceptional, the poor conditions and abuses there are not aberrations.

A Department of Justice report indicated that around 4 percent of female state prison inmates and about 3 percent of female federal prison inmates were pregnant when they were admitted.[110] Of pregnant women in state prisons, only 53.9 percent received prenatal care. Professor of gynecology and obstetrics Carolyn Sufrin explains that prisons and jails pose risks for pregnant people: "The stress and conditions in jails and prisons, including lack of consistent access to standard prenatal care and mental health care, poor diets, poor sanitation, infestations with bugs and vermin, poor ventilation, tension, noise, lack of privacy, [and] lack of family and community contact, can be detrimental to physical and mental health which can result in poor pregnancy outcomes for both the mother and the baby."[111] Sufrin discusses her work as an expert witness reviewing pregnancy cases, writing "As an expert witness, I personally have reviewed cases from other county jails where pregnant women's bleeding was ignored, and they miscarried or gave birth to still- and live-born babies in their jail cells.[112]

Defendants described their experiences in jail and prison, commonly mentioning the lack of quality medical care, unhygienic conditions, fear, and a sense that prisons and jails just weren't appropriate for pregnant or postpartum people. In the deposition one Black woman explained, "It was disgusting. I can't even describe it. It was a cell with bars and it was a toilet that was filthy dirty. The floors were filthy dirty. The bench that had—that I had to sit on was filthy dirty. And it was—it was stink. It was disgusting." Another woman was freezing cold but didn't want to use the provided blanket, testifying that it "looked like somebody else done used the blankets and wiped their back sides with them." Postpartum women also reported being denied menstrual products in jail and discussed the shame and disgust they felt after they bled through their clothing. One woman talked about being afraid that somebody would hurt her in the jail.[113]

Angela Waters, who earlier described wearing an open-back hospital gown upon her arrest, explained what happened when she arrived at the jail:

ATTORNEY. Describe the cell.

WATERS. It was cold. It was—I don't have no shoes on. The shoes I had was paper shoes.

ATTORNEY. Paper shoes?

WATERS. From the hospital.

ATTORNEY. Continue.

WATERS. The commode had other people waste on it. Blood. And I want to urinate so bad.[114]

One woman was held in the Laurens County Jail, in South Carolina, for the entire seventh month of her pregnancy. In the deposition she explained,

> I was placed in a small one-room cell with ten and sometimes as many as 15 other women. I was forced to sleep on a mat on the floor, sometimes near the overflowing toilet. Never being allowed out of the cell, I could do nothing more than stand, squat, or lay for the entire 30 days. I was not allowed milk or juice because the other inmates could not have the same. It being the month of August, temperatures were soaring. There was no air conditioning or even a fan. I was truly miserable. I repeatedly requested medical attention, but to no avail. . . . They would promise that I would see the jail doctor the next day, but tomorrow never came.[115]

In contrast to the crowded jail cell, pregnant people incarcerated at Tutwiler are typically held in a dorm for sick people. Apparently, one incarcerated woman gave birth on a gurney in the hallway of a prison. Alysia Santos of the Marshall Project writes, "According to several prisoners, the nurses sent her back to the dorm after she went to the medical unit multiple times to report that she was in labor."[116]

Most of the people arrested for crimes against their own pregnancies had already given birth and so entered jail during their postpartum period. In 26 cases defendants were arrested on the same day that they gave birth. In 128 cases arrests occurred within a week of birth, and 264 were arrested within thirty days. Dr. Hytham Imseis, a specialist in maternal and fetal medicine in North Carolina, emphasized the importance of the period immediately following birth: "Separation of mothers from their infants increases the risk of postpartum, and mental health disorders, including postpartum depression, postpartum anxiety, postpartum traumatic stress disorder and postpartum psychosis." He continued, "Early separation of mothers from their infants also has adverse impacts on infant and child development with ramifications that stretch into adulthood."[117] One study found that mothers who lost custody of a child to foster care experienced much higher rates of depression, substance use, and mental illness than parents who had survived the death of their child.[118] Murphy and Rosenbaum found that when the women in their study lost custody of their newborns, they "usually spiraled downward into drug-fueled destructive cycles of self-blame."[119]

Regaining child custody is especially difficult for parents who are incarcerated. Roberts writes, "In the vast majority of states, inmates' newborns are automatically placed in foster care immediately after delivery.

Moreover, federal law governing child welfare practice encourages the termination of incarcerated mothers' parental rights, and local policies do too little to keep these mothers in contact with their children or to support their families after they are released from prison."[120]

One woman talked about being arrested when she tested positive for marijuana not even ten days after giving birth: "I was still going through postpartum . . . still bleeding. Still had stitches down there." She reported that the nurses at the jail were kind, but it took almost a whole day to receive pads to absorb postpartum bleeding, and she never received the pain medication she needed for her pelvis. Another woman went to the hospital with premature labor and was then sent to jail for the next three weeks until she delivered. She explained, "They told me I was under arrest for distributing to a minor. They put me in handcuffs and shackles and put me in a wheelchair and took me to jail." During her time in jail, she received no substance use counseling or treatment.[121]

Katie Darovitz, the woman who was arrested after using marijuana to manage her epilepsy, described being held in suicide watch in the jail, because she was so distraught over getting in trouble for the first time and being separated from her newborn. Bleeding from birth and lactating, she was held in the solitary of suicide watch with no soap, or blanket for the week it took for her family to make her $7,500 bail. By the time she was released from jail, Darovitz was "close to catatonic."[122]

Another defendant, who spent the last twenty weeks of her pregnancy in jail, related the pain of lying on a hard floor in her cell and described the conditions of the prison in a letter to her judge: "I have not been in no trouble and it is easy to get into trouble here. Do you no *[sic]* that they have wine here, weed, people sniff pills, soboxin *[sic]*. . . . I don't do it. I even done seen crack but I have been strong cause I want to go home I know if I go home and don't do right my kids will be taken back away and I will come back to this hell whole *[sic]*. As I'm writing you, they just took 8 people to seg for dirty pee."[123]

Many of the sentences included drug court. Touted as a less punitive innovation to respond to the reality of substance use disorder, drug court is court mandated, and sometimes court-designed, drug treatment.[124] The Drug Policy Alliance asserts that, among other things, "Drug courts have made the criminal justice system more punitive toward addiction—

not less."[125] In a 2019 report, the United Nations decried drug court, asserting, "Drug treatment courts, or 'drug courts,' are meant to offer court-supervised treatment for drug dependent people who would otherwise go to prison for a drug-related offence. Evidence shows, however, that 'in many States these courts have not achieved their intended results, have failed to conform to a public health approach, and do not tackle mistreatment and human rights violations that occur in treatment centers.'"[126] A deferred sentence to drug treatment can be viewed in some ways as an indeterminant sentence. Even if a court-ordered drug treatment program is designed to take a prespecified number of months, breaking the rules or relapsing can extend the program. A 2017 study by Physicians for Human Rights found that, overall, drug courts, framed as a blend of criminal punishment and therapeutic treatment, "largely failed at providing treatment to those who truly needed it, and filled up limited treatment spaces with court-mandated patients who didn't always need the care." The study continued, "In many cases, court officials with no medical background mandated inappropriate treatment not rooted in the evidence base."[127] Pregnant or postpartum people were placed in various drug-rehabilitation programs on pretrial diversions. It is not clear that all of them needed drug treatment, as a single positive drug test does not demonstrate that a person has substance use disorder.

Research has shown that pregnancy can motivate pregnant people with substance use disorder to seek treatment and that the vast majority of women who use drugs make an effort to reduce their consumption during pregnancy out of concern for the fetus.[128] Despite indications that pregnancy could be a critical moment for connecting pregnant people to drug rehabilitation or substance use treatment, it can be difficult to access in the United States, especially for people who are pregnant. Quality, accredited care is even harder to find. Tami Mark, William Dowd, and Carol Council found that only 50 percent of drug treatment facilities offered medications for substance use disorder, testing for infections, self-help groups, employment assistance, and transportation assistance—all elements that federal agencies have defined as indicative of higher-quality care. Only 51 percent of facilities were accredited.[129]

Many drug treatment facilities in the United States are religiously oriented, offering "faith-based" treatment services. Professor of criminal justice Hung-En Sung and his colleagues found that Christian-oriented treatment facilities approached treatment differently than secular treatment facilities. Christian treatment providers were more likely to see human nature as "fundamentally perverse and corrupt." They also felt that the top contributors to substance use were "separation from God" and "lack of meaning and purpose in life," while secular treatment providers ranked neurological and genetic factors as leading contributors. Echoing old Puritan values, the Christian treatment providers saw pharmacological strategies, advocacy, and empowerment as the least important treatment interventions, while "spiritual or religious needs" and "self-control and discipline" skills were ranked as the most important interventions.[130]

It is clear that at least a few of the people in my study were sent to religiously affiliated drug treatment programs. One such facility is called Hosanna Home, operated by a Christian group called Harvest Evangelism and described as a "Christian discipleship" treatment program. Their website explains, "The purpose of Hosanna Home was to give a place of restoration to women who are 19 years+ that are suffering from life controlling issues. Primarily some form of addiction such as drugs, alcohol, men, etc. Hosanna Home is a one-year program that allows women a safe refuge while repairing past mistakes and building a new relationship with our Lord and Savior." It continues, "Hosanna Home prays to send [the patients] out as Godly wives, mothers, daughters in the way they were created by God." Hosanna Home bans the use of any psychotropic medications, including antidepressants, antipsychotics, mood stabilizers, and stimulants and requires all patients to volunteer in the Hosanna Home–affiliated thrift store.[131]

Though religiously affiliated drug treatment programs may be useful or comforting to some, not everyone sentenced to receive care in such facilities believes in the premise or finds the treatment effective, and it is worrisome that a government institution would sentence someone to complete a religiously oriented treatment program. New Life for Women, another Christian rehabilitation program, is described as a "long-term, intensive, Faith-based, experiential treatment program for women who need help in overcoming their addiction to drugs and alcohol"[132] One woman was kicked out of this program twice for being out of "compliance." The first time she was medically discharged because "her psychological wellbeing was a concern." According to a note in the case file, the "client disclosed during an in-house AA [Alcoholics Anonymous] meeting that she didn't trust anyone at the facility including counselors. Client even went further to disclose that she had thoughts of running away from the facility and going to the truck stops in hopes that someone would kidnap and kill her. At no time did client ever disclose any of these feelings with her counselor." Her probation officer arranged a meeting with a doctor, who put her on some kind of medication and sent her back to New Life for Women. Her second discharge relates to her, apparently, not taking the Christian orientation of the treatment plan seriously. The facility noted, "One Saturday client was reprimanded for being dressed inappropriately and her response was, EVERYONE ELSE IS DOING IT. Sunday she was caught laughing and giggling with another client during Sunday School. And on Monday night we had a guest speaker and [the defendant] spent the time writing and passing notes with another client."[133]

Some defendants never received drug treatment at all, even when they wanted it. For example, in South Carolina in 2002, a woman was arrested and held in jail after she gave birth. She apparently got no offer of drug treatment at the hospital after she was tested or upon arriving at the jail. Indeed, even as she remained incarcerated, she was given no information about the amnesty program. Her own defense attorney is the one who ultimately was able to find drug treatment for her, though the solicitor's office tried to take credit for treatment they had obstructed through her immediate arrest and incarceration.[134] Law professor Wendy Bach's 2022 study of the fetal assault law in Tennessee showed that "few women actually got access to treatment through prosecution. Instead, they got what the criminal justice system always delivers; they were placed on probation, they went to jail, and they found themselves owing sometimes thousands of dollars in criminal debt."[135]

Issues finding accessible drug treatment options appeared over and over again in arrest cases. One woman was ordered to attend treatment as a condition of her release from jail on bond. She went to an inpatient treatment center, but then she started having seizures. Unequipped to care for her, the facility medically released her. The medical discharge, however necessary, meant that the defendant was out of compliance with the terms of her bond arrangement, and she was sent back to jail.[136]

There are many barriers to accessing drug treatment, including limited access to transportation, lack of health insurance, financial issues, homelessness, and bureaucratic challenges related to insurance and scheduling. Legal epidemiologist Sarah Roberts and clinical professor of public health Cheri Pies also attribute difficulties in accessing care to the drugs themselves. One woman in their study reported that her drug use made it hard for her to get an "appointment because by the time I found out I was pregnant, I had zero dollars, zero friends, a car that I couldn't drive, I didn't have internet, I didn't have telephone, and finding services to get the ball rolling in that way. Then in the phone book it doesn't exist. So if you don't have internet access, you're kind of in the dark."[137] Some of the people in my study had their deferred sentences terminated because they did not report to drug rehab when they could not find care for their children, as drug treatment facilities generally do not permit parents to bring their children along. Professor of public health Chandni Joshi and her colleagues found that barriers to treatment for women included lack of transportation and long travel time, lack of child care, judgmental clinicians, insufficient access to MOUD, health insurance not covering postpartum treatment, programs not accepting public insurance, insufficient funding, structural and institutional stigmatization, and criminalization of substance use during pregnancy.[138]

Prosecutors seemed unaware of, or indifferent to, the availability or accessibility of drug treatment options in their area—that it wasn't their responsibility. Solicitor Charles Condon insisted that there were enough drug treatment programs available but that the women who had been arrested "simply haven't taken advantage of them." My analysis of arrest cases indicated that this just wasn't true. For example, one woman had two different chemical endangerment charges from two different pregnancies. After being charged and arrested, she was released on bond on the condition that she start drug treatment. She did her best to comply with the orders. As she explained in a handwritten letter to her judge, "I am writing you this letter to hopefully express to you my desire for help. I understand that it looks bad a pregnant addict, but I was sincerely trying to get into treatment before my daughter was born." She called the inpatient drug treatment center every day to see if there was an open bed for her, but every day was told no.[139]

She made other efforts to change her life. She explains, "I was following new [DHR] plans and doing everything they asked of me. I had returned to church and was starting back into my singing ministry." Because she couldn't find treatment, she was arrested again, about a month after giving birth to her second child. The judge granted her furlough so she could be at her mother's death bed. She explains, "We had a visit. I got to say goodbye and promise her that she didn't have to worry about me, that I was gonna do good and not fall back into that bad lifestyle that I had recently been in . . . and I WILL keep my promise to her." She was motivated to attend drug treatment—to keep her promise to her mother and to be a good mom, but treatment just wasn't available. She wrote the judge begging to be released from prison: "I am asking if you would please give me the opportunity to do my time on community corrections, so I can continue to get my weekly visits with my baby at DHR, and go to church, and work on my addicts for Christ meetings that I have been going to. . . . I am asking you sir for this one chance and I promise I will use it like I am supposed to and do right so I can raise my little girl and be the mother she needs me to be."[140]

Another woman wrote a letter to her judge literally begging to attend rehab, motivated to be a better mother to her children than her own mother had been: "I realized I messed up, but the night I got arrested really took a toll on me because my babies got took from me and it was the worst pain I've ever experienced. I don't want to follow in my mother's footsteps and I'm breaking away now. . .. If I can go to rehab while waiting for court in May, then I should be able to complete my program."[141]

Still others were held in jail indefinitely when there were no beds available at the local treatment facilities—an unconstitutional practice. A twenty-three-year-old white woman who tested positive for marijuana early in her pregnancy was arrested and held in the county jail in Etowah, Alabama. Her pregnancy was considered high risk, as there was a history of miscarriage in her family. Her jail cell was crowded, and the only bed space available to sleep on was a top bunk, which was not safe for her to use, given her condition. Arrested at six weeks of pregnancy, she was taken to the local hospital six weeks later when she started bleeding. She was diagnosed with subchorionic hematoma. Back at the jail, she kept bleeding for another five weeks, while she suffered from hunger and slept on the floor. Another woman was arrested six days after giving birth, while visiting her baby at the NICU, because she had a false positive test for methamphetamines and was taking prescription Subutex (a medication that helps prevent opioid withdrawals). She too was held in the jail when no bed at a treatment facility was available for her. Her boyfriend told reporters that in addition to being robbed of the opportunity to bond with her newborn, she wasn't given pads to absorb her postpartum bleeding. Instead, she resorted to stuffing paper towels in her pants to absorb the blood. She was held in jail for about three months.[142]

Medical treatment in these facilities also varied significantly, as the regulation and oversight of drug treatment programs are haphazard. Some facilities advertised that they provided medication for opioid use disorder but did not provide these services once the women were enrolled. One woman reported,

> When I went there, oh my god, [the treatment center] was awful. I wouldn't send my dog there. I went there during the day and the lady was really nice. "Oh, we'll help you, we'll give you something to ease the withdrawal and to help you sleep and we'll keep you comfortable." I'm like, okay, this is what I need, this is where I need to be. And that night, they refused to give me anything to help with the withdrawals and I was freaking out and I was sick and I had just had it. Two o'clock in the morning, I ended up walking out of there. They wouldn't help, they just basically looked at me like I was some horrible drug addict.[143]

Drug treatment for pregnant people can be more complex than drug treatment for people who aren't pregnant, creating a disincentive for centers to treat pregnant people—they are considered a liability. Professor of nurse midwifery Julia Phillippi and her colleagues conducted a secret-shopper–style study, calling drug treatment programs in an attempt to arrange care. They found that the prospective clients "frequently experienced long hold times, multiple transfers, and difficult interactions. Clinic receptionists were often mentioned as facilitating or obstructing access."[144] Dorothy Roberts writes, "Most hospitals and programs that treat addiction exclude pregnant women on the grounds that their babies are more likely to be born with health problems requiring specialized prenatal care. Program directors feel that treating pregnant addicts is worth neither the increased cost nor the risk of tort liability should a woman sue the clinic for harm to the baby." She continues, "A congressional survey of hospitals in large metropolitan areas showed that two-thirds had no place to refer pregnant women for drug treatment."[145] Very few inpatient treatment programs in South Carolina, Alabama, or Tennessee specialized in treating pregnant people, accepted Medicaid, and allowed parents to bring young children. Researchers from *America Tonight* contacted all the treatment programs listed on the Tennessee Department of Health and Human Services website that claimed to offer services for pregnant women. In the entire state, "they found five clinics that would allow pregnant women to enroll in their program and accepted Medicaid. Two of the programs were full, leaving fewer than 50 beds available" in the entire state.[146]

Furthermore, pregnant women who were referred for opioid use treatment by criminal justice agencies were less likely than women referred through other sources to receive nonreligious treatment.[147] Stigma contributed to the negative experiences for people seeking care. Phillippi and her colleagues' secret-shopper study found that pregnant people had negative experiences on the phone related to their pregnancy status. For example, one secret shopper was told "that if I did not follow [their] protocol, I would go into convulsions and possibly kill the baby." Another caller was told she should stop using because "I have another life to think about." Callers were also sometimes told they could not be seen because "the clinic did not have the 'correct' medication and/or remarks about previous poor experiences with pregnant patients." Pregnant callers were sometimes denied treatment because the providers were "afraid," "didn't feel comfortable," or because pregnant people were "too much of a high risk." One pregnant caller was told, "Whoaaaaah, we don't do that here, I won't get into that mess again."[148]

In another study one woman reported, "It was just the whole, I guess liability issue of the miscarriage associated with treatment and withdrawal of the pregnancy that really scared people. And even when I went to [the local hospital] and said, 'Can you guys watch me while I detox?' and they said no, I mean, I even—and then they ended up sending me home and I was like, 'I'm sick, can you at least send me home with some Vicodin or something?' and they were like, no, so I said, 'So you're going to send me home to have a miscarriage then.'" She continued to use heroin while she looked for other possible treatment options. By the time she found treatment, she was thirty weeks pregnant.[149] Because of the shortage of drug treatment facilities, pregnant people may be subject to long waiting periods before space becomes available. For example, a Tennessee woman called the only local facility that treats pregnant people and was told that "the wait list . . . was like, three, four weeks—and that's for a pregnant woman."[150] What does it mean to mandate drug treatment to avoid incarceration when drug treatment just isn't available?

AFTERMATH

Even when cases were dismissed without sentencing or people completed their sentence, the trouble was not over. They faced the trauma of what they went through, the humiliation that they were exposed to, and the scorn that their communities have for them. When Kimberly Blalock's case was finally dropped, after over a year of wondering and waiting, she still struggled. Though she is no longer facing the threat of a criminal penalty, and her baby is "healthy, loving, and super smart," Blalock and her family are still struggling with the aftermath of everything that happened. Her two teenage sons, traumatized from the police raid, "still get scared when [they] pass a police car on the highway."[151] Blalock explained to journalists, "Ever since a group of armed police officers showed up at our home, my children have lived in fear that their mother would be taken away from them."[152] The children have also contended with bullying and harassment at school, due to local knowledge about their mother's case. Seeing mean comments people have made about her case online and feeling judged by their community, Kimberly's family no longer attends church as often.[153]

Some of the MUSC defendants in the *Ferguson* case discussed their fear and the feeling of being trapped when, after being treated so terribly during their pregnancies, they were forced by limited options to return to MUSC for care. One woman reported that, since she was jailed after birth, "It's hard for me to sleep at night anymore because I'm so afraid somebody is coming to get me. So I have to drink just go to sleep, to go through with it. . . . With no other options for medical care, one woman was left with the choice of either returning to this hospital where she was being surveilled and treated disrespectfully or losing a limb to cellulitis, a skin infection that can be deadly if untreated.[154]

Several who had been arrested at MUSC mentioned their disillusionment with authority and their fear or mistrust of health-care providers. One woman said, "I will never trust a doctor or a physician again. That they just—they just tormented—tormented me. I never understood why." Another woman explained, "As I go forward with my life now, I—I'm more precautious of where I get my medical treatment from and who I talk to. If I talk to anybody. I don't—this experience to me, has made me see that people will do anything they want to with or without your consent. . . . My life is still devastated every time I look at my little girl to know that she was almost conceived in jail." A woman who needed regular medical care for hepatitis described how challenging it was for her to get that care after experiencing medical trauma. When she even thought about going to the doctor's office, she explained, "I have anxiety and panic attacks and it's—they have gotten worse."[155]

Casey Shehi, the woman who was arrested for taking a single tablet of Valium over two nights, one half at a time, explained that after her arrest she felt ostracized from her community: "I feel like everywhere I go, people just kind of look at me and shame me like I'm a monster, like, 'how could you do that to your baby." Living in a relatively small town, Shehi described running into people who were involved in investigating and prosecuting her. Her child goes to the same day care as the lead investigator on her case, and they run into each other sometimes at drop-off or pickup.[156]

As can be imagined, defendants in these cases had other things happening in their lives when they were arrested for crimes against their own pregnancies. Relying on court documents and media stories offers only a glimpse at their lives beyond the criminal charges, but an examination of these has revealed some commonalities worthy of discussion—child-care and family obligations, jobs, abusive relationships, and financial struggles. For example, at least two arrest cases involved women who were unhoused. Several people were identified as having done street-based survival sex work, one of them starting as a thirteen-year-old.[157]

Several of the Black women from the *Ferguson* case in South Carolina spoke in their depositions about the impact that Hurricane Hugo had on their lives and on their ability to access medical care, like prenatal care or drug treatment. Hugo made landfall in South Carolina as a category 4 hurricane in September 1989. The storm was devastating, knocking out electricity for 80 percent of the state. The National Weather Service estimated that Hugo damaged 79,000 homes and killed thirty-five people in the state.[158] This destruction had an impact on people who were pregnant and in need of care. For example, a Black woman talked about how the hurricane essentially leveled her community, homes and vehicles alike. She was supposed to get medical care some distance away, but because her car, and the cars of her family members, had been totaled in the storm, she was unable to make her appointments and was eventually arrested. She explained, "It was right after Hugo cuz I—after Hugo came in September, since I lost everything that I had, I didn't have any home or no transportation to keep up with my appointment back and forth to medical. Everybody in the area had lost everything they had too." She describes a family member using the insurance check that she received to cover the expenses associated with flood damage to bail her out of jail: "My cousin got a bondsman and my mother used the only insurance money that we had gotten off our house, we had insurance on the furniture, so she used that. . . . That was from after Hugo my house was destroyed, and that was the insurance money we had things insured in the house. So she had to use that."[159]

It was evident that some of the people in the study were struggling with abusive relationships. One woman had an abusive ex-boyfriend attempt to use her chemical endangerment arrest as evidence that she was an unfit parent. After violating a protection order at least twenty times, he tried to break into her home while armed with a handgun and sent threatening text messages. The woman reluctantly called the police, who shot and killed him. The bond for her chemical endangerment arrest was $10,000, but the highest bond her ex ever faced was $3,000. The woman told a reporter that she wondered if her chemical endangerment arrest impacted the way officials handled her ex-boyfriend's violence.[160]

One woman told law enforcement that she used drugs after she was assaulted by a man out of state.[161] Several others struggled after they gave birth at home. Another woman said that her common-law husband beat her when she told him she was pregnant. He helped deliver the baby at home in their trailer. Once the baby was born, she said that he wrapped the baby in a blanket, walked out of the room, and then denied the existence of the baby, who was later declared dead due to head trauma. Apparently her friend came to visit and check in after the birth and had to literally fight her way past the common-law husband to enter the trailer. The woman lost a lot of blood during the birth and needed medical attention that her husband wouldn't have allowed her to have without her friend's intervention.[162]

Several of the defendants discussed their familial obligations, mostly in caregiving roles. Hiring a care worker, such as a home aide, can be prohibitively expensive, leaving the labor of care to family members. Some women were worried after they were incarcerated because they were the only ones available to give care to elderly family members. One woman was tasked as the sole caretaker for her elderly father, and another was the primary caretaker of her disabled stepfather.[163] What would happen to them?

The implications of these findings are many, beginning with the idea that not only are these charges used against people who are pregnant—they can be used against anybody who *looks like* they could become pregnant. Pregnancy policing works to surveil, regulate, and control those who seem like they *could* have the capacity for pregnancy, whether they are actually pregnant or not. The policing is then run through a discretionary filter that is time and location specific—the decision by health-care providers to administer a drug test, the decision to report health information to social workers or directly to law enforcement, the decision to file a criminal complaint, the decision to make an arrest, the decision to prosecute, and the decision to convict. People's county, race, age, health status, birth outcome, relationship status, social class, and type of drug they may test positive for all determine their chances of being tested, reported, and criminally charged for actions that *only* people with the capacity for pregnancy are charged with.

As Angela Davis and her colleagues write, "The criminal legal system so profoundly masks the harm that it produces that even when people are not helped by the system, the system is never held responsible for its failings and the individual is instead at fault."[164] By examining the experiences of the people charged with pregnancy-specific crimes, we are better able to understand the direct impact of test, report, and arrest policies and of arrests for crimes against a person's own pregnancy. The experiences and case outcomes indicate that these arrests and prosecutions are very much felt as punitive treatment that is humiliating, denigrating, traumatizing, and medically inappropriate. Instead of encouraging drug treatment for drug-related arrests, these policies incentivized *hiding from, avoiding, or evading* health care, a direct *opposite* outcome of the stated goal of pushing people to treatment. A lack of workable and culturally and medically appropriate drug treatment options meant that people who desperately *wanted* to enroll in treatment and even people who were arrested and ordered to treatment couldn't find treatment that worked for them. Some defendants keenly, and perhaps accurately articulated a sense that they had lost their rights when they noticed they were being treated differently than people who weren't pregnant. While "drug scare" narratives focus on overstated harms and villainize people being targeted for arrest to justify punitive treatment, examining the experiences of the pregnant and postpartum people who are punished unmasks the very real harms being caused by the punitive policies themselves.

6 Wielding the Velvet Hammer

In the context of highly sensationalized drug scares, the pregnancy police were motivated to do something about drug use during pregnancy, specifically about pregnant people using politically salient and racialized drugs. South Carolina got started during the crack crisis in the late 1980s and early 1990s; Alabama designed its policy around the methamphetamine crisis of the midaughts, and Tennessee responded to the opioid crisis of the 2010s. Prosecutors played a central role in this process. They provided "teeth" for the policy—using their prosecutorial authority to solve a public health problem as a criminal justice problem. In their view all they needed to do was use the threat of punishment to coerce pregnant drug users into treatment. Instead of the heavy hammer of the law, they'd use a "velvet hammer," that, to quote law professor Khiara Bridges, "would softly pummel pregnant women."[1] Health-care providers, social workers, law enforcement, prosecutors, and judges built a system that relied on coercion—the threat of criminal penalties—and that could function only if pregnant people were understood to have fewer rights than other similarly situated people.

In this chapter I explore the goals of prosecutors, judges, and law enforcement in policing pregnancy and the tactics they've used to achieve these goals. I'll also explore the outcomes, or consequences, of their work.

Indeed, while many initially spoke of a desire to help pregnant people with substance use disorder and their newborns, this often gave way to judgement of and disdain for people who use drugs during pregnancy. Many of the actors who work in the criminal justice system fundamentally misunderstand substance use disorder and are uninformed about or biased against the most effective treatment options.[2] Additionally, because these cases involve many different departments or institutions and the people involved in policing pregnancy are responsible for and sometimes only aware of their small part, they are able to insulate themselves from the consequences of their involvement.

GOALS

Many of those involved in policing pregnant people spoke to a sense of urgency. Judge Tim Dwyer explained to reporters, "I'm just trying to do something when other people aren't doing anything."[3] Deputy district attorney general Jennifer Nichols explained, "I think what we are finally doing is trying to mount an effort to address the problem that has been present and very real in our state and across the country for a long time." They weren't alone. Other prosecutors and law enforcement officers shared the opinion that prenatal drug use was especially harmful and that not enough was being done about it. Chris Connolly, a district attorney in Lauderdale County, Alabama, described neonatal withdrawal as "horror." In 1991 Catherine Christophilis, an assistant solicitor in Greenville, South Carolina, described seeing children in a NICU who were apparently in withdrawal. She said, "If you see these little kids, it's just an image in my head that will never . . . Of these babies in withdrawal, just all the shaking and all. You're talking about these little teeny babies, through no fault of their own, having to go through that the rest of their lives. That's wrong." Amy Weirich, a district attorney in Shelby County, Tennessee, told reporters, "These babies that are born with these drug addictions are going to have[,] some of them[,] physical, emotional, and psychological side effects because of the drugs their mothers ingest while pregnant."[4] Tennessee representative Terri Weaver understood this harm to be lifelong and devastating: "These babies are born and their lives are totally destroyed."[5]

Angela Hulsey, an assistant district attorney in Colbert County, Alabama, explained that it is hard to know the full scope of the harm but implied it could be even worse than initially anticipated: "What's really scary is once these babies are born and test positive for certain drugs, it's hard to say at that point how much of an impact it's going to have on that child because that's going to depend on the drug and how much of the drug the child was exposed to. So they could have longer lasting effects than we would even be aware of at the beginning when they first test positive." Danny Reid, a police lieutenant in Pleasant Grove, Alabama, shared these sentiments, suggesting that even infants who *seem* normal and healthy at birth could be hiding damage from drugs: "You won't know you've truly victimized this child until much later in life when she has trouble in school, trouble functioning." Even decades after the policies were first implemented, some felt not enough was being done to solve the problem. In 2019 Detective Robert Smith, of the Columbia Police Department, said, "These are terrible drugs and we don't know the lasting effects. We could be melting babies' brains, and we are just letting it go."[6]

All the prosecutors I interviewed said that their ultimate goal was to help the baby and the pregnant person by incentivizing drug treatment with the threat of prosecution and were emphatic that locking up pregnant women was not their goal. Prosecutor statements from news articles also reflected this. Julia Graham, who started the first testing policy in South Carolina, described the need for an approach that addressed the mother and her child together:

> How can we get to the bottom of this . . . and protect the children but also get the mothers well? Because from the get-go, we did not want the State of South Carolina to become the parent, but we wanted to try and come up with [a] way in which to . . . outreach for the moms and the other family and to keep the babies safe. So, trying to do these goals together . . . because the goal was just like I said, to protect the children and get the mothers well and get us out of their lives.[7]

District attorney Chris Connolly echoed this sentiment, telling reporters, "Our goal in these cases is to offer [the mothers] drug treatment and give them an opportunity to turn their lives around." In another interview Connolly said, "Our goal is not to try to put her in jail but to insist she get drug treatment." Similarly, Greg Gambril, a district attorney in Covington County, Alabama, explained, "We are doing this for the sole purpose of trying to make sure both the mother and the child have a healthy pregnancy. . . . We're not trying to throw these women in jail. That's absolutely not the goal of it."[8] Deputy district attorney general Jennifer Nichols said, "The goal is to help them kick their habits, get rehabilitation that they need and at the end if they successfully complete drug court then it is expunged meaning taken off."[9] Jimmy Harp, a district attorney in Etowah County, Alabama, said, "I think we all have the same goal, and that's to make sure a child is born to a mom and dad who are clean and drug free, and that child is born drug free, and lives in a happy and safe environment."[10] District attorney Walt Merrell mentioned that he wanted pregnant mothers with substance use disorder to ask for help from them *directly*. DA Merrell told reporters, "What we want is for that addicted mother to come in my office and say they need help. If an addicted woman came into my office right now and said that she was addicted to whatever and that she needed help, then my only effort would be to get her into a clean environment."[11] Despite all these words to the contrary, a deeper dive shows that more punitive attitudes lie just beneath the surface.

Some prosecutors articulated a sense of tension between helping the baby and punishing the mom, weighing polar interests like protection and punishment or the rights of the pregnant person versus the rights of the fertilized egg, embryo, or fetus. ADA Hulsey told journalists, "It's a terrible situation to see because you have multiple interests that are competing interests that you have to balance out and work with these cases. Obviously, you want to do what you can to make sure the child is protected and justice is served, but you also want to see some treatment for the mother as well." Her statement indicates a primary concern with the fetus and a secondary concern with the pregnant person. Sixteenth Circuit solicitor of South Carolina, Tommy Pope, explained "the need to balance those interests: the desire to prosecute and punish a child abuser, versus the desire to not scare away expectant mothers from prenatal care." DA Harp expressed some frustration with the public response to the prosecutorial approach: "You had terrible [newspaper] pieces about how prosecutions invaded a woman's right to do this and that. . . . My goal is certainly not to infringe on the constitutional rights of anybody. It's simply to save a life."[12] Even if it wasn't the goal, the policies being used to achieve that goal necessitated the infringement on constitutional rights.

Prosecutors also articulated a belief in the maternal-fetal conflict: that the fetus was an innocent victim and needed to be protected from its mother. This seemed to open the door to more punitive attitudes. For example, Todd Entrekin, a sheriff in Etowah County, Alabama, told reporters, "In this county, we will continue to protect those innocent lives that cannot yet protect themselves. . . . Pregnant women will be arrested for endangering their child's life. If they have not received this message yet, they will soon find out."[13]

Prosecutors and law enforcement emphasized the tininess and helplessness of the fetal victims, both attempting to humanize them and singling them out as uniquely small and vulnerable. District attorney Bill Veitch of Bessemer, Alabama, said, in 2016, "My whole point in all of our arguments in court is that we have to protect those who cannot protect or defend themselves. When you are addicted to this extent, even your own child is expendable. We have to defend the children." Detective James Heaton of the Clarksville Police Department in Tennessee explained, "The child can't say, 'No, mommy, I don't want to do this.'" Christophilis told reporters, "We're talking about babies that are addicted, in my opinion one of the most helpless groups of citizens in the country and we're just not going to put up with that."[14] By describing the fetus as "innocent," they draw a contrast with the pregnant person, who is *not* seen as innocent. Attorney Bobby Hood, who represented the Medical University of South Carolina (MUSC) in the *Ferguson* case, told reporters that the appropriate focus should be on the protection of the fetus, saying, "These women are pathetic human beings, they lead pathetic lives, and they need help. The mother and the fetus both have rights, but society has a duty to protect the weaker of the two."[15]

Many law enforcement officers and prosecutors compared drug use during pregnancy to graphic physical abuse. Mitch Floyd, an assistant district attorney in Marshall County, Alabama, said, "Child abuse—whether physical, sexual, or chemical—is the worst of crimes."[16] Hood compared maternal drug use to "taking a pistol and shooting the baby right through the mother's stomach or taking a knife and sticking it in there."[17] In research interviews prosecutors compared prenatal drug use to drunk driving, planting and then detonating a bomb in a building, lacing baby formula with drugs, injecting drugs into a child with a syringe, and driving without a seatbelt.[18] Solicitor Pope compared prenatal drug use to kidnapping, explaining, "The victim is, in essence, held hostage by the defendant for nine months." Sheriff Leon Lott from Richland County, South Carolina, told reporters, of someone who experienced a pregnancy loss, "Every time she used drugs, she was killing that child—a little more each time."[19] Note that some of these analogies require the transformation of the pregnant person into an object, like a car or a building.

These negative attitudes creep into judgements about appropriate motherhood. For example, ADA Floyd explained, "Addiction is a 'very powerful force . . . however there's a force that's more powerful than that to me, and that child is helpless, and God has put one person on this planet to be the last-line defense, to be the fiercest protector of that child, and that is its mother. My wife would literally claw someone's eyes out—fight you to the death for our children. I mean, that's just what mothers are supposed to do. When that child's ultimate protector is the one causing the harm, what do you do." He continued, "It's a shame that babies need to be protected from their own mothers, but sometimes they do, and that's our job. . . . It upsets me and offends me at the same time."[20] Representative Terri Weaver explained to the Tennessee House Criminal Justice Subcommittee, "Let's just focus on the children and not make excuses for some of the parents that, my idea is and I'll put this on the record, have no business being parents. They know how to make 'em but they do not know how to be parents."[21] Assistant solicitor Phil Smith said, "I can't think of a mother intentionally hurting her child."[22] Sheriff Gene Mitchell told reporters, "It's a reckless and selfish act for a mother to use drugs while pregnant."[23] Lieutenant Reid explained, "I'm doing my damndest to try to prevent any future damage to this child, since it's obvious the mother doesn't seem to care."[24] John Andrews, a district attorney in Butler County, Alabama, said, "It is unbelievable to me that a mother-to-be would take that kind of chance with the life of their unborn child."[25] While wanting to get healthy for children can be motivating for some people in treatment for substance use, it is simply not true that the "mothering instinct" alone can overcome substance use disorder.

Sociologists Sheigla Murphy and Marsha Rosenbaum conducted a qualitative interview-based study of pregnant women who use drugs.

Their findings challenge the idea that crack users lose the impulse to mother, writing that these women "felt a strong responsibility for their children as well as deep shame when they failed."[26] Letters written by defendants in my study that are included in their case records undermine the idea that they don't care about their children. For example, in Alabama's Gulf Coast, one white woman begged to be released from jail so she could attend her daughter's kindergarten graduation. A Black woman in Alabama explained that she had completed some required programming in jail and asked to schedule a court date soon so she could be home with her six kids for the holidays.[27] In a letter to her judge, one white woman in Alabama begged for drug treatment while she was in jail so that she could regain custody of her children before they were taken away forever: "My kids need me but meth had a hold on me. . . . I have been away from my babies for 5 months too long and while I'm sitting here [in jail] that's just longer for me to be away from them. At rehab I can be around my kids. I need this opportunity. I'm young. I need to be with my kids. I need them. . . . Please sir, I miss my kids and I need them and they need me."[28]

Rosemary Cleveland, a Black woman in Alabama, sent letters and a photograph of her two children to the judge. In some of the letters, she shared intimate aspects of her life and begged to be reunited with her children. Just before Rosemary was arrested, her eldest daughter, a fourteen-year-old, had given birth. Rosemary's three-year-old son may have been sexually abused by another child in foster care. In her letter she begs, "I'm trying to go home please. I have a grand baby and I'm missing all her life. I have five more kids I'm trying to go home to. Please, I'm missing everything with them." In another letter she explained,

> It hurted me so bad when my 1yr old came to visit me and didn't even know me and didn't even want me to touch her. . . . Do you know how it feel to be without your family? It killing me. Every time I call home they want me to come home and I can't. Could you help me please, Mrs. [Judge?] . . . I been talking to my grandy and kids and what hurt me so bad is that my son he 3 and they was in foster care. And he was complaining that his butt area was hurting. . . . My only son done possibly got hurt and I was not there to protect him. And I feel bad. I need to be with all of them now. I don't want nothing else to happen. My 8 yr old will be starting being a misses soon. I need to be there. . . . I need them and they need me.[29]

A white woman in Alabama was arrested the day after she gave birth. She would spend the first year of her daughter's life at the Julia Tutwiler Prison for Women. She wrote a letter to her judge, which reads,

> I just recently had a baby girl Monday morning. . . . She is so beautiful! I made the biggest mistake of my life and did some drugs with her father right before I went into labor unaware I was about to have her. I'm in jail for chemical endangerment of a child. My bond is $200,000. I need to go to rehab and I will do whatever it takes to be a good mama to my baby. This is my first child and she is 3 days old. She is so beautiful. I need rehab and I know I do, but I would like to be with my beautiful baby girl so I can bond with her. I don't want to not be there to bond with my daughter. I will do anything and everything it takes but I really would like to be able to be with my baby until I get into [a drug treatment program]. Please, please let me spend this most important time with my baby. I will take drug tests every day if you want. I will do anything.[30]

A Black woman in Alabama, who was held in prison from the time she was four months pregnant and who gave birth in custody, wrote a judge begging for help. She was allowed to spend about fifteen hours with her infant son before she was removed from the hospital and returned to the prison: "I's about to lose the last little piece of mind that I have left. Please hear me out. . . . Now I'm hurting very badly judge. I had a handsome son. . . . I had to leave my baby at the hospital 15 hours after I had him and it's killing me. . . . Please. Help. Can you imagine how it must feel to give a baby away after 15 hr of holding him, carrying him for 9 months of labor and having him with no med. Naturally."[31]

In case documents and depositions, others describe their roles as mothers to other children, expressing the intense concern they had for their kids after they were arrested—they hadn't been given the chance to arrange for someone else to pick the children up from school, hadn't explained to the children that they would be going away for some time, and hadn't been able to arrange child care. In a deposition Dorothy Blackburn, a Black woman in South Carolina, shared her experience:

ATTORNEY. When you left your children that morning . . . did you say good-bye to your children?

BLACKBURN. No.

ATTORNEY. Did you tell them that you would be gone for three or four weeks?

BLACKBURN. No, I thought I was going right home.

ATTORNEY. Did you go right home?

BLACKBURN. No, I went to jail.[32]

Another Black woman in South Carolina was arrested after having a miscarriage.[33] Her children were incredibly upset when they witnessed her being arrested, reportedly screaming for their mother and crying, "They are going to kill her!"[34] Though the stated purpose of these arrests was child protection, witnessing a parent's arrest can be harmful to children. One study conducted by professor of human ecology Julia Poehlmann-Tynan found that "witnessing the parent's arrest was associated with missed milestones in children's development, especially in the area of early academics . . . as well as less than optimal health." She continues, "It should be noted that most of the young children were described as reacting to witnessing the arrest with intense distress." Poehlmann-Tynan also found that witnessing a parent's arrest can cause "toxic stress—strong or prolonged activation of the body's system that regulates stress," which has "adverse impacts on the structure of the developing brain, especially when toxic stress occurs during early childhood."[35] Another study found that witnessing a parent's arrest was associated with higher rates of "internalizing behavior" concerns like depression and anxiety, especially for children under eight years old.[36]

A Black woman in South Carolina worried about her children needing someone to hold them or give them a hug.[37] Gabriela Flores, a twenty-two-year-old mother of three, who was arrested for self-managing an abortion, told deputies, "I was very afraid for my kids because they were going to be left alone."[38] A Black woman in South Carolina asked, when she was being arrested, if she could go home to talk to her child about what was happening. In a deposition she explained, "I asked if I could be escorted home just long enough to talk to my son. Because I'm very close to my son, he has never really been away from me before other than to go to his grandparents' on the weekend or something, but he always knew where his mommy was. . . . I just wanted to be able to explain to him, you know, that mommy was going in the hospital. And just to make arrangements to make sure he would be okay while I was in the hospital." She wasn't allowed to. Another Black woman in South Carolina worried about who would look after her children while she was gone.[39]

Though it is clear that many of the people arrested for crimes against their own pregnancies had complicated lives and that they would have benefited from additional resources and support, these stories and anecdotes belie the notion that pregnant people who use drugs are uniformly dangerous, uncaring villains set on harming their children. Neither the angel nor antimother images reflect the reality that mothers are, in fact, human beings. They have personalities, desires, flaws, and histories. They were people before they became mothers, and they are people after. However, the failure to measure up to cultural expectations resulted in a sharp descent in the eyes of the pregnancy police, from angel to antimother.

TACTICS

The prosecutors I spoke with all invoked a similar strategy, which they referred to as "carrots and sticks" or "velvet hammers." They used their prosecutorial authority to create networks of health-care providers, law enforcement, and social workers to find prenatal drug users and offer two options: prison or drug treatment. The understanding was that, prior to their policy innovation, there was no incentive for women to access available services to help themselves. The prosecutors offered a *disincentive*—the threat of prosecution. As DA Weirich explained, she and her colleagues supported the fetal assault law "not because any of us care anything about locking up mothers who are addicted to drugs. I think all of us in the room would agree that that doesn't serve the public any good. What we have to do is fix that addiction, and do what we can to encourage women to do that. And far too often if we could just encourage them with a gentle word that would be enough but unfortunately it is the 'velvet hammer' of prosecution that sometimes inspires them to do the right thing and get into those programs."[40]

George Lester, a district attorney in Alabama, expressed a similar sentiment. Before prosecutors got involved, health-care providers would inform social services of any positive drug tests. Parents might lose custody of their children, but they weren't being prosecuted for pregnancy-related offenses. Lester felt that the threat of prosecution would encourage women to get off drugs. He explained, "The prosecution side, to me, gives you teeth to affect behavior that you probably can't do as successfully through a social service. . . . You know, what can *they* do? The worst they can do is take your kid, right? I mean . . . so what? But we can put you in prison."[41] Lester's glib statement about removing children from their families is contradicted by research evidence showing the harm caused by family separation and by statements from the people in this study who were devastated after they lost their children.

Rob McBurney, spokesperson for the South Carolina Attorney General's Office, said, "These women generally are not going to go to treatment unless there is something to hold over their heads. That's why the amnesty program has worked so well."[42] Graham explained, "The ultimate goal was to use the, sort of, the heavy hammer of the law. . . . That would hopefully, you know, scare the mothers into, uh, at least trying to complete their treatment plan."[43] Defendants would be offered deferred sentences. The deal was if they completed drug court and probation, then they would not have to serve time in prison and could regain custody of their child. Ninth Circuit solicitor for South Carolina David Schwacke said, "It's extremely geared toward treatment options prior to any arrests. . . . The beauty of the plan is that it is both a carrot and a stick. Treatment is better than a prosecution."[44] Detective Heaton told reporters, "Most of the time, when they walk in [to drug treatment programs], they'll stay a few days and then walk out. . . . We hope the threat of jail time will give us a little leverage to see they stay until they are clean."[45] Weaver demonstrated her paternalistic attitude when she compared threatening pregnant people with prosecution to spanking a child: "I liken that to being a parent. You know, you have parameters, you have borders, and you say to your baby or your child or your toddler, 'Little Johnny, don't do that! Don't do that, Little Johnny, or you're going to get a little spanking on your butt! And they test you and they test you, and then you have to spank them, and you've got some accountability there because you're trying to train them. This bill, in its heart and in its intent, is not punitive."[46] It is interesting that Weaver interprets substance use during pregnancy, but not hitting a child, as child abuse.

For all the talk of carrots, some prosecutors emphasized the role of the stick, explaining what would happen if someone relapsed or failed to comply with orders. Joey Rushing, a district attorney in Franklin County, Alabama, explained that he'd had "cases where pregnant women were using drugs and we required them to stay in a drug treatment facility until the baby was born to get them both off drugs." Judge Jack Guedalia said, "I felt like I had to put her under some sort of control so she would not harm the unborn child. . . . I had to think, how can I stop this woman."[47]

Some of the pregnancy police hoped that these "carrot and stick" policies would deter future drug use. Surely, if the people who chose to do drugs during pregnancy knew they would be punished and maybe publicly humiliated with mugshot photos in local news media or would be led through the hospital by law enforcement, in shackles, they would choose to stop. Gary McAliey, a district attorney in Coffee County, Alabama, urged, "It's important for society to know that it will be prosecuted and dealt with severely."[48] Detective Wes Martin told reporters, "We've had enough of it, we're going to do something about it, and if you don't want your name in the paper, we suggest you get your life straight."[49] US attorney William C. Killian said the prosecutions send the message that "should a child, born or unborn, be exposed to a substantial risk of harm . . . we will pursue any available enhancements at sentencing."[50] Public knowledge about the punitive policies may have contributed to avoidance of medical care more than they actually deterred substance use.

Many members of law enforcement and prosecutors talked about the intentional creation of interagency networks to accomplish the goals of the policies, involving health-care providers and social workers in their effort to coerce pregnant drug users into treatment. These networks could be considered a prototype for a future pregnancy police force. In this way health-care providers and social workers join the ranks of the pregnancy police, collecting evidence and reporting their patients and clients to law enforcement. Sheriff Scott Walls explained the role of social workers: "Most often, we get a call from DHR [Department of Human Resources]. . . . When a child is involved like this, DHR usually takes custody of the child and places that child in foster care or the care of a relative until the situation is resolved."[51] Law enforcement would collect the information gathered by health-care providers and social workers and use it to build a case for criminal charges against the pregnant person. Prosecutors and judges would use their velvet hammers and their carrots and sticks.

DA Connolly told journalists, "Our department and law enforcement are working hand in hand with the human resources department on these." DA Gambril explained, "We do it hand in hand with pediatricians here, the OB-GYNs here, with the doctors. . . . Everybody seems to be consistently on board." DA Harp said, "The three departments [the prosecutor's office, the sheriff's department, and the Department of Human Resources] have been in talks for about two weeks on how to work to both prosecute those responsible, and also see that they get counseling help." As a solicitor, Trey Gowdy was involved in building "a committee of law enforcement officers, prosecutors, religious leaders, social workers, and alcohol and drug counselors to develop guidelines for hospitals and law enforcement officials to follow after a woman tests positive for drugs." DA Harp announced "a concerted effort by all to make sure that the lives of unborn children are not being abused while in the womb." In 1989 D. L. Butler, a police detective, explained, "A meeting is planned next week among . . . DSS [Department of Social Services] officials, the solicitor's office and the hospital to work out a formal system for handling these drug cases."[52]

Graham spoke at length about the benefits of the team approach to detect, report, and pressure pregnant drug users to seek treatment. She developed both a response team and a review team that included prosecutors, law enforcement, hospital personnel, doctors, and hospital social workers, as well as representatives from the Department of Social Services. Graham's teams worked to develop response plans tailored to the pregnant women's needs: inpatient or outpatient drug treatment and programs like parenting classes and job training. Graham said, "It wasn't a cookie-cutter way to deal with these cases. It was an individual way to deal with them." The response team was involved in developing the initial treatment and safety plan, while the review team was responsible for fine-tuning and tailoring the plans to meet the women's needs through trial and error. The health-care providers on the team developed the protocol indicating when a drug test should be made. The prosecutors used the threat of prosecution to coerce women into drug treatment. The social workers developed safety plans and handled child custody.[53]

Using the team approach also allowed some of those involved to distance themselves from the ultimate outcome of a case or to deny responsibility for (or even knowledge of) what happened next. Health-care providers initiated the vast majority of arrest cases, usually by making a report to social services. Doctors weren't sending their patients to jail—they were simply making a report to social services. Amy Dugger, a nurse practitioner at Andalusia Regional Medical Center, told reporters that hospital officials were bound by Department of Human Resources guidelines requiring the reporting of possible child abuse. "We just work with DHR. . . . We don't call law enforcement. DHR does that." Pediatrician Joel Pedigo explained, "When there is evidence of drug use, we notify DHS. Where the case goes from there is not up to us." Police chief Jeff Helms explained, "There's kind of a moral issue, and we've toyed with that. . . . But if this baby came through a hospital and they are obligated to call DSS, and DSS is obligated to call us, it seems pretty clear what we have to do. . . . We're going to act on it."[54]

Alabama district attorney David Campbell was very attentive to existing precedent, most notably from the *Ferguson* case, on privacy and the collection of medical information to use as criminal evidence. He intentionally left the drug-testing protocol up to health-care providers, in part for legal reasons. "That wasn't a state action. And so I didn't have to worry about the legality of how they acquired the results of the test. . . . Had we gone to them and said, 'You need to start testing all babies,' that's a different story."[55]

Sometimes, when prosecutors were uncertain about the legality of what they did, they relied on the expertise and clout of another network. South Carolina solicitor Charles Condon, in 1996, asked law enforcement agencies "to hold off on making arrests until he can meet with doctors and social workers to discuss how to approach prosecutions." Until Condon issued the guidelines, local prosecutors let health-care providers and hospital administration make decisions about reporting to law enforcement.[56] Even actors in the same field were sometimes unaware of how their actions had influenced events down the line. For example, district attorney Michael Miller, who was working in private practice by the time the *Ankrom* case was heard at the state supreme court, expressed shock when I told him the court's decision: that it applied for any substance that could potentially harm a pregnancy, at any stage of pregnancy. Miller yelled out, "But that could be *coffee!*"[57]

Legal Interpretations

Prosecutors used a variety of different legal interpretations to support their actions, though some expressed a desire for a more explicit law. The prosecutors who were among the first to pursue pregnant drug users, prior to formal criminalization, argued that the laws already on the books permitted these new policies. Graham felt that existing legislation and case law gave her everything she needed. Though South Carolina at this point had never explicitly defined a pregnant person as a potential perpetrator against a pregnancy, the state had already extended victimhood status to the fetus in case law. DA Lester explained, "We thought we were on solid legal ground charging it that way. And that we were doing good. That we were helping the community."[58]

DA Gambril interpreted Alabama's chemical endangerment statute, which criminalized having children in "environments" where drugs, drug paraphernalia, or drug precursors were kept, to apply to uterine environments. He told reporters that the purpose of the statute was to guarantee that a child has a safe environment: "When drugs are introduced in the womb, the child to be is endangered. No one is to say whether that environment is inside or outside the womb." Marshall County's district attorney Steve Marshall, who is now the Alabama attorney general, acknowledged, "We have clearly used it a little bit different than it was designed. That, in and of itself, doesn't mean it's wrong."[59] Marshall explained his rationale for prosecuting drug use during pregnancy while attempting to avoid questions about the legal status of the fetus. Instead, he argued, "If the mother does drugs while the child is still attached to the umbilical cord and the baby is exposed and tests positive, the statute applies."[60] In other words, he argued that the traces of drugs in a pregnant person's blood, pulsing through the umbilical cord to the newborn infant, in the moments before it is cut, constituted the crime of delivery of drugs to a minor.

Law enforcement and prosecutors even had legal strategies for charging residents of their own states who gave birth elsewhere and charging residents from other states who gave birth in their jurisdictions. For example, in 2019 a twenty-seven-year-old white woman from South Carolina gave birth in North Carolina and then returned home with her baby. Four days later she was arrested in South Carolina and charged with unlawful neglect.[61] The arresting detective in the case told reporters, "Even though the baby was born in another state, the crime happened in [his jurisdiction]."[62] People with the capacity for pregnancy who lived in other states but who gave birth in the three study states could be arrested and charged too. At least two defendants lived in other states at the time of their arrest, arguably having committed the crime of prenatal drug *use* in their home states, but were still charged and arrested in the jurisdiction where they ended up giving birth. Cases like these are potentially illustrative of how prosecutions might work against those who travel to other states for legal abortion care.

Although many prosecutors may have believed in their own interpretations of the law, they couldn't be certain that there wouldn't be legal challenges or critiques. Responding to claims that MUSC's drug-testing policy violated constitutional rights, Attorney Hood told reporters, "We have not violated anyone's constitutional rights, least of all the baby in the woman's tummy. It's no big deal. The police officers who came to the hospital wore plain clothes and covered the woman in a blanket after they'd chained her ankles so they couldn't run."[63]

Some prosecutors and law enforcement expressed uncertainty about their interpretation of the law and explained work-arounds meant to bolster potentially shaky legal arguments. ADA Floyd said of one case, "We worked hard to get this negotiated plea because, frankly, we were in uncharged waters here. . . . There has never been a case like this tried in Marshall County, or anywhere. We don't have any precedents to look back on."[64] DA Miller discussed another strategy for avoiding a legal challenge: "All you do is, you add a count of 'attempt,' which lowers the case one level. We're back to the Class A Misdemeanor, which has all the leverage you need. . . . And this is a little cynical, so get ready, but, talk about a way to avoid ever having to be held accountable on appeal! Because you're pleading every case out in a far less, uh, serious level."[65] District attorney Dave Clark, from Anderson County, Tennessee, said he sought two indictments as alternatives because there's some uncertainty about case law involving the "recognition of [the] viable fetus as a crime victim."[66]

Solicitor Pope wanted clarification from the state on how pregnant drug users should be treated. Cases in his jurisdiction were starting to add up, and he wanted to know how to proceed. He told reporters, "We're playing the game while we're trying to establish the rules." He explained that the "prosecutions are relatively new and haphazard." He also seemed to understand the broad implications of such policies and, without legislation, wasn't sure how far he was supposed to go. He told reporters, "There is also the question of limits.... Are alcoholic mothers as neglectful as women using cocaine? How about heavy smokers?" He continued, "In certain senses it opens a Pandora's box, but you can't ask law enforcement to look the other way.... There is a need for some consistency" in the law.[67]

DA Gambril hoped that legislation would provide more clarity as to the legality of these prosecutions: "It's obviously a close call under the law.... We would like the matter cleared up with a statute." The deputy district attorney for Tennessee's Thirteenth District, Gary McKenzie, explained, "This will be the practice of our judicial circuit to pursue these cases.... It is hoped that the legislature will address the problem of innocent children being exposed to methamphetamine, and give us more tools to work with."[68]

District attorneys George Lester and David Campbell both sought formal legal clarification. Of the Alabama Supreme Court decision ruling in favor of the policy, Lester said, "I'm glad it wasn't from my circuit, but, I mean... we wanted a ruling on that." Though Campbell did feel confident that he was interpreting the law fairly, he still thought it would be better if there was a law explicitly defining the application of criminal laws to the fetus, not only to reduce the likelihood of a successful appeal of a conviction, but also because he thought it was important to standardize the policy throughout the state. He said, "Everybody's been prosecuting these things all over the state, but no one seemed real interested in, in trying to, to get a clarification of the law and putting in [the treatment-defense] safeguard." He noticed that in some jurisdictions people weren't being given the opportunity to seek treatment before being sent to jail. Working together with a district attorney from another Alabama county, Campbell found a legislator who had personally encountered a death attributed to prenatal drug exposure and was "determined to try to get some legislation passed." Campbell presented the bill before the House Judiciary Committee, but that legislative term "nothing was getting passed. And so, it, as well as about 80 percent of the bills that went into the hopper that year, died on the floor. Never even got heard."[69] He hoped to try again the following legislative term, but he lost his reelection before he had the chance.

CONSEQUENCES

Once their policies had gone into effect, some prosecutors confronted unexpected consequences. Especially in the precriminalization period, policies and practices concerning the criminal prosecution of pregnant people were all over the place, and some were more punitive than others. Graham spoke about how the city of Charleston, in South Carolina, inspired by her county's new policy, developed one of their own. Graham recalled, "They just had a different approach from different leadership."[70] South Carolina solicitor Matthew Payne used stronger words: "I can't remember what Charlie Condon's protocol was. I remember looking at it and thinking it was . . . not right. I don't know about unconstitutional or . . . but I remember specifically saying, you know, 'I think what we're doing is safer, better.'"[71]

DA Campbell introduced his policy to other district attorneys at the annual statewide conference of prosecutors and ultimately came to regret what he saw as inappropriate prosecutorial discretion stemming from the disdain that many people have for pregnant drug users. He recalled, "When we did this, my concern was [my] county. And perhaps it was naivete on my part to not realize that other counties were going to look at what we were doing, and they were gonna start doing it their way." After winning an award for the work he did to establish this policy, other district attorneys reached out to him with comments that he found troubling. "I was having people come up to me and say, 'Those women should rot in Hell!' And I'd be like, 'Whoa, whoa, whoa!' You know, 'No, no, no, that's not what we're after.'"[72]

Interagency Ruptures

Though prosecutors and law enforcement expressed a desire to use the threat of criminal prosecution to drive people to seek drug treatment, it seems that, once they learned more about drug treatment, they weren't so sure. For example, Judge Tim Dwyer said, "I think that suboxone is like substituting one drug for another."[73] Some prosecutors expressed a willingness to investigate or even prosecute people receiving medication-assisted treatment. Sixty-six arrest cases involved some kind of medication for opioid use disorder, and I confirmed that in some cases it was legally prescribed. Sheriff Entrekin told reporters, "We're going to look all the way back. If there's someone at the hospital that's addicted to methadone and they're getting it legally, I'm not saying that my office is not going to look at that. We're going to follow it back to the root of the problem."[74] Despite the policy's stated intent of pushing pregnant drug users into treatment, Entrekin's statement is indicative of punitive attitudes that actually reject and criminalize substance use treatment.

DA Veitch is clear in his criticism of the highest-quality treatment facilities available to low-income pregnant or postpartum women. Preferring a more punitive approach than drug treatment, he complained that patients weren't incarcerated at the treatment center, telling reporters, "The [treatment center], while well intentioned, does not have control of its patients, who use their sympathy and lack of control to simply walk away when they get the slightest urge to use drugs."[75] The urge to punish and control fundamentally conflicts with treatment.

Though the drug-testing policies indicated that the threat of criminal prosecution would be used as an incentive to receive treatment, statements made by some law enforcement officers and prosecutors suggest a lack of knowledge about substance use disorder and a lack of belief in treatment. The rhetoric of choice was especially present in these more punitive views: both that pregnant people were *choosing* to use drugs and that fetuses or newborns didn't have a *choice,* positioning fetuses as innocent and pregnant people as culpable because of their choices. Medical anthropologist Kelly Ray Knight notes that the current "understanding of addiction as a 'complex brain disease characterized by compulsive, at times, uncontrollable drug craving, seeking, and use despite devastating consequences' runs directly counter to liberal notions of free will that apply broadly to matters of criminal intent or negligence." In this context the use of the word "choice" is troubling, as pregnant people with substance use disorder "would have little or no choice over choosing to continue their addicted behaviors. Yet the question of choice, whether to stop or to continue using drugs, maintains social traction even as the science of prenatal substance use exposure and emergent neurobiological understandings of the course of addiction complicate questions of both 'willpower' and 'environment.'"[76]

Sheriff Entrekin told reporters, "A disturbing tragedy is occurring weekly in Etowah County as pregnant women are choosing to chemically endanger their unborn child. . . . We will stand together as concerned law enforcement and social service professionals to fight this troubling issue." DA Andrews explained, "I always have and will continue to prosecute any woman who chooses to do drugs while pregnant with a child. . . . We have programs available for these women, and we are here to help them. If they choose not to help themselves, then I have no sympathy whatsoever for them." DA Harp told reporters, "Ninety percent of the addicts we have aren't bad people, they just make bad choices." Christophilis, then the South Carolina attorney general's director of drug prosecutions, explained, of a case where someone continued drug use, "It's just one of those cases where you offer the help, and you offer the treatment, but there comes a point where a person has to take responsibility for their own actions." Solicitor Condon said, "These women do not care what happens to their child. . . . They do not respond to warnings; instead they choose to abuse drugs.'"[77]

Some invoked the language of choice to describe the helplessness of fetuses or newborns. This mirrored the language of choice often deployed by antiabortion advocates—fertilized eggs, embryos, and fetuses are innocent victims who do not *get* to choose. It is likely that this view is indicative of antiabortion attitudes as well. The sheriff of Butler County, Alabama, Kenny Harden, told reporters of a specific case, "This baby never had a choice."[78] DA Gambril said, "The unborn children are not making the choice. . . . It's the mothers who are making the choice to do it to them."[79] Lieutenant Reid said, "Let's not lose sight that the unborn baby is the victim here. . . . She had no choice in being brought unnecessarily into a fight where she was relying on her mother for protection."[80] Franklin County sheriff Larry Plott said, "It's an emotional case 'because newborns just don't have a choice and they aren't in control. It really pulls at your heart strings.'"[81]

The idea that substance use disorder is a matter of mere choice and willpower certainly influences what would be seen as appropriate treatment solutions. For pregnant people with opioid use disorder, medication-assisted treatment is considered part of the standard of care.[82] Medication-assisted treatment uses regular doses of substances like buprenorphine, methadone, and naltrexone to bind with opioid receptors without causing the high.[83] The Substance Abuse and Mental Health Services Administration reports that medication-assisted treatment is associated with improved patient survival, increased treatment retention, and improved birth outcomes.[84]

While the punitive policies were generally designed as collaborations between health-care providers, social workers, law enforcement, and prosecutors, these varied institutions didn't always fit together seamlessly. Sometimes the interests and goals of various parties in these institutions came into conflict with one another. In one case the tension between punishment and treatment came to a head. Alexandra Laird, a white woman in Alabama, was arrested twice. The first time, in March 2015, she was only nineteen years old. She gave birth at the University of Alabama at Birmingham (UAB) Medical Center and tested positive for opiates and amphetamines. Laird was arrested about a month later, charged with chemical endangerment of a child, and granted a $5,000 bond. She tested positive for opioids and pregnancy about a year later, when she was drug tested as a condition of her bond for the first arrest. Now a twenty-one-year-old, and between eighteen and twenty weeks pregnant, this second charge meant that the bond from the first charge would be revoked, and she would be sent back to jail. Laird was arrested on September 8, 2016, and was going to be held in the Bessemer County Jail until she went into labor.[85]

Laird had opioid use disorder, and, while in jail custody, she received no medications to manage withdrawals. Not long after arriving at the jail, she fell and hit her head, potentially due to withdrawals, and she was hospitalized. Laird was prescribed Subutex, a drug that helps prevent withdrawals from opioids, which is considered the standard of care for a pregnant person with opioid use disorder. Circuit court judge David Hobdy ordered Laird back to prison, but her doctors at UAB wouldn't comply with the order. They argued that the jail wasn't a safe place for a pregnant person with an opioid use disorder. They wanted Laird to be sent to

Aletheia House's program for pregnant drug users, one of the only programs in the state that specializes in working with pregnant people and that accepts Medicaid. Dr. Peter Lane, medical director of the Addiction Recovery Program at UAB, spoke about the need not only for medication but for counseling and other resources.[86]

Initially, Bessemer County Jail was reluctant to treat Laird with medications for opioid use disorder (MOUD), explaining that Subutex was a valuable drug and Laird could sell it in jail instead of using it herself.[87] Whether this was standard jail policy or a decision about Laird as an individual, this decision indicates a fundamental distrust of the people being held in jail, many of whom have not been convicted of any crime, and also demonstrates the desperate financial need of the people being held there. Though Bessemer County Jail eventually agreed to treat Laird with Subutex, Lane still didn't want her sent there. "Sending somebody back to jail is traumatic. . . . Without anything else, it just makes it more likely for them to use"[88] DA Veitch disagreed. He didn't trust that Laird wouldn't just leave the drug treatment facility and wanted to make sure she was kept in jail through the rest of her pregnancy.[89] The Jefferson County Sheriff's Office's chief medical officer, Dr. Michael Chandler, told reporters that the jail in Bessemer County was an adequate place to spend a pregnancy: "The mother might not be as happy but the baby doesn't know the mother's in jail."[90] In the end Lane got his way. Laird spent the rest of her pregnancy in the hospital and gave birth in January 2017.[91]

Incentivizing Abortion

Several of the prosecutors told me that some critics of test, report, and arrest policies were concerned that they incentivized abortion. Campbell told me, "I remember meeting with, uh, the governor, and his first question was 'Well, aren't you afraid that once it's clarified like this, that we're gonna have this great increase in abortions?'" Campbell didn't share the governor's concerns:

> The one thing that I tried to explain is that the people who are drug addicted, and that are carrying a child, have already made the choice to keep the child. . . . It was always hard to try to get so many of the more conservative-

> minded folks to get off of that high horse of, you know, "abortion, abortion, abortion!" . . . You know, they're not gonna go get an abortion because of this law. You know, if they wanna keep the child, they're gonna keep the child. They're gonna say, 'I can beat this!' And then, unfortunately, while they're through their pregnancy, they find they can't.[92]

However, DA Miller felt differently and explained how that incentive would operate: "A lot of these people, certainly in Alabama Supreme Court, . . . and in Alabama by and large, they are very antiabortion, and these kinds of interventions, in many cases, probably led to some women saying, 'Oh, fuck this. I'm not gonna risk going to jail. I'll just go. . . . It's completely lawful for me to go terminate this pregnancy. I'll go do that.'"[93] Abortion was still federally protected during much of my study period. The arrest of pregnant people in their first and second trimesters of pregnancy was a legal puzzle. Applying the logic of fetal protection or fetal personhood, it was legal to *intentionally "kill"* your pregnancy, but it was not legal to *possibly, unintentionally, harm* your pregnancy.

While some of the pregnancies in these cases were unplanned, only a handful of cases report that the pregnancy was unwanted. The majority of the people arrested for crimes against their pregnancies wanted to give birth and parent their children. However, when faced with the possibility of being charged with a felony for continuing a pregnancy or for giving birth, abortion became the only way out. While I have no evidence of this happening, in addition to creating a legal contradiction, it is possible that it had incentivized abortion in some cases. This demonstrates another way that these punitive policies could be coercive and may generate medically or legally risky evasive responses—avoiding prenatal care, unsafely self-managing abortions, or attempting to flee the state while in labor—from those who do not want to go to jail or lose custody of their children.

One prosecutor confronted the contradiction between abortion legality and criminal charges for pregnant people's behavior with respect to their own pregnancy head on. In July 2015 a twenty-nine-year-old woman referred to as Jane Doe was charged with chemical endangerment of a child after she told her probation officer she was in her first trimester of pregnancies and tested positive for drugs while on probation for a prior crime. Apparently, she admitted to using amphetamines, including methamphetamine and Adderall. Jane Doe was arrested and placed in jail.

Prior to her arrest, Jane Doe had been planning to have an abortion. Even then, when abortion was still legal in Alabama, this would have been no easy feat, costing several hundred dollars and requiring a ninety-minute one-way drive and at least two trips to a clinic—one to receive state-mandated counseling and another for the procedure itself. Doe was arrested before she could have the abortion she wanted. Time was ticking. She would be able to legally access abortion in her state for only a few more weeks. While in custody, she demanded that she be permitted to have the abortion.[94] In response district attorney James Palmer filed a motion to terminate Doe's guardianship over the fetus, under the theory that when she used drugs, she had abused the fetus.[95] In other words, Palmer asserted that Doe had abused her child and as such should lose custody of it *while it was still inside of her and part of her own body,* a violation of Doe's right to abortion, her right to receive medical care while incarcerated, and her human rights more broadly.

What happened next is contested by Palmer and the American Civil Liberties Union attorney. According to Palmer, Doe was one of their "frequent flyers," having given birth to three or four children who had tested positive for drugs: "We monitor jail calls. . . . And one of the reasons we, that I, filed what I filed is I knew from her. . . . She was talking to her mother from jail. . . . Almost immediately after making the demand . . . she was telling her mother on the jail calls, 'I don't want an abortion. I can't tell my [other child] that.' . . . I don't know if she was, she just didn't, you know, she didn't want it." Palmer contended that if Doe had truly wanted to have an abortion, she could have simply made a request at the jail. Instead, lawyers got involved. Palmer felt that Doe's court-appointed attorney wasn't "mindful of what the girl really wanted." Instead of representing Doe's interests, he said the defense attorney worked "with the ACLU's help to get this abortion thing stirred up." Palmer said, "I found out that the ACLU was looking for a test case in Alabama involving chemical endangerment cases, to try to challenge the constitutionality at the Supreme Court level. But, anyway, so they made a big hullabaloo about it and sued. They sued the sheriff in federal court."[96]

That's when Palmer says he filed a motion to appoint a guardian ad litem for the fetus and an attorney to represent Doe in the parental rights case. Appointed representation is not typical in family court, and, by its very nature, prosecutors arranging legal representation for people they may prosecute draws concern about conflicts of interest. If the person trying to take your child away was the same person who set you up with a lawyer, would *you* trust that the lawyer had your best interests in mind? Palmer's legal theory was that if Doe lost custody of the fetus, she would be legally unable to have an abortion. Palmer admitted, "We oppose [abortion] morally. . . . It is the policy of the State of Alabama to protect all life—born or unborn."[97] And all this happened while abortion was still legal in Alabama.

Doe's original defense attorney and the ACLU attorney share a *very* different account. They contend that Doe had already been in the process of trying to obtain an abortion when she was arrested, and that the sheriff's office was refusing to transport her to the abortion clinic. In her ACLU declaration, Doe stated, "I am very distraught. I do not want to be forced to carry this pregnancy to term." She went on to say that "getting an abortion in Alabama is always a lengthy process, requiring a visit to a clinic for abortion counseling at least 48 hours before the procedure itself." She continued, "I do not know how long I will be in jail, but it could be several months," at which point she might be beyond the legal gestational limit for abortion in the state. The ACLU and Doe's defense attorney argued that Palmer was attempting to create a public spectacle by announcing to the media that he was charging the woman with chemically endangering her fetus and that he sought to terminate her parental rights to prevent her from having an abortion.[98]

Two days before rulings were expected in the custody-termination case and the suit against the county sheriff, Doe abruptly, apparently, changed her mind. While it was, of course, well within her rights to do so, the considerable pressure she was under and the legal threats she faced raise concerns about coercion. In an affidavit she wrote, "After much consideration and counsel, I . . . have decided that I no longer desire to pursue an abortion procedure and intend to carry the unborn child to full term and birth. I have arrived at this decision of my own volition and choosing . . . without any undue influence, duress or threat of harm."[99] This concerned the attorneys representing Doe in the federal case. The appointed family court attorney, James McMahon, who is the chancellor and attorney for a faith-based Christian school and day care, worked with Doe to submit the affidavit. The legal director for the Alabama ACLU told reporters, "The circumstances under which this affidavit was obtained are highly suspicious and raise serious red flags." After Doe withdrew her request to have an abortion, the federal judge dismissed the suit against the county sheriff, and Palmer withdrew his motion to terminate Doe's parental rights. He also offered Doe the opportunity to avoid prison by staying in, and completing, an available in-patient drug treatment program for the duration of her pregnancy.[100]

Doe's ACLU lawyer told reporters, "The amount of pressure that can be brought to bear on an individual held in jail by officials is indeed heavy pressure." But McMahon countered, "She wasn't promised anything, she wasn't threatened with anything. This was a decision she made on her own." The ACLU questioned Doe's discussion of the federal case with McMahon, stating, "He was there representing her on a petition to terminate her parental rights and while he was talking with her, they talked about the federal case."[101] The ACLU lawyer suggested that Doe was given appointed representation for the custody trial by the prosecution so that he could convince her to cease her attempt to have an abortion—something Palmer denied at the time but confirmed in our interview, where Palmer explained that the guardian ad litem and Doe's appointed attorney "became allies of ours in trying to save the baby."[102]

In any case, even in the absence of an explicit quid pro quo, Doe was faced with several powerful incentives to not have an abortion. If she agreed to continue her pregnancy, the attempt to suspend her parental rights would be ended. If she completed a drug treatment program, the criminal charges would be dropped. On the other hand, if she were granted a medical furlough in federal court and could access the abortion she had been seeking, Palmer says he still would have tried to prosecute her for chemically endangering the fetus prior to the abortion. In our interview Palmer stated, "If she has an abortion, that's the fetus in our chemical endangerment case. So we had an interest in . . . getting that fetus for an autopsy." Palmer would have attempted to collect the products of conception from the abortion clinic to be used as evidence against Doe in a chemical endangerment case. Doe spent the rest of her pregnancy at an inpatient drug treatment facility by court order. She gave birth to a healthy child and, subsequently, relapsed. She was then sent to prison to complete her original sentence.[103]

Failure and Success

In interviews I conducted, the prosecutors' assessment of their own programs was varied, though all expressed some uncertainty about the success or failure of the policies—troubling considering the extent to which the policies infringe on the rights of pregnant people. Christophilis thought the prosecutions were working, based on the numbers of newborns testing positive in the program. She explained to reporters, "The people who test positive during pregnancy are being referred to Department of Social Services and treatment, and their babies are not testing positive."[104] ADA Floyd said he saw success in drug court participation: "They are some of the best drug court participants we have ever seen. . . . So far, we have not had any of them re-offend up to this point. All of them are either still in the program or have finished it."[105]

Dr. Melvin Thornbury, a physician from Marshall County, Alabama, wasn't sure. While he saw fewer people testing positive at his hospital, he thought it may have been because patients were deterred from care. "I think, and I really want to believe, that our testing program is actually getting some people to stop doing drugs. I hope it is. It's either that or they have chosen to go elsewhere to deliver where they know they aren't going to be tested."[106] DA David Campbell said that he saw fewer reports of children born exposed to drugs but didn't know "if that's because of the statute or if it's because of . . . the number of people being arrested for meth, all the meth education that we were doing in the county."[107] Payne reported uncertainty as well. When asked about whether the program was effective, he responded, "[I] have no idea. You know, I mean, I'm being honest. . . . I asked that question. And I know that we . . . I'm pretty sure we dismissed a lot of cases." He went on, "I don't think you could ask anybody whether we kept statistics beforehand versus afterwards or not, so . . . But somebody may have. . . . I can't tell you it *wasn't* effective."[108] Rather than relying on facts about the success of the program, Weaver relied on the "fact" *of her own opinion*, telling reporters, "I'm just going to stand my ground on the fact that I believe wholeheartedly this bill *does* help . . . these women that are in situations that never would have gotten the help they needed."[109]

Prosecutors were generally less hesitant to label specific cases successes or failures, with a few exceptions. Graham saw the most success come from women who could stay with their children while attending drug court.[110] Other prosecutors described cases in which they could control the pregnant person until birth. DA Lester recalled a particular case: "We had a relatively successful outcome, in that we actually jailed her when she was, I think, six months pregnant. She stayed in jail, and . . . the baby was delivered. And the baby's healthy and all that." But, after the birth of the healthy baby, the defendant seemed to fall through the cracks. Lester continued, "The idea was get her back in connection with the Department of Human Resources, so that they could work to reunify her with this baby . . . while the baby's a small child. And . . . that didn't work. But, at least, in my mind, it was a 'success' because we didn't have a drug-addicted child born in that case."[111]

Lester's contact with one of his defendants seemed to have an impact on his attitudes. After giving birth and completing drug treatment, the defendant relapsed and was sent to prison, having violated the terms of her deferred prosecution by using drugs again. Lester emphasized that she was different from other pregnant drug users, in his estimation, recounting, "I was really disappointed in that girl. . . . She was, like, the valedictorian of one of the county high schools, and . . . a smart girl and all that kind of thing, you know. Just . . . a tragic story about meth." He went on, "Am I gonna send this girl to prison, now that we've saved her baby? . . . Or do you give her the hundredth chance." This defendant is currently incarcerated in one of the most notoriously violent women's prisons in the United States, the Julia Tutwiler Prison. Lester confessed, "Do you know? I'd still be willing to help her. And I guess I'm conflicted with her because I looked her in the eye in the courtroom and said to her, 'You screw this up, and you're going to prison.' 'Yes, sir, Mr. [Lester]! I understand. I'm not gonna let you down this time.' That kills you when they do."[112] Lester saw her as someone who, at least before she used drugs, was respectable, which seemed to stir more compassion than he had for most of the other defendants. Other prosecutors expressed fewer concerns about people who continued using drugs. DA Connolly said, "We have had some success with these cases in the past, but unfortunately some [people] don't change and they end up in jail."[113]

The prosecutors that I interviewed asserted that their ultimate goal was to help pregnant women and their children, not to punish them.

However, the ability of prosecutors to affect this kind of change is questionable, even with the purest intentions. Prosecutors decide to prosecute or to not prosecute. Their job is to demonstrate, beyond a reasonable doubt and on behalf of the state, that a person is guilty of a crime. They use the system of law to do this. Their effort to use "carrots and sticks" or a "velvet hammer" to coerce people into drug treatment does not align with the reality of how treatment for substance use disorder works: MOUD is the standard of care for opioid withdrawal, relapse is part of the process for many people, and the treatment of traumas at the root of substance use disorder is essential.[114]

It's not at all evident that, even if all the law enforcement officers, prosecutors, and judges had carried out their role in the test, report, and arrest policies perfectly and equally and only with the idea of protection in mind, that they would have ultimately helped or protected anyone. There is evidence showing that punitive approaches to health problems drive people away from care.[115] In the cases examined, the kinds of support that *are* shown to help were not expanded or made accessible in a meaningful way.[116] For a wide variety of reasons, pregnant people who use drugs are already less likely than other women to seek prenatal care—even in the absence of punitive policies.[117] Many medical organizations and public health advocacy groups oppose these punitive measures for fear that they will only aggravate disparities in medical care. For example, the American Medical Association suggests that "pregnant women will be likely to avoid seeking prenatal or other medical care for fear that their physicians' knowledge of substance abuse or other potentially harmful behavior could result in a jail sentence rather than proper medical treatment."[118]

A study by legal epidemiologist Sarah Roberts and professor of public health Cheri Pies indicated that "one of the reasons why pregnant drug users don't use care is because they are afraid that they will be reported to CPS [Child Protective Services] and that their children will be taken away," belying assumptions that people who use drugs during pregnancy do not care about their children. One of the women included in their study said, "When you're using and you think about prenatal care, you're nervous and you're scared because you don't want anybody to take your baby. That's the first thing on your mind." Another woman confessed, "That whole time, that whole 9 months, you're like, I cannot go to this doctor because if I do, they're gonna take my kid or put [me] in jail for the rest of [my] 9 months just to take the baby when [I deliver]."[119]

Though a positive drug test cannot tell us if someone is a good parent, a positive drug test can be interpreted as grounds to remove children from their families, and it can be especially difficult for parents to regain custody of their children. Child custody records related to these cases are not made public, but it is clear that many of the birthing people who were tested, reported, and arrested lost custody of their children for at least some time and that some of their children entered foster care. In 2021, a total of 2,709 children entered foster care in South Carolina. About 13 percent of those children were less than a year old. In 2021, 3,504 children entered foster care in Alabama, and 21.9 percent of them were less than a year old. In Tennessee in 2021, 9,227 children entered foster care, and 14.1 percent of these children were less than a year old.[120]

Though the stated purpose of removing children from parents who test positive for drugs is to prevent harm, there is substantial evidence that doing so actually causes harm. Children in foster care experience physical and sexual abuse. Children also experience neglect in their foster homes—the same kinds of neglect that often results in removal from their families. For example, one study found that 22 percent of foster children were not getting enough food and that 26 percent did not have seasonally appropriate clothing. Foster children are also substantially less likely to receive medical care than children not in foster care. The very act of separating children from their family is itself harmful and traumatizing.[121] Trauma, mental illness, interpersonal violence, and social isolation are understood as some of the underlying factors that contribute to substance use disorder.[122]

In their area of South Carolina, Della Bricker and Maureen Gimlet work to provide holistic care for pregnant women and to remove as many barriers as possible for their recovery. Gimlet explained, "So that's everything from domestic violence [counseling] to financial counseling to [local colleges] helping them to get, um, their GED if they didn't finish high school, helping them move forward with job skills." The services that Bricker and Gimlet offered at their facility included psychotherapy, twelve-step meetings, life-skills classes, medications for opioid and alcohol use disorders, and services to help patients prepare a safe home for their coming babies. They offer child care, allowing patients to bring their babies with them. They also provide advocacy in court and in health-care settings, where pregnant drug users frequently face disparaging comments and judgment. At the time of our interview, Gimlet reported, "Now, to date, we've had 117 healthy, drug-free babies through what is now a residential program."[123]

PUTTING DOWN THE VELVET HAMMER

One South Carolina solicitor ultimately stopped prosecuting arrest cases in his circuit. Peter Hermann recalled that when he started as a solicitor, he was elected as a "law and order" candidate. He solidified that reputation after he successfully prosecuted a murder case that received attention nationally and internationally. He was not a "soft on crime" kind of prosecutor. He explained, "When I worked down in [another city] years ago, they had a drug court, and I kind of laughed. I said, in my younger mind then, I knew what drug court was. You had court at night, and you prosecuted more drug dealers [laughter]. . . . But at some point later in my career, I *started* a drug treatment court." Hermann felt that he never would have won his first election campaign if he had favored drug court at that time, but, after he established himself as a stern prosecutor, "people were receptive, because they trusted me, because I'd been the guy that prosecuted people. You know, I wasn't just giving everybody a hug."[124] Hermann saw his shifting attitudes about substance use disorder and prosecution as a kind of prosecutorial maturation. "What I noticed was, as I maybe matured as a prosecutor and took to the role, is I could keep putting people in jail, but at some point, if I can affect a change . . . "

Della Bricker, one of the directors of the drug treatment facility in Peter Hermann's South Carolina circuit, recalled, "[Solicitor Hermann] was part of [the prosecutions] initially" and asserted "I will take credit for helping him to understand that this is a disease."[125] Maureen Gimlet, executive director of that same treatment facility, recalled, "[Della] worked very closely with [Hermann], because he certainly was instrumental in making sure that we received the referrals."[126] Hermann explained his new view of the issue by sharing a story that a family court judge told him:

> There's two guys fishing on the bank, and a basket comes by, kind of like Moses, with a baby in it. And one of the guys puts his fishing rod down and walks out and gets the basket and takes it out. And, you know, they start fishing again. And another basket comes by, same thing. Puts the fishing rod down, walks out, takes it again. Third time, a basket comes by, the guy puts his fishing rod down and starts walking up the bank. And the other guy says, "Hey, where you going? You're not gonna go out and get that baby?" And he says, "No, I'm gonna walk up and see who's putting these babies in the water." Well, that's kind of the same thing. I think it's smart policy on anything.[127]

Hermann came to believe that arresting and prosecuting people for substance use during pregnancy wasn't addressing the underlying problems that can contribute to substance use disorder—something that, with Bricker's encouragement, he came to understand as an illness. Instead of fetching floating basket after floating basket (arresting people as they test positive), a more appropriate policy approach would involve addressing the underlying reasons that people use drugs and connecting pregnant people to treatment and services *before* they gave birth (before the basket is put in the river). Hermann explained, "You're kind of faced with a problem that maybe needs a scalpel, maybe needs surgery, and all you've got's a machete to do it with, ya know? If you're going to do a deterrent but you don't provide services, you're not doing anybody much favors."[128] Dr. Deborah Frank, a pediatrician and director of the Boston Medical Center Children's Clinic, put it even more starkly: "To simplify a complex medical and psychosocial issue into a criminal issue is really just like using a hammer to play the piano."[129] Solicitor Hermann came to recognize that the threat of criminal prosecution was inadequate. Substance use disorder is more complex than a mere matter of willpower, and quality drug treatment wasn't always available. Why hack away at a problem that needs a much more sophisticated, intricate solution?

Instead of prosecuting pregnant drug users who were reported to his office, he would refer them to treatment with Bricker and Gimlet. After this shift in perspective and practice, Hermann lost a member of his own family to an overdose during pregnancy. He knew how much this relative cared about her expected baby, and this experience drove home the message that substance use disorder isn't a form of child abuse, and it is not something you can prosecute your way out of.[130]

My analysis suggests that in many cases the policies were *not* carried out as intended. While some of the prosecutors who got involved in the policies may have displayed less punitive attitudes, they ultimately work in a punitive position, and the tools at their disposal are punitive. They were unable to contain the spread of and the subsequent, perhaps, *misuse* of their policies that enacted punitive responses. The sense that they were needed to address an urgent problem and negative judgments about pregnant drug users drove the creation of policies that required the suspension of fundamental rights, with no evidence that they would be effective. Using interdisciplinary teams allowed law enforcement to skirt issues of legality and allowed members of the pregnancy police to insulate themselves from the outcomes or even from knowledge of the outcomes. They could account for some so-called success stories—the birth of a healthy baby or someone who is in recovery postpartum—but they were less likely to acknowledge that the success stories themselves were riddled with potentially traumatizing events and circumstances. They distanced themselves from the fact that these policies were ineffective: many people relapsed after they gave birth, violated the terms of their probation, were unable to access treatment, and were forced to serve the prison sentences that were *supposed* to be only motivating threats.

Responding to and producing panic and remaining largely misinformed of the true medical impact of substance use on fetuses, pregnancy policing created policies that, in at least South Carolina and Alabama, ultimately changed the law; defined pregnant people as belonging to an exceptional, lesser class of person; and established fetal personhood. Perhaps part of what made this possible is that the criminal justice apparatus was used to target some of the most stigmatized, marginalized people in our society, many of whom were suffering from a very misunderstood disorder. Now, without federal constitutional protections for abortion rights and the increasing criminalization of abortion in the United States, it is plausible that the networks created to serve test, report, and arrest policies will also be used to systematically punish people who self-manage abortion and those who help them. When all you have is a hammer—even a velvet hammer—everything looks like a nail.

7 Conclusion

The pregnancy police aren't new. They were at work in restricting the labor of people with the capacity for pregnancy in the early 1900s, in institutionalizing and sterilizing people deemed unfit in the 1920s and 1930s, and in sterilizing marginalized people of color deemed financially and sexually irresponsible through the 1960s and 1970s. The ideology of fetal personhood breathed new life into policing pregnancy, framing the people who gestate these fertilized eggs, embryos, and fetuses as the most significant threat to their own pregnancies. Even as other threats, like pervasive intimate partner violence, generated concern for the well-being of (certain kinds of) pregnant people and their pregnancies, this too has ultimately contributed to the policing of pregnancy and to the treatment of pregnant people as mere vessels for the production of children. Despite claims that punitive policies are necessary to protect the unborn and, to a lesser extent, to protect the well-being of the pregnant person, these claims are undermined by the documented harms caused by these punitive policies.

Test, report, and arrest style cases involving drug use during pregnancy represent the vast majority of arrest cases included in this study, but they do not represent the full scope of pregnancy criminalization. My research has shown that, in addition to the criminalization of drug *use,* arrests and prosecutions of people with the capacity for pregnancy also have the effect of criminalizing actions such as failing to take care of a pregnancy, being shot in the abdomen, surviving attempted suicide, rejecting medical treatment, failing to bring the products of conception to a coroner after a miscarriage, driving or running, and self-managing abortion.[1] The criminal prosecution of pregnant people for crimes against their own pregnancies is an expected extension of pregnancy exceptionalism into the criminal realm. By defining people with the capacity for pregnancy as a separate class of persons in need of regulation, for their own benefit, for the benefit of their potential offspring, or for the overall benefit of society, we have reduced their legal status as a class of persons.

This controlling approach to pregnancy thrives both within and outside the scope of the law. Pregnant people are charged with crimes against their own pregnancies when there are no laws defining these pregnancy crimes. They are even charged with crimes against their own pregnancies when there are explicit legal prohibitions of such prosecutions. Official criminalization by way of legislation or court findings was unable to reduce the dramatic racial disparities and disproportionate focus on racialized and politically salient drugs. Indeed, the laws themselves are undergirded by assumptions about good and bad mothering practices coded in raced and classed terms.[2]

Efforts to establish fetal personhood in the criminal code crept in through legislation that purported to help protect (certain kinds of) pregnant people from violence, usually intimate partner violence. This emphasis on violence committed by individuals against other individuals appropriates feminist appeals to protect women from violence and also obscures the reality of *state* violence. The project to use the criminal legal system to address violence is one of the things that have made pregnant people even *more* vulnerable to violence. As Angela Davis and her colleagues write, "Capitulating to a carceral feminism that calls upon the state to 'protect' women from gender violence would replicate the very conditions that needed to be challenged." They continue, "The pretext of ending gender violence allows the state to determine the nature of the problem, to decide on 'reasonable' solutions, and to categorize people as either deserving to be free from injury or not. These are the same tactics that people who cause harm in intimate relationships use: arbitrary authority, attributions of blame to justify punishment, and expulsion of those who are objectionable, threatening, or obsolete."[3] In other words, when the state was tasked with protecting people from their abusive partners, the state essentially became another abuser—or at least had access to a new form of abuse.

After the murder of George Floyd, yet another horrific murder of a Black man by law enforcement, calls to defund the police gained national attention and political salience. If police don't keep us safe, and in some cases are the very ones causing harm, why should their budgets be so bloated? A 2020 study found that the United States "spends twice as much on law and order as it does on cash welfare."[4] So instead of addressing the causes of crime, tax dollars fund a criminal legal system that has failed to keep people safe because it meets nearly any social or public health problem with arrest and incarceration after the fact. Calls to defund the police ask that police budgets be redistributed to fund other public services and goods—housing, food stamps, health care, and social workers.

While I am amenable to propositions to defund the police, I am also concerned that this will not have the effect of limiting the already overgrown institutional apparatus and philosophy of policing embedded in other state agencies and programs. Contact with state agencies opens the door to state surveillance, regulation, and control.[5] Legal historian Dorothy Roberts writes about the child welfare system as a form of family policing for poor people of color, arguing that the prison-abolition framework must expand to include the state violence of the "family-policing system."[6] My analysis of arrest cases of pregnant people for crimes against their own pregnancies found that health-care providers and social workers were involved in the policing. Other individuals participate as well—neighbors or friends who heard about a pregnancy loss and decided to report it. Bounty-hunter–style abortion bans, like the one in effect in Texas, similarly deputize random people to police those with the capacity for pregnancy, allowing them to collect $10,000 from anyone who assists in the provision of an illegal abortion. A lawsuit is already underway: an abusive ex-husband is suing the three women who helped his ex-wife have an abortion.[7] How can the police be truly defunded when police are already present seemingly everywhere?

Advocates have cautioned that the success of the antiabortion and fetal personhood movements would lead to the increased criminalization of pregnancy. Attorney Lynn Paltrow, founder of National Advocates for Pregnant Women (now Pregnancy Justice), writes, "I believe that attacks on *Roe v. Wade* and efforts to treat fertilized eggs, embryos, and fetuses as separate legal persons will establish a system of law in which women who have abortions will go to jail." Paltrow emphasizes the dramatic expansion of the criminal justice system in the years since *Roe v. Wade* was decided, writing that this "makes it far more likely today than in 1973 that if Roe is overturned women will themselves be arrested and jailed."[8] *Roe has* been overturned, putting people with the capacity for pregnancy in an even more precarious position. The removal of constitutional rights for abortion has the potential to permit not only restrictions on abortion but the further criminalization of abortion. Research has shown that criminalizing abortion does not end efforts to abort pregnancies.[9] As abortion becomes more criminalized in the states, people seeking to end their pregnancies will be forced to take more legal risks. Even in the absence of laws providing penalties for pregnant people, other legislation could be applied. For example, Alabama attorney general Steve Marshall, who brought chemical endangerment charges against pregnant people back when he was the district attorney of Marshall County, Alabama, commented that people who use medication abortion to end a pregnancy could be charged with chemical endangerment of a minor.[10]

The three states in this study have had many decades to practice policing pregnancy on the bodies of women and birthing people of color and poor white people. These states provide models for other states to learn from and rapidly adopt. With the overturn of *Roe,* millions of people have lost the legal right to abortion and are put in a position where they may be forced to confront this now well-practiced, if unofficial, police force in the state where they live, work, go to college, or go on vacation.

But *Roe v. Wade* wasn't only a case about abortion. To the extent that *Roe v. Wade* also emphasized the legal personhood of pregnant people prior to fetal viability, overturning the opinion opens the door to other constraints on the legal personhood of pregnant people. In my analysis of pregnancy crime legislation, the bills introduced after *Dobbs* have become even more punitive—removing "maternal" exemptions from criminal responsibility in feticide statutes, creating new crimes against the fetus, and increasing penalties for pregnancy loss. Some states are exploring the adoption of so-called fetal personhood in their legal code, and Georgia has already taken the plunge. These laws make fertilized eggs, embryos, and fetuses the legal equivalent of born children, potentially expanding opportunities to apply charges against pregnant people. In research interviews some prosecutors expressed that they felt somewhat constrained by *Roe v. Wade* in applying charges, particularly in applying charges for previability pregnancies. With *Roe* gone prosecutors are free to apply charges from the earliest moments of pregnancy. Not only does this expand the period over which pregnant people's actions could be seen as criminal, but it also means we may see an increase of still-pregnant people in jails and prisons.

My study shows some limited evidence that some prosecutors, like district attorney Peter Hermann, may be persuaded away from prosecuting for pregnancy-related crimes.[11] However, when an individual prosecutor leaves office, the replacement can begin the practice all over again. Working to elect prosecutors who refuse to prosecute pregnancy cases is similarly fraught, as new legislation is currently being introduced to remove this discretionary power from prosecutors and to even create criminal penalties for prosecutors who don't pursue convictions for pregnancy cases.

This doesn't have to be inevitable. Organizations around the country, dedicated to the principles of reproductive justice, have been working for decades to support individual people with the capacity for pregnancy and to fight the laws and institutional structures that do harm to and limit their rights. These organizations, such as SisterSong Women of Color Reproductive Justice Collective, Healthy and Free Tennessee, SisterReach, Pregnancy Justice, and If/When/How have been aware of the political storm brewing and have been preparing for this moment. Though the array of looming reproductive oppressions may feel impossibly vast, the reproductive justice framework's demands for the freedom to have children, the freedom to not have children, and the freedom to raise our children in safe and healthy environments provide real opportunities for political alliances and coalitions.

Pregnant people can be advised to limit what information they share with their health-care providers, to be mindful of their electronic footprint, and to refuse consent for drug testing. Patient advocates like doulas, who support pregnant, birthing, and postpartum people, may be able to provide rights advocacy in medical settings. Health-care providers can be encouraged to practice civil disobedience in support of their ethical responsibility to not harm patients, by not drug testing patients, not recording results of drug tests, and not making reports claiming that substance use during pregnancy is a form of child abuse.

Ultimately, however, the work needed to assert the personhood of people with the capacity for pregnancy and to support their physical and mental well-being is much deeper. This study has indicated that people with the capacity for pregnancy are often coping with abuse, poverty, and compounded trauma, which can all contribute to substance use disorder and negative birth outcomes. The elimination of the pregnancy police is not enough to remedy this suffering and injustice. Access to quality housing, abuse intervention, living wages, support for families and children, and comprehensive health care, among other things, are all necessary to ensure the well-being of pregnant people and their families.

The pregnancy police exist outside of the law. They are in our attitudes and beliefs. They are in our moralizing, our respectability politics, and our strategic silence and distancing from marginalized people deemed unworthy of care or too politically risky to publicly support. Unless these social and cultural attitudes can be changed, the pregnancy police will still exist, and people with the capacity for pregnancy will continue to be surveilled, controlled, and punished.

Afrofuturist author Octavia Butler wrote that "there is nothing new under the sun, but there are new suns."[12] Stepping away from the historical urge to treat people with the capacity for pregnancy as a class of persons with reduced legal status and to control, punish, and surveil them requires us to envision new possibilities—to find a new sun. Just as these oppressive and harmful systems are created and sustained, *new* ways of being, oriented around human rights and social justice, can be envisioned, created, and sustained. In the words of friend and mentor Dr. Monica McLemore, "We can make this all different." Indeed, we must.

Appendix 1: Methodology

This is a mixed-method study. The benefits of using mixed methods are numerous. Jennifer Greene, Valerie Caracelli, and Wendy Graham outlined five strengths of multimethod research, including triangulation, complementarity, development, initiation, and expansion.[1] Doren L. Madey writes that "combining quantitative and qualitative research helps form a conceptual framework, to validate quantitative findings by referring to information from the qualitative phase of the study, and to construct indices from qualitative data that can be used to analyze quantitative data."[2] Mixed-methods research can also provide a bifocal lens, allowing for study at both the macro and micro levels.[3]

To chart the legislative behavior of states with regard to pregnancy-specific crimes, I first searched for all the introduced bills on the state legislative online archives by year, between 1973 and March 2023, using a fixed set of search terms.[4] After identifying 1,171 bills, I coded them for legislative content, bill status, and the names of bill sponsors and sorted them into four legal typologies (1) the criminalization of harm to fertilized eggs, embryos, and fetuses; (2) the definition of pregnant people as a unique class of crime victim; (3) the criminalization of abortion; and (4) the prosecution of pregnant people for crimes against their own pregnancies. I further coded these bills for content on the gestational age at which they were applied and, finally, coded the bills for legal exceptions in the areas of medicine, abortion, and the pregnant person's actions or inactions. I omitted from the analysis fetal personhood bills that were abortion focused but contained no explicit criminal content. Bills with a civil rather than criminal focus, such as those concerning parental custody or damages for certain prenatal harms, were also omitted. Next I conducted full-text searches of the legal code for each state, as of March 2023, using the aforementioned set of search terms. These statutes were coded for content using the same scheme detailed earlier.

I also collected case records for arrests of pregnant people for crimes against their own pregnancies in South Carolina, Alabama, and Tennessee, occurring from 1973, post-*Roe v. Wade,* through 2022.[5] The data is most robust through 2020, as this is the final year of arrest cases shared with me by the legal advocacy organization Pregnancy Justice (formerly National Advocates for Pregnant Women). I identified 1,116 confirmed pregnancy-related arrest cases: 267 cases in South Carolina, 747 cases in Alabama, and 102 cases in Tennessee. This is, no doubt, an undercount. The case identification and collection process presented many challenges. Because this study includes an analysis of arrests conducted *prior* to criminalization, the charges brought against defendants can vary significantly, from reckless endangerment to delivery of drugs to a minor to aggravated assault and even homicide, to name a few. Though these documents are on the public record, the nonexistence of a uniform charge greatly reduces the feasibility of a freedom of information request for a list of pregnancy-related criminal charges.

My first steps in the search for case documents involved outreach to nonprofit organizations such as the National Advocates for Pregnant Women and to journalists, public defenders, media outlets, police blotters, and internet search tools. I also established a set of Google alerts using key terms so that relevant news stories would be sent directly to my inbox, which helped me identify additional cases reported by local news outlets, including police blotters.[6] I continue to pursue new avenues for case identification. Tennessee has proven to be the most challenging state to study, as it has no online uniform case-lookup system, and arrests have been made under a wide variety of charges. As such, I present some general findings for Tennessee but am unable to make claims as to the impact of formal codification on arrest and prosecutorial practice from the state based on case data.

Once a case was identified, I used case record–retrieval software, such as Alabama's Alacourt and South Carolina's Public Index search tools, to collect summary information about cases and defendants, including their race and age, who has jurisdiction in their case, dates of arrest, and so on. I also contacted county clerks' offices and individual police departments to collect relevant case documents, which included arrest reports, warrants, affidavits, and sentencing sheets. This was an expensive process, requiring a paid subscription to Alacourt, per-page charges for court documents, and sometimes an additional charge for the retrieval of the records. Occasionally, these files also included medical records, interview transcripts, and handwritten letters from jail or prison.[7] I coded these documents for many variables about the nature of the cases: the kind of crime and what defendants were charged with; how the cases came to the attention of law enforcement; the birth outcome or pregnancy status of the defendants; if they were accused of using drugs; whether they had a public defender; how their cases concluded; and what their sentences were. I also coded the data to indicate whether the arrest occurred prior to formal criminalization or after.[8] The coded case data was contextualized by census data on state and county demographics, state-level data on nonpregnancy-specific drug charges, and Substance Abuse and Mental Health Services Administration survey data on substance use and drug treatment admissions.

I originally intended to conduct research interviews with the people who have been most impacted by the criminalization of pregnancy—those who were arrested. However, given their stigmatized position, vulnerable legal status, the likelihood that their experience was traumatizing, and the reality that many of them have *already* had intimate aspects of their private lives shared against their will, the idea of using their public criminal records to track them down for interviews felt too invasive and potentially triggering of their trauma. At the same time, they are the true experts. Nobody knows what it feels like to be arrested for a crime against your own pregnancy more than they do. But I don't want to expose people who want to maintain their privacy. As such, I share only the names and identifying details of individual defendants when they have already received and participated in major media coverage or when they were a named subject of a major, precedent-setting court case.

I do my best to share their voices in this book, including excerpts from case records, letters written to judges, statements from depositions, and quotes from media interviews. I share only details that are on the public record. This means that I frequently do not know or will not share details about the children of those arrested or about how these criminal interventions have impacted custody arrangements, which are handled by the civil court system. Existing research shows that pregnant drug users frequently lose custody of their children, at least temporarily, based on the understanding that drug use during pregnancy is a form of child abuse.[9]

Preliminary research indicated that district attorneys and solicitors, government prosecutors who work at a local, substate level, played a central role in the criminal prosecution of pregnant people, working as a conduit between different state and county agencies with an interest in pregnancy and substance use. Even before explicit criminalizing legislation was passed or state courts ruled that nonspecific legislation could be applied to pregnancy, prosecutors were using nonpregnancy-specific law to bring charges. In South Carolina and Alabama, prosecutorial interpretation of the law is what ultimately made it possible for state supreme courts to set precedents explicitly permitting these prosecutions. After coding arrest data by county, year, and prosecutor, I ranked prosecutors by the year of their first pregnancy-related prosecution and their total number of prosecutions, to find those who were the earliest and most active adopters of the punitive approach. I received Institutional Review Board approval to conduct inductive semistructured interviews with prosecutors about their motivations and goals for pursuing criminal action. Starting with the earliest, most active prosecutors, I found professional contact information and began the process of recruiting prosecutors for research interviews. Our initial point of contact was typically over the phone, followed by email exchanges.

During June and July 2016, I traveled to Alabama and South Carolina to conduct in-person, audio-recorded, semistructured interviews that averaged from sixty to ninety minutes in length. We discussed legal interpretations, policy development, goals and motivations, challenges, and the legal strategies used to overcome these challenges. I transcribed the interviews and imported the transcripts into NVivo, a qualitative analysis software, which I used to inductively code the interviews for themes. I interviewed six prosecutors who were among the first to adopt the policies in their states. One prosecutor referred me to a local drug rehabilitation facility that specializes in the treatment of pregnant women, the founders of which heavily influenced the prosecutor's approach to the issue of prenatal substance use. (This research approach is called snowball sampling.) I interviewed the two women who started the rehab program for prenatal substance use.

Several notable actors from South Carolina could not be interviewed for this project. One, Charles "Charlie" Condon, was the solicitor for Charleston, South Carolina, and was one of the major parties involved in developing the drug-testing protocol at the Medical University of South Carolina that was challenged in the *Crystal Ferguson v. City of Charleston* case. He eventually became the state attorney general. He did not respond to my invitation to participate in a research interview. Another, Robert "Bobby" Hood, was the attorney who represented the Medical University of South Carolina in the *Ferguson* case. Though he was willing to have an off-the-record conversation at his law office in Charleston, he did not consent to participate in a research interview. In lieu of audio-recorded interviews, I draw from statements that Condon and Hood gave to the media.

I was unable to recruit prosecutors from Tennessee in June and July 2016. Contact information for relevant actors was less readily available, as apparently some of these individuals are now retired (many of the earliest arrests included in the study came from Tennessee). Furthermore, at the time when I was recruiting subjects and conducting interviews, the Tennessee law had just "sunset," or expired, and its supporters were unwilling to speak with me at that time. However, because the Tennessee law was formally codified by the legislature and not by the state court, there were other sources of information available. Videos of the legislative hearings in which the bill was debated and discussed are available online, and these include explicit statements of intent and support from the district attorneys involved in developing and advocating for the law. In lieu of interviews with Tennessee prosecutors, I include analysis of the statements that prosecutors made at these legislative hearings.

In the summer of 2022, I attempted to conduct another round of interviews with prosecutors to understand variations in how they approached these pregnancy-related cases and to discuss the possible impact that the end of *Roe* would have on prosecution for pregnancy loss, but this proved fruitless. When I conducted the first round of interviews, I was a graduate student and had no trouble arranging interviews with prosecutors in South Carolina and Alabama—some of them even seemed eager to talk to "the girl from the college." Six years later things are a little different. My professional reputation and media presence, perhaps in addition to some degree of increasing political polarization in the intervening years, hurt my ability to recruit subjects for interviews. Additionally, several of the prosecutors involved in the earliest arrests died before the summer of 2022. As such, instead of using interviews, I pivoted to conducting an analysis of media interviews of both prosecutors and law enforcement. These were inductively hand-coded for themes in NVivo.

Appendix 2: Court Cases

Buck v. Bell, 274 U.S. 200, 47 S. Ct. 584, 71 L. Ed. 1000 (1927) tested the constitutionality of a 1924 Virginia law that permitted the compulsory sterilization of certain people deemed unfit by the state. A woman named Carrie Buck had been deemed "feebleminded" and was the first candidate for sterilization under the Virginia law. The court argued that the precedent underlying mandatory vaccinations and the war draft supported compulsory sterilization law—the forced sterilization of the unfit would serve a public good that justified the infringement on personal liberty. The opinion asserted that three generations of Carrie's family deemed to be imbeciles—Carrie's mother, Carrie's daughter, and Carrie herself—were "enough."

DeGraffenreid v. General Motors Assembly Division, etc. 412 F. Supp 124 (E.D. Mo. 1976) demonstrated the difficulty of making legal claims on the basis of intersectional identities in the US legal system. While General Motors didn't hire black women until 1964, it *did* hire *white* women (read as a neutral, raceless legal category), and it *did* hire Black men (read as a neutral sexless legal category). When the company adopted a last-in, last-out layoff policy that disproportionately impacted Black women, five Black women sued. The court dismissed their sex discrimination suit as not legally actionable, essentially because white women weren't similarly impacted. The five Black women were encouraged to join a racial discrimination lawsuit with Black men, but the men's lawsuit did not reflect the discrimination they experienced as Black women.

Dobbs v. Jackson Women's Health Organization, 142 S. Ct. 2228, 597 U.S., 213 L. Ed. 2d 545 (2022) tested the constitutionality of a Mississippi law that banned abortion outright after fifteen weeks of pregnancy. Outright abortion bans prior to viability would be considered undue burdens under the precedent set in *Roe v. Wade* and *Planned Parenthood v. Casey*. However, in this case, the court overturned both precedents. The court asserted that because the right to privacy is not named *explicitly* in the US Constitution, because abortion was not a part of the history and tradition of the nation, and because some people believe that abortion is the taking of a human life, *Roe* and *Casey* had been decided improperly. The court ruled that states are now free to pass any abortion regulations they see fit.

Eisenstadt v. Baird, 405 U.S. 438, 92 S. Ct. 1029, 31 L. Ed. 2d 349 (1972) tested the constitutionality of a Massachusetts law that criminalized the giving away of "any drug, medicine, instrument, or article whatever for the prevention of conception." During a lecture Baird had exhibited contraceptive devices, and he gave a young woman a package of contraceptive foam. He was convicted of violating this law. Baird argued that the Massachusetts law violated the rights of single people, as *Griswold* had allowed married couples to use contraceptives. The US Supreme Court agreed. This case extended *Griswold*'s right to privacy to unmarried couples, allowing them to use contraceptives.

Ex parte Ankrom, 152 So. 3d 397 (Ala. 2013) determined the (state) constitutionality of applying the Alabama chemical endangerment law to pregnancy. In this case two women found guilty of violating the Alabama chemical endangerment statute for using drugs during pregnancy appealed their convictions. They argued that, as the law didn't mention its application to fetuses, it was unconstitutionally vague for the purposes of pregnancy-related arrests. The Alabama Supreme Court disagreed, arguing that the statute applied to fertilized eggs, embryos, and fetuses.

Ex parte Hicks, 153 So. 3d 53 (Ala. 2014) addressed Sarah Hicks's conviction for chemical endangerment of a child when she used drugs during her pregnancy. Hicks appealed her conviction, arguing that the chemical endangerment law's application to pregnancy was unconstitutionally vague. The Alabama Supreme Court affirmed its decision in *Ankrom,* upholding Hicks's conviction.

Ferguson v. City of Charleston, 532 U.S. 67, 121 S. Ct. 1281, 149 L. Ed. 2d 205 (2001) addressed a policy adopted by the Medical University of South Carolina that required drug testing of pregnant patients. People who tested positive for drugs were to be offered a choice: drug treatment or prosecution. Health-care providers from the hospital, along with law enforcement personnel, developed a list of criteria specifying when drug tests would be administered. Crystal Ferguson, one of the people who was drug tested, reported, and arrested under the law, sued. The US Supreme Court found that, because the hospital had developed its testing protocol for law enforcement and because the drug tests had been administered for nonmedical purposes with no warrant or probable cause, that the policy was unconstitutional and violated the Fourth Amendment prohibition on unlawful searches and seizures.

Fowler v. Woodward, 138 S.E.2d 42, 244 S.C. 608 (1964) concerned a civil action for damages in the wrongful death of a viable fetus. A woman died in a car accident and subsequent fire when she was eight months pregnant. A wrongful death lawsuit was brought against the man who was found to be at fault in the accident. The South Carolina Supreme Court was asked to decide if wrongful death statutes applied to viable fetuses. The court found that, for the purposes of civil actions, viable fetuses counted as persons.

General Electric Co. v. Gilbert, 429 U.S. 125, 97 S. Ct. 401, 50 L. Ed. 2d 343 (1976) tested the constitutionality of General Electric's disability insurance, which excluded pregnancy coverage. Gilbert represented a class of women who argued that the exclusion of pregnancy was unlawfully discriminatory for violating Title VII of the Civil Rights Act. The US Supreme Court argued that pregnancy discrimination was not the same as sex discrimination, as not all women can become pregnant, and not all women are pregnant all the time. The exclusion of pregnancy from the insurance plan was deemed lawful.

Griswold v. Connecticut, 381 U.S. 479, 85 S. Ct. 1678, 14 L. Ed. 2d 510 (1965) tested the constitutionality of Connecticut law that criminalized the use of "any drug, medicinal article or instrument for the purpose of preventing conception." Griswold, the executive director of Planned Parenthood of Connecticut, and Buxton, a physician and professor at the Yale School of Medicine, "gave information, instruction, and medical advice to married persons as to the means of preventing conception" and were found guilty of violating the Connecticut law. Griswold and Buxton argued that the Connecticut statute violated the Fourteenth Amendment and appealed to the Appellate Circuit Court and the Supreme Court of Errors, which both affirmed their conviction. Finally, they appealed to the US Supreme Court, arguing that constitutional amendments indicate that there is a right to privacy. The court argued that the married couple who received contraceptive counseling was within that "zone of privacy." As such, the Connecticut law was found to be unconstitutional, permitting married couples to be counseled on and to use contraceptives.

Laube v. Haley, 234 F. Supp. 2d 1227 (M.D. Ala. 2002) concerned a lawsuit brought by female inmates at three facilities operated by the Alabama Department of Corrections, alleging that the overcrowding, inadequate supervision, improper inmate classification, inmate violence, availability of weapons, small number of segregation cells, inadequate living space, inadequate ventilation, and extreme heat conditions at the prison violated the Eighth Amendment prohibition on cruel and unusual punishment. The court agreed that the understaffing and overcrowding in inmate dorms at the Julia Tutwiler Prison for Women were unconstitutionally unsafe. The court found against the other allegations, including all allegations against the other two facilities.

Lochner v. New York, 198 U.S. 45, 25 S. Ct. 539, 49 L. Ed. 937 (1905) questioned the constitutionality of a New York law, the Bakeshop Act, which imposed maximum working hours on professional bakers to promote public health. Lochner, the owner of a bakery, was charged with violating that law. Lochner argued that the Bakeshop Act was an unconstitutional violation of the rights of employees and employers to contract working conditions and requirements. The court found in favor of Lochner, arguing that the New York law wasn't a public health law but rather a labor law in disguise.

McKnight v. State, 661 S.E.2d 354, 378 S.C. 33 (2008) addressed the conviction of Regina McKnight for giving birth to a stillborn baby who tested positive for cocaine metabolites. Regina was convicted for homicide by child abuse. She filed a petition for postconviction relief, arguing ineffective assistance of counsel, but the court rejected the petition. Appealing to the South Carolina Supreme Court, McKnight argued that her attorney failed to bring more expert witnesses and to emphasize that the stillbirth may have been caused by infection and not drug use, and the court failed to properly instruct the jury that they needed to find beyond a reasonable doubt that the death had been caused by "circumstances showing extreme indifference to human life." The court reversed the PCR court's denial for relief.

Muller v. Oregon, 208 U.S. 412, 28 S. Ct. 324, 52 L. Ed. 551 (1908) concerned the constitutionality of an Oregon law that placed limits on the number of hours female employees could work each day. The Grand Laundry had required a woman to exceed the limit, in violation of the law. The employer was sentenced to a ten-dollar fine, and he appealed to the Oregon Supreme Court, which affirmed the conviction. The employer then appealed to the US Supreme Court to determine the constitutionality of the Oregon law. The employer argued that the law was an unconstitutional infringement on the right to contract. The court found that a woman's "physical structure" and "the performance of maternal functions place her at a disadvantage in the struggle for subsistence," especially if she is a mother. Even if she is not a mother, the court found that "as healthy mothers are essential to vigorous offspring, the physical well-being of woman becomes an object of public interest and care in order to preserve the strength and vigor of the race." As such, the Oregon law placing maximum-hour limitations is justified and constitutional.

Nelson v. Norris et al., No. 07-2481 (8th Cir. 2009) involved the shackling of an incarcerated pregnant woman while she gave birth. Shawanna Nelson was incarcerated by the Arkansas Department of Corrections when she was six months pregnant. When she was in labor she was transported to the hospital, and her legs were shackled to opposite sides of the bed for hours of labor. Nelson sued ADOC, arguing that the shackling violated her Eighth Amendment right against cruel and unusual punishment. A federal district judge ruled that Nelson's case should be considered by a jury, but, before a jury was empaneled, a three-judge panel of Eighth Circuit Court of Appeals judges dismissed the lawsuit outright, ruling that the shackling had not violated her constitutional rights. At a subsequent hearing before the full Eighth Circuit Court of Appeals, this time with ACLU representation, the court found that her shackling was unconstitutional.

Planned Parenthood of Southeastern Pa. v. Casey, 505 U.S. 833, 112 S. Ct. 2791, 120 L. Ed. 2d 674 (1992) concerned the passage of state laws that directly conflicted with the trimester framework established by *Roe v. Wade,* with regulations beginning in the first trimester. Contested abortion regulations in Pennsylvania included handouts of state-mandated and state-designed informed-consent materials that required a twenty-four-hour waiting period before having an abortion; a requirement that people seeking abortion notify their husbands before the procedure could be performed; a requirement that minors get consent from at least one parent before an abortion could be performed; a change in the state definition of medical emergency that narrowed the instances in which abortion exceptions apply; and reporting and record-keeping requirements imposed on abortion providers. Striking down *Roe*'s trimester framework, the court created a new standard by which to evaluate the constitutionality of state abortion regulations: the undue burden standard. Regulations deemed to pose an "undue burden" on people's exercise of their right to abortion would be deemed unconstitutional. Otherwise, regulations were permitted at any stage of pregnancy. With the undue burden standard, the only Pennsylvania regulation found to be unconstitutional was the spousal-notification requirement.

Roe v. Wade, 410 U.S. 113, 93 S. Ct. 705, 35 L. Ed. 2d 147 (1973) found that abortion is a constitutionally protected fundamental right based on the right of privacy established in *Griswold v. Connecticut.* The court established the "trimester framework" to spell out when and what kind of abortion regulations states can implement. In the first trimester, no state regulations can be applied to abortion—the decision should be left to a woman and her doctor. In the second trimester, some regulations may be applied, but only those in the interest of protecting the pregnant person. In the third trimester, the fetus is considered viable, and at this stage states may favor their interest in the fetus above their interest in the pregnant woman's fundamental rights. In the third trimester, states may ban abortion completely, with exceptions for protecting the life and health of the pregnant person and for pregnancies resulting from rape and incest.

Skinner v. Oklahoma ex rel. Williamson, 316 U.S. 535, 62 S. Ct. 1110, 86 L. Ed. 1655 (1942) concerned the constitutionality of an Oklahoma law, the Habitual Criminal Sterilization Act, which ordered the involuntary sterilization of "habitual criminals"—persons who had been convicted of two or more crimes "amounting to felonies involving moral turpitude." The act prohibited the sterilization of people who had committed two or more offenses involving "prohibitory laws, revenue acts, embezzlement, or political offenses." Skinner was convicted of stealing chickens and then for robbery with firearms and then a third time for another robbery with firearms. Skinner challenged the constitutionality of the Oklahoma law on the basis of the Fourteenth Amendment. The Oklahoma Supreme Court ruled against Skinner, and he appealed to the US Supreme Court. The court found that, as the law permitted sterilization only for certain crimes and not for others, it was discriminatory and thus unconstitutional.

State of West Virginia v. Stephanie Elaine Louk, 786 S.E.2d 219, 237 W. Va. 200 (2016) addressed the criminal conviction of Stephanie Louk for child neglect resulting in death. Louk injected methamphetamine when she was thirty-seven weeks pregnant and subsequently experienced breathing difficulties. An emergency cesarean section was performed, and doctors determined that Louk's breathing difficulties deprived the fetus of oxygen, resulting in death. Louk was sentenced for three to fifteen years in prison. Louk appealed her sentence, arguing that prenatal acts were not included in the West Virginia child neglect statute. The West Virginia Supreme Court agreed with Louk, emphasizing that the court's role is not to make legislation but to enforce the plain language of the law. They reversed Louk's conviction.

State v. Horne, 319 S.E.2d 703, 282 S.C. 444 (1984) determined the (state) constitutionality of applying the South Carolina murder statute to an "unborn child." Terrance Horne had been convicted of assault and battery with intent to kill and voluntary manslaughter after he stabbed his estranged wife, Deborah, who was nine months pregnant. Deborah was rushed to the hospital to treat wounds in her neck, arms, and belly. The fetus did not survive. Building on the precedent set in *Fowler v. Woodward,* the court found that "it would be grossly inconsistent for us to construe a viable fetus as a 'person' for the purposes of imposing civil liability while refusing to give it a similar classification in the criminal context." The South Carolina murder statute did apply to viable fetuses.

West Coast Hotel Co. v. Parrish, 300 U.S. 379, 57 S. Ct. 578, 81 L. Ed. 703 (1937) addressed a Washington law that set a minimum wage for female employees. The West Coast Hotel argued that this was an unconstitutional violation of the right to contract, citing *Lochner*. Citing *Muller*, the US Supreme Court found that the law was constitutional, as it was in the public interest to protect women, writing, "What can be closer to the public interest than the health and protection of women and their protection from unscrupulous and overreaching employers?"

Whitner v. State, 492 S.E.2d 777, 328 S.C. 1 (1997) concerned South Carolina's child abuse and endangerment statute in the children's code. Cornelia Whitner pled guilty to child neglect after her baby tested positive for cocaine metabolites after birth. Whitner was sentenced to eight years in prison and filed for postconviction relief, arguing that the child abuse and endangerment statute did not specify that it applied to pregnancy, which her defense attorney should have asserted at trial. The petition was granted, and the state appealed to the South Carolina Supreme Court, which found that the court granting postconviction relief had erred, as it did not have subject-matter jurisdiction. Whitner's conviction was reinstated, and she was forced to serve the rest of her prison sentence. In effect this case permits the criminal prosecution of pregnant people for crimes against their pregnancies.

Notes

INTRODUCTION

1. Case record on file with author; Calhoun (2012). I am sensitive to the privacy concerns of those who have had their pregnancies criminalized. While the information about arrests and prosecutions are on the public record, this does not mean those involved asked for their names or lives to become topics of discussion or academic discourse. Some people have expressed that they felt humiliated by press coverage of their case. As such, I disclose only the parties named in major court cases or who participated in major press coverage.

2. I do not know what ultimately happened to Heather's children. Child-custody arrangements are part of the civil legal system and are not on the public record.

3. Roberts (1990, 1991, 1992, 1996, 1997, 2000a, 2000b); Flavin (2008); Flavin and Paltrow (2010); Paltrow and Flavin (2013); Murphy and Rosenbaum (1999); Mohapatra (2011); Goodwin (2014, 2021).

4. Paltrow and Flavin (2013).

5. Cox (2008).

6. Colb (2011).

7. Navarro (2022).

8. See Denbow (2015).

9. Howard (2019); Skinner v. Railway Labor Executives' Assn., 489 U.S. 602, 109 S. Ct. 1402, 103 L. Ed. 2d 639 (1989). There is a large body of case law

limiting the ability of health-care providers to share medical information with state entities like law enforcement. In the early 1990s, HIPAA extended that to include private entities as well. The legality of tests and reports of pregnant people to law enforcement is complex and debatable.

10. Howard (2019).

11. There are some state benefits for pregnant people. The Women, Infants, and Children Program (WIC) offers education and food to pregnant people throughout pregnancy and for six months after birth. Pregnant people may also enjoy some nonlegal privileges, like priority admissions in drug treatment facilities (that is, if the facility actually treats pregnant people) or the social privilege of others offering their seat on public transit.

12. Ross (2006).

13. Crear-Perry et al. (2021); Bray and McLemore (2021); Stevenson, Root, and Menken (2022). In the United States, the maternal mortality rate has been rising since 2000. From 2018 to 2019, the rate increased from 17.4 to 20.1. From 2019 and 2020, it spiked 18.4 percent, to 23.8 deaths per 100,000 live births. The maternal mortality rate in the United States is far higher than that of any other industrialized country, with France at 8.7, Sweden at 4.3, and New Zealand at 1.7, for example. Additionally, the rate for Black mothers is three times higher than that of white and nonwhite Hispanic mothers, at 55 deaths per 100,000 live births versus 19 and 18 respectively (Hoyert 2022).

14. Ross and Solinger (2017).

15. Roe v. Wade, 410 U.S. 113, 93 S. Ct. 705, 35 L. Ed. 2d 147 (1973); Planned Parenthood of Southeastern Pa. v. Casey, 505 U.S. 833, 112 S. Ct. 2791, 120 L. Ed. 2d 674 (1992).

16. "Last Five Years" (2016).

17. Dobbs v. Jackson Women's Health Organization, 142 S. Ct. 2228, 597 U.S., 213 L. Ed. 2d 545 (2022).

18. McCann et al. (2022).

19. Kinnard (2022); Robertson (2022); Belluck (2022). Sepsis is a condition where the body has a severe response to an infection and limits organ function. It can be fatal.

20. González-Rojas (2016).

21. "Reproductive Justice" (n.d.); Ross (2020).

22. Kaye et al. (2016).

23. Goodwin (2021, 567).

24. Supreme Court (2021).

25. Eisenstein (1988, 79).

26. Quoted in Baer (1999).

27. Mink (1998, 18).

28. 1997 Wisconsin Act 292, Wisconsin Statutes § 48.193, enables pregnant people to be treated in this way.

29. Carroll (2019).

30. Baer (1999, 55); MacKinnon (2007, 147); Mink (1998, 18).

31. Quoted in Eisenstein (1988, 80–81).

32. Eisenstein (1988, 81).

33. Quoted in Yurcaba (2022).

34. Geduldig v. Aiello, 417 U.S. 484, 94 S. Ct. 2485, 41 L. Ed. 2d 256 (1974); General Electric Co. v. Gilbert, 429 U.S. 125, 97 S. Ct. 401, 50 L. Ed. 2d 343 (1976).

35. George (2020).

36. Pérez (2007).

37. See Price (2018); Thomsen and Morrison (2020); Fixmer-Oraiz and Yam (2021); and Thomsen (forthcoming).

38. Howard (2019, 349n8).

39. Wood, Carrillo, and Monk-Turner (2022); Seely (2021); Bindman et al. (2022); Dolan et al. (2020); Lovell, Luminais, and Flynn (2018).

40. Young (2012).

41. Jacobs (2014); S. Brown (2015); Bell, McNaughton, and Salmon (2009); Goodwin (2014); Oaks (2015); Ladd-Taylor and Umansky (1998); Feldstein (2018).

42. Crenshaw (1989, 141, 142, 140); DeGraffenreid v. General Motors Assembly Division, etc. 412 F. Supp 124 (E.D. Mo. 1976).

43. See Kolder, Gallagher, and Parsons (1987); Gallagher (1987); Roberts (1991); Paltrow and Fox (1992); Daniels (1996); Gómez (1997); Ikemoto (1998); Nelson and Marshall (1998); Roberts (1997); Adams, Mahowald, and Gallagher (2003); Cherry (2007); Samuels et al. (2007); Fentiman (2006, 2009); Flavin (2008); Cantor (2012); and Bach (2022b).

44. Morone (2004, 32, 35).

45. Mink (1998, 30).

46. Murphy and Rosenbaum (1999, 134).

47. Jordan-Zachery (2009, 51–52).

48. "Alcohol Use" (2022); Riley, Infante, and Warren (2011).

49. Forray (2016); Behnke et al. (2013).

50. Committee on Obstetric Practice (2017); Einarson and Riordan (2009).

51. Forray (2016); Behnke et al. (2013).

52. Ogawa, Takeshima, and Furukawa (2018); Zwink and Jenetzky (2018).

53. Jansson (n.d.).

54. Behnke et al. (2013); "Contraceptive Deserts" (n.d.); Andrade (2018); Forray and Foster (2015); Gorman et al. (2014); Huybrechts et al. (2018); Shah et al. (2012); Wright et al. (2015).

55. Forray (2016); Behnke et al. (2013).

56. Martin and Osterman (2023); Corey et al. (2020); Alhusen et al. (2015); Perrotte, Chaudhary, and Goodman (2020).

57. Shah, Balkhair, and Knowledge Synthesis Group (2011); Perera et al. (1998); Perera et al. (2003); Taylor, Golding, and Emond (2015); Wai et al. (2017); Amereh et al. (2022); Ragusa et al. (2021).

58. D. Davis (2019a, 2019b); D. Davis (2020); Owens and Fett (2019); Bridges (2020).

59. Margerison et al. (2022).

60. Goldstick, Cunningham, and Carter (2022).

61. Davis et al. (1992, 289); Olshan and Faustman (1993, 196); Lindbohm et al. (1991); Savitz (1994); Stellman, Stellman, and Sommer (1988); Daniels (1997); Petrelli et al. (2000); Daniels (2008).

62. Widra and Herring (2021).

63. Roberts (2022, 172, 21).

64. Roberts (2022, 22, 23, 29).

65. M. Mitchell (2016).

66. Roberts (2022, 230).

67. Krauthammer (1989).

CHAPTER 1

1. Wakeman (2017).

2. R. Miller (2021); Goodman (2022).

3. D. Johnson (2004).

4. Unborn Victims of Violence Act, 18 U.S.C. § 1841 (2004).

5. Margerison et al. (2022).

6. St. George (2004).

7. Bearak et al. (2020).

8. My count of state laws aligns with the findings in "Fetal Homicide Laws" (2022).

9. Kim (2022); Nash and Guarnieri (2022); Keveney (2022).

10. The thirty-eight states are Alabama, Alaska, Arizona, Arkansas, California, Florida, Georgia, Idaho, Illinois, Indiana, Kansas, Kentucky, Louisiana, Maryland, Massachusetts, Michigan, Minnesota, Mississippi, Missouri, Montana, Nebraska, Nevada, New Hampshire, North Carolina, North Dakota, Ohio, Oklahoma, Pennsylvania, South Carolina, South Dakota, Tennessee, Texas, Utah, Virginia, Washington, West Virginia, Wisconsin, and Wyoming.

11. Quoted in Coleman (2007).

12. "Governor Denies" (2018).

13. Reeves (2017).

14. Asmussen (2004).

15. "Man Who Partied" (2004).

16. Goldstein (2004); *House Hearing* (2003).

17. "Family Members" (2004).
18. Hegeman (2006).
19. Page (2011).
20. "Family Members" (2004).
21. Morone (1997).
22. Lawn and Koenen (2022); James, Brody, and Hamilton (2013); A. Davis (1981).
23. Bridges (2019a, 778). While possessing, selling, or manufacturing certain substances and operating a vehicle under their influence are considered crimes, mere *using* as documented by a positive drug test is not generally considered a crime.
24. Bridges (2019a, 808).
25. Beckett (1995, 588); Ocen (2017, 1163).
26. Ferguson v. City of Charleston, 532 U.S. 67, 121 S. Ct. 1281, 149 L. Ed. 2d 205 (2001).
27. See Roberts (1996); Marshall (2016).
28. Roberts (1997, 187).
29. Roberts (1997, 174).
30. US Const. amend. IV.
31. *Ferguson,* 532 U.S. 67 (2001) at 68.
32. *Ferguson,* 532 U.S. 67 (2001) at 68.
33. *Fowler v. Woodward,* 138 S.E.2d 42, 244 S.C. 608 (1964) at 611.
34. It is unclear why the first name of "Baby Fowler" wasn't invoked in this case, as it was in other cases where legislation was passed to recognize the fetus as a crime victim. It is possible that, as this was a civil court action and not a social movement to push for a legislative change, that the use of a first name was less necessary. It is also possible that the couple hadn't yet picked out a name for their baby or that the court did not want to release the first name of the baby in its opinion for purposes of confidentiality of the (albeit deceased) minor.
35. State v. Horne, 319 S.E.2d 703, 282 S.C. 444 (1984).
36. Whitner v. State, 492 S.E.2d 777, 328 S.C. 1 (1997).
37. Tantibanchachai (2014).
38. "Crack Mom" (1998).
39. *Whitner,* 492 S.E.2d 777.
40. Tantibanchachai (2014).
41. "Crack Mom" (1998).
42. *Whitner,* 492 S.E.2d 777 at 5.
43. *Whitner,* 492 S.E.2d 777.
44. *Whitner,* 492 S.E.2d 777 at 8.
45. Unborn Victims of Violence Act, S.B. 1084, 116th S.C. G.A. (2005) at 3.
46. "Search for Killer" (2014).
47. G. Mitchell (2006).

48. M. Brown (2019).
49. Romo (2019).
50. Patterson (2019).
51. Szekely (2019).
52. "Ala. Code 1975" (2006).
53. Archived news article on file with author.
54. Todd (2013).
55. Case record on file with author.
56. Calhoun (2012); "Quickfacts: Coffee County" (n.d.).
57. Case record on file with author.
58. Calhoun (2012).
59. Case record on file with author.
60. Calhoun (2012).
61. Case record on file with author.
62. Ex parte Ankrom, 152 So. 3d 397 (Ala. 2013).
63. Calhoun (2012).
64. Case record on file with author.
65. Wong et al. (2021).
66. The reason why the obstetrician ordered a drug test is unclear. It is possible that drug tests are ordered in every infant death as a diagnostic tool. It is also possible that this test was ordered at the discretion of the doctor because Kimbrough disclosed that she used drugs or the doctor suspected that she used drugs. Calhoun (2012).
67. Case record on file with author.
68. Calhoun (2012).
69. Pilkington (2015); Morris, Wald, and Watt (1999).
70. *Ankrom,* 152 So. 3d 397.
71. *Ankrom,* 152 So. 3d 397.
72. *Motion for Leave* (n.d.). Other amici, or friends of the court, include the American Public Health Association, National Association of Social Workers, Alabama Women's Resource Network, American College of Obstetricians and Gynecologists, American Psychiatric Association, Black Women's Health Imperative, Child Welfare Organizing Project, Harm Reduction Coalition, International Center for Advancement of Addiction Treatment of the Beth Israel Medical Center, Baron Edmond de Rothschild Chemical Dependency Institute, Global Lawyers and Physicians, International Doctors for Health Drug Policies, International Mental Disability Law Reform Project, Legal Action Center, American Academy of Addiction Psychiatry, American Society of Addiction Medicine, Center for Gender and Justice, Child Welfare Organizing Project, Citizens for Midwifery, Global Lawyers and Physicians, Institute for Health and Recovery, International Center for Advancement of Addiction Treatment, National Association of Nurse Practitioners in Women's Health, National Coun-

cil on Alcoholism and Drug Dependence, National Latina Institute for Reproductive Health, National Organization for Women–Alabama, National Women's Health Network, Our Bodies Ourselves, and Southern Center for Human Rights.

73. *Ankrom,* 152 So. 3d 397.

74. "Our View" (2015).

75. *Ankrom,* 152 So. 3d 397.

76. *Ankrom,* 152 So. 3d 397.

77. Case record on file with author.

78. Ex parte Hicks, 153 So. 3d 53 (Ala. 2014) at 66. Roy Moore gained a place on the national stage over repeated controversies in his career as a judge and politician. These included the construction of a large granite replica of the Ten Commandments that he installed outside of the judicial building; ethics violations and ultimately a suspension from the bench regarding same-sex marriage and his noncompliance with *Obergefell v. Hodges,* the case that offered constitutional protections for gay marriage; and credible child sexual abuse allegations against him. He later ran for the US Senate seat vacated by Jeff Sessions, ultimately losing to Democrat Doug Jones.

79. Archived news article on file with author.

80. Yurkanin (2022a).

81. Nowell (2022).

82. Equal Justice Initiative (2021).

83. Nowell (2022).

84. Yurkanin (2022a).

85. Yurkanin (2022a).

86. Nowell (2022).

87. Nowell (2022).

88. Nowell (2022).

89. Nowell (2022).

90. Yurkanin (2022a).

91. Nowell (2022).

92. Yurkanin (2022a).

93. Nowell (2022).

94. "2010 Tennessee Code" (2010).

95. "Public Chapter No. 1006" (2011).

96. Medically speaking, the term *fetus* is only applicable starting ten weeks after the last menstrual period. Before the tenth week, the correct term would be embryo, blastocyst, or fertilized egg, depending on the stage of the pregnancy. "Tennessee Senate Bill 3412" (2012) at 1.

97. "Tennessee Senate Bill 0459" (2013) at 1.

98. Hale (2014).

99. Paltrow and Flavin (2013).

100. "West Virginia Senate Bill 146" (2005) at 2.

101. State of West Virginia v. Stephanie Elaine Louk, 786 S.E.2d 219, 237 W. Va. 200 (2016).

102. "Texas Criminal Code" (2021).

103. Newman (2010b).

104. Paltrow and Flavin (2013).

105. See Grayned v. City of Rockford, 408 U.S. 104, 92 S. Ct. 2294, 33 L. Ed. 2d 222 (1972).

106. See Cantwell v. Connecticut, 310 U.S. 296, 60 S. Ct. 900, 84 L. Ed. 1213 (1940).

107. See Winters v. New York, 333 U.S. 507, 68 S. Ct. 665, 92 L. Ed. 840 (1948).

108. Weir (2006); Waggoner (2017); Daniels (1996); Duggan (2016); Muller v. Oregon, 208 U.S. 412, 28 S. Ct. 324, 52 L. Ed. 551 (1908) at Syllabus.

109. Hobbes (2010).

CHAPTER 2

1. Martin (2014).

2. See Harrison (2022).

3. Bei Bei Shuai v. State, 966 N.E.2d 619 (Ind. Ct. App. 2012).

4. Newman (2010a).

5. M. Brown (2019).

6. Morone (2004, 225).

7. E. M. Armstrong (2003, 47).

8. Morone (2004, 222).

9. McClintock (1993, 62).

10. Fineman (1991, 289–90).

11. Morone (2004, 225, 223).

12. Hancock (2004, 30).

13. Morone (2004, 225, 226).

14. Lochner v. New York, 198 U.S. 45, 25 S. Ct. 539, 49 L. Ed. 937 (1905).

15. Drawn from the Fifth and Fourteenth Amendments, substantive due process prevents government infringement on fundamental rights. In the *Lochner* era, this fundamental right was the right to make contracts.

16. For foreign corporations, see Allgeyer v. Louisiana, 165 U.S. 578, 17 S. Ct. 427, 41 L. Ed. 832 (1897). A yellow-dog contract is one made between employers and employees, where employees agree as a condition of employment that they will not join or remain in a labor union. Yellow-dog contracts weaken the collective bargaining ability of workers; see Adair v. United States, 208 U.S. 161, 28 S. Ct. 277, 52 L. Ed. 436 (1908); and Coppage v. Kansas, 236 U.S. 1, 35 S. Ct. 240, 59 L. Ed. 441 (1915). For the coal industry, see Carter v. Carter Coal Co., 298

U.S. 238, 56 S. Ct. 855, 80 L. Ed. 1160 (1936); and for child labor, see Hammer v. Dagenhart, 247 U.S. 251, 38 S. Ct. 529, 62 L. Ed. 1101 (1918); and Bailey v. Drexel Furniture Co. 259 U.S. 20 (1922).

17. But see Adkins v. Children's Hospital of DC, 261 U.S. 525, 43 S. Ct. 394, 67 L. Ed. 785 (1923). Justice George Sutherland asserted that *Adkins* was fundamentally different from *Muller,* in that the maximum-hours law in *Muller* still permitted employees to negotiate their wages, whereas the minimum-wage law in *Adkins* did not, restricting the employer in negotiating employment contracts. Additionally, Sutherland asserted that the passage of the Nineteenth Amendment had essentially erased the political differences between women and men, and, as such, the special protection given to women in the *Muller* decision was no longer necessary. Muller v. Oregon, 208 U.S. 412, 28 S. Ct. 324, 52 L. Ed. 551 (1908).

18. *Muller,* 208 U.S. 412.

19. Other exemptions to the prohibition on labor regulation included safety, morality, and "general welfare." *Lochner,* 198 U.S. 45 (1905) at 53.

20. *Muller,* 208 U.S. 412 (1908) at 421.

21. *Muller,* 208 U.S. 412 (1908) at 421, 422.

22. West Coast Hotel Co. v. Parrish, 300 U.S. 379, 57 S. Ct. 578, 81 L. Ed. 703 (1937) at 379.

23. Lombardo (2022, 128).

24. Morone (2004, 226).

25. Roberts (1995, 100).

26. Brake and Grossman (2013).

27. General Electric Co. v. Gilbert, 429 U.S. 125, 97 S. Ct. 401, 50 L. Ed. 2d 343 (1976).

28. Brake and Grossman (2013).

29. Quinnell (2021); "PDA" (n.d.).

30. Pregnancy Discrimination Act of 1978, 42 U.S.C. § 2000e(k) (2012).

31. Daniels (1996, 62).

32. E. M. Armstrong (2003, 194).

33. Buklijas and Hopwood (2014).

34. E. M. Armstrong (2003, 195).

35. Daniels (1996, 3).

36. Pfohl (1981); Erickson (2000).

37. Erickson (2000).

38. Roberts (2022, 41).

39. Neuspiel (1996, 47).

40. Erickson (2000).

41. Roberts (2022, 172).

42. Roberts (2022); Chasnoff, Landress, and Barrett (1990).

43. Knight (2015, 12).

44. Beckett (1995, 589).
45. Roberts (1997, 40–41).
46. Roberts (1997, 40).
47. Murphy and Rosenbaum (1999, 104).
48. Roberts (1997, 178).
49. Archived news article on file with author.
50. Original interview on file with author. George Lester is a pseudonym.
51. Archived news article on file with author.
52. Faulk (2013).
53. Archived news article on file with author.
54. Thompson (1979).
55. Griswold v. Connecticut, 381 U.S. 479, 85 S. Ct. 1678, 14 L. Ed. 2d 510 (1965).
56. "Summary" (2022).
57. Pfohl (1977, 319).
58. Quoted in Erickson (2000, 79).
59. Pfohl (1977).
60. Erickson (2000).
61. Eisenstadt v. Baird, 405 U.S. 438, 92 S. Ct. 1029, 31 L. Ed. 2d 349 (1972) at 453.
62. Roe v. Wade, 410 U.S. 113, 93 S. Ct. 705, 35 L. Ed. 2d 147 (1973).
63. Siegel (2010, 1901).
64. Waggoner (2017, 101).
65. Nussbaum (2004, 153, 154).
66. Bridges (2017, 207).
67. Balmer (2022).
68. Kolbert and Kay (2021).
69. Planned Parenthood of Southeastern Pa. v. Casey, 505 U.S. 833, 112 S. Ct. 2791, 120 L. Ed. 2d 674 (1992) at 966.
70. "Abuse" in this case refers to obstetric violence or violence and neglect in prisons and jails for what amounts to status crimes.

CHAPTER 3

1. Gould (1985, 333).
2. Cohen (2016, 24, 20).
3. Gould (1985, 335).
4. Buck v. Bell, 274 U.S. 200, 47 S. Ct. 584, 71 L. Ed. 1000 (1927); Gould (1985); Cohen (2016, 24).
5. Gould (1985, 335).
6. Lombardo (2008, 59, 61).

7. Galton (1883).
8. Galton (1904).
9. Roberts (1997, 60, 9).
10. Dickens (2004, 24).
11. Gould (1985, 332).
12. Bridges (2019a).
13. Morone (2004, 274).
14. Isenberg (2017, 192, 195).
15. Morone (2004, 274–75).
16. Bridges (2019a, 830).
17. E. M. Armstrong (2003, 29).
18. E. M. Armstrong (2003, 54, 55).
19. Cohen (2016, 301).
20. Bridges (2019b, 464).
21. Lombardo (2022).
22. Gould (1985).
23. Roberts (1997, 61–62).
24. Gould (1985, 332).
25. Lombardo (2022, 128).
26. Lombardo (2008, 3, 14, 15).
27. Lombardo (2008, 65, 67, 65, 67, 65).
28. Lombardo (2008, 67, 65, 76–77).
29. Roberts (1997, 65, 67).
30. Gould (1985, 332).
31. Gould (1985, 332).
32. General Assembly (2020).
33. *Buck*, 274 U.S. 200.
34. Gould (1985, 336).
35. Cohen (2016, 291).
36. Gould (1985, 336).
37. Bridges (2019b, 455).
38. Cohen (2016, 98).
39. Bridges (2019b, 455).
40. Cohen (2016, 196–98).
41. Gould (1985, 332).
42. Roberts (1997, 69).
43. Roberts (1997, 69).
44. *Buck*, 274 U.S. 200.
45. Gould (1985, 335).
46. Howard (2013).
47. Wray (2006, 19, 37, 46).
48. Hartigan (2005).

49. Isenberg (2017, 180).

50. Hartigan (2005).

51. Isenberg (2017, 187, 180).

52. Gould (1985, 336–37); *Buck,* 274 U.S. 200; see also Schoen (2005).

53. R. Robinson (2022).

54. Byrd (2019, 535).

55. R. Robinson (2022).

56. Anglin (2016); Appalachian Land Ownership (1983); Blauner (1969); Lewis, Johnson, and Askins (1978); Ada Smith (2016).

57. Skinner v. Oklahoma ex rel. Williamson, 316 U.S. 535, 62 S. Ct. 1110, 86 L. Ed. 1655 (1942); Stern et al. (2017).

58. Stern (2022, 356).

59. Klautke (2016, 36).

60. Stern (2001, 226).

61. Roberts (1997, 89, 90, 92).

62. Roberts (1997, 206, 207).

63. Hancock (2004).

64. Roberts (1997, 92).

65. Quoted in Stern (2001).

66. Stern (2005).

67. Andrea Smith (2015).

68. López (2008).

69. "Forced Sterilization" (2022).

70. Roth and Ainsworth (2015).

71. Manian (2020).

72. Gould (1985).

73. Lombardo (2008, 51, 198, 43).

74. Many contemporary disability rights groups use identity-first language to reject the negativity associated with the disability label and to emphasize the social model of disability, suggesting that the problems they face aren't due to impairment but to a society that disables them ("Forced Sterilization" 2022, 2).

75. "Forced Sterilization" (2022).

76. Lipton and Campbell (1988); Arthur (1992); Roberts (1992).

77. Case record on file with author.

78. Case record on file with author. Sandra Simon is a pseudonym.

79. Quoted in "Elofson" (2010).

80. Archived news article on file with author.

81. Murphy and Rosenbaum (1999, 50).

82. Murphy and Rosenbaum (1999, 52, 53, 4, 50).

83. "Contraceptive Deserts" (n.d.).

84. Gomez, Fuentes, and Allina (2014, 171).

85. “National Unintended Pregnancy” (n.d.).

86. “Alabama State Policy Information” (n.d.); “Tennessee State Policy Information” (n.d.); “South Carolina State Policy” (n.d.).

87. Mark and Wu (2022).

88. Luker (2007, 69).

89. Florida Chapter 2023-105, Committee Substitute for House Bill No. 1069, Laws of Florida, 1000.21, 1000.071, 1003.42 1003.46, 1006.28.

90. Martinez (2020).

91. Morone (2004, 275).

CHAPTER 4

1. Murch (2015, 164).
2. Fellner (2009, 262).
3. L. Miller (2015).
4. Murch (2015); L. Miller (2015).
5. L. Miller (2015, 193, 194).
6. Tonry (1994).
7. Alexander (2020, 6).
8. Grogger and Willis (2000).
9. Murch (2015, 166); Grogger and Willis (2000).
10. Kennedy (2011, 10).
11. Quoted in Murch (2015, 169).
12. Murch (2015, 162).
13. Grogger and Willis (2000, 520).
14. Murch (2015).
15. Chitwood, Murphy, and Rosenbaum (2009, 34).
16. Murch (2015, 170).
17. Jordan-Zachery (2009, 56).
18. Quoted in Murch (2015).
19. Beckett (1995).
20. Morone (1997, 1009).
21. Roberts (1997, 155).
22. Morone (1997).
23. Murch (2015, 164).
24. Alexander (2020, 68, 224, 7); Tonry (1994).
25. Jordan-Zachery (2009, 56).
26. Roberts (1997, 155).
27. Chasnoff et al. (1985, 666).
28. Quoted in Winerip (2013).
29. Beckett (1995, 590).

30. Roberts (1997).

31. Murphy and Rosenbaum (1999, 8).

32. Roberts (1997, 155, 156).

33. Carpenter (2012); Jordan-Zachery (2009).

34. Roberts (1997, 153).

35. Roberts (1997).

36. Chasnoff, Landress, and Barrett (1990).

37. Goodwin (2021, 543).

38. Murakawa (2011, 221); see also Paltrow and Jack (2010); and Roberts (1997).

39. Roberts (1997, 179).

40. Murakawa (2011).

41. R. Smith (1986).

42. Krauthammer (1989).

43. Blake (2004, 10).

44. Winerip (2013).

45. Roberts (1997, 156).

46. Quoted in Winerip (2013).

47. Blakeslee (1989).

48. Roberts (1997, 157).

49. Trost (1989).

50. Winerip (2013).

51. Morgan and Zimmer (1997).

52. Koren et al. (1989).

53. Betancourt et al. (2011, 36).

54. Hurt et al. (2009).

55. Quoted in FitzGerald (2013).

56. Murphy and Rosenbaum (1999, 141).

57. Original interview on file with author. Julia Graham is a pseudonym.

58. Archived news article on file with author.

59. Original interview on file with author. Matthew Payne is a pseudonym.

60. Archived news article on file with author..

61. House Criminal Justice Subcommittee (2016, 1:01:00).

62. Behnke et al. (2013); "Methamphetamine Abuse" (2011); Andrade (2018); Gorman et al. (2014); Huybrechts et al. (2018); Ladhani et al. (2011); Wright et al. (2015); Good et al. (2010); "Principles of Harm Reduction" (2020).

63. Case record on file with author.

64. "Quickfacts: South Carolina" (n.d.).

65. "South Carolina Crime Statistics" (n.d.).

66. *Combating Methamphetamine Proliferation* (1999).

67. Hunt, Kuck, and Truitt (2006, iii).

68. E. G. Armstrong (2007, 437).

69. E. G. Armstrong (2007, 435).

70. Byram (1998).

71. Solotaroff (2003).

72. E. G. Armstrong (2007, 436).

73. Knight (2015, 162–63).

74. The Faces of Meth campaign is run by the Multnomah County Sheriff's Office in northwest Oregon and was originally created for use in an educational slideshow for Oregon high school students. "Mug Shot Match-Up" (n.d.).

75. Linnemann and Wall (2013).

76. Murakawa (2011, 219).

77. E. G. Armstrong (2007).

78. Chitwood, Murphy, and Rosenbaum (2009).

79. Kirkpatrick et al. (2012, 783).

80. Shoblock et at. (2003, 359).

81. Chitwood, Murphy, and Rosenbaum (2009).

82. Hart et al. (2012).

83. Caldwell and Brown (2003, 8).

84. Shanker and Duenwald (2003).

85. McCabe et al. (2005, 96).

86. Warren (2014); "Excessive Alcohol Use" (2013); Warner et al. (2016). The measure of methamphetamine-related deaths was not limited to deaths caused by methamphetamine alone. For example, of the 3,728 methamphetamine-related deaths in 2014, 45 percent involved another drug, most often an opioid. A total of 734 meth-related deaths involved heroin, and 300 involved morphine (Warner et al. 2016).

87. "Results" (2010, table 1.1A).

88. "Results" (2016, table 1.1A).

89. Original interview on file with author. Peter Hermann is a pseudonym.

90. Original interview on file with author. David Campbell is a pseudonym.

91. Original interview on file with author.

92. Archived news articles on file with author.

93. Original interview on file with author. Julia Graham is a pseudonym.

94. Original interview on file with author.

95. Archived news article on file with author.

96. Archived news article on file with author.

97. Original interview on file with author.

98. Rawls (2008).

99. Archived news article on file with author.

100. Archived news articles on file with author.

101. Behnke et al. (2013); Andrade (2018); Forray and Foster (2015); Gorman et al. (2014); Huybrechts et al. (2018); Ladhani et al. (2011); Wright et al. (2015); "Principles of Harm Reduction" (2020).

102. Original interview on file with author. Michael Miller is a pseudonym; original interview on file with author.

103. "Drug Crimes" (n.d.); "Statewide Drug Crimes" (n.d.).

104. "Alabama Epidemiological Profile" (2018).

105. "Treatment Episode Data Sets" (2013, 2017).

106. America Counts Staff (2021).

107. "Drug Overdose Deaths"(2023).

108. "Overdose Prevention Strategy" (n.d.).

109. Altekruse et al. (2020).

110. "Opioid Overdose Epidemic" (2023).

111. "Opioid Epidemic" (2016).

112. *Role of Purdue Pharma* (2021).

113. Cicero et al. (2014).

114. "Fentanyl" (2023).

115. Rudd et al. (2016).

116. Stroud (2016); Cicero et al. (2014, 825).

117. Netherland and Hansen (2016, 675, 673).

118. Weller et al. (2021).

119. Quoted in Bridges (2019a, 796).

120. Bridges (2019a); Welle-Strand et al. (2013).

121. Bridges (2019a).

122. "Contraceptive Deserts" (n.d.); Behnke et al. (2013); Lind et al. (2017); Bada et al. (2005); Cleary et al. (2011); Cleary et al. (2012); Hulse et al. (1997); Wurst et al. (2016); "Principles of Harm Reduction" (2020).

123. "Contraceptive Deserts" (n.d.); "Principles of Harm Reduction" (2020).

124. Smith and Lipari (2017); Committee on Obstetric Practice (2017); "Prenatal Drug" (2022).

125. Wilson and Shiffman (2015).

126. House Criminal Justice Subcommittee (2013, 52:54).

127. Senate Judiciary Committee (2014, 2:13:05).

128. Carey (2014).

129. Case record on file with author. I could not determine how she had violated her probation.

130. Case record on file with author.

131. Bach (2022a).

132. Case record on file with author.

133. Archived news article on file with author.

134. The *New York Times* "Chronicle" (2012) data tool indicates that there were 108 articles mentioning crack cocaine in 1996.

135. Bridges (2019a, 777).

136. Roberts and Nuru-Jeter (2012); Jarlenski et al. (2023).

137. Tonry (1994, 25).

CHAPTER 5

1. Talvi (2003).
2. SIA Legal Team (n.d.).
3. Talvi (2003).
4. SIA Legal Team (n.d.).
5. McKnight v. State, 661 S.E.2d 354, 378 S.C. 33 (2008).
6. *McKnight,* 661 S.E.2d 354.
7. Herbert (2001).
8. *McKnight,* 661 S.E.2d 354.
9. SIA Legal Team (n.d.).
10. Case record on file with author.
11. Goodwin (2014, 794).
12. Patrick et al. (2012).
13. Martin (2015).
14. Chasnoff, Landress, and Barrett (1990).
15. Martin (2015).
16. Ferguson v. City of Charleston, 532 U.S. 67, 121 S. Ct. 1281, 149 L. Ed. 2d 205 (2001) at 71.
17. Case record on file with author.
18. Archived news article on file with author; case records on file with author.
19. Case record on file with author.
20. Silva (2017).
21. Stack (2017).
22. Silva (2017).
23. Bollinger (2005).
24. Friedman (2006).
25. Bollinger (2005).
26. "Farm Maid's Tale" (2005).
27. Bollinger (2005).
28. Bollinger (2005); Friedman (2006).
29. "Medical Management" (2018).
30. Bollinger (2005).
31. "Farm Maid's Tale" (2005).
32. Case record on file with author.
33. "Farm Maid's Tale" (2005).
34. Brundrett (2005).
35. "Farm Maid's Tale" (2005).
36. Bollinger (2005).
37. Case record on file with author.
38. Case record on file with author.
39. Case record on file with author; archived news article on file with author.

40. Case record on file with author.
41. Archived news article on file with author.
42. Case record on file with author.
43. Case record on file with author.
44. Case record on file with author.
45. Case record on file with author.
46. Case record on file with author.
47. Martin (2015).
48. Case record on file with author.
49. Martin (2015).
50. Case record on file with author.
51. Case record on file with author.
52. Archived news article on file with author.
53. Grossman, Berkwitt, and Osborn (2020).
54. Finnegan (n.d.).
55. Case record on file with author.
56. Doyle (1996); Blondel and Kaminski (2002); Giuffrè and Corsello (2012).
57. Archived news article on file with author.
58. See Waggoner (2017).
59. Case record on file with author.
60. Goshin et al. (2019, 28); Dignam and Adashi (2014).
61. Nelson v. Norris et al., No. 07-2481 (8th Cir. 2009); Sussman (2008); Sichel (2007).
62. Case record on file with author. Diamond Jones is a pseudonym.
63. Lang, Farnell, and Quinlan (2021).
64. Case record on file with author.
65. Case record on file with author.
66. Huss (2022).
67. Case record on file with author.
68. Atkins and Durrance (2020); Kozhimannil et al. (2019); Meinhofer et al. (2022); Poland et al. (1993); Roberts and Nuru-Jeter (2010); Austin, Naumann, and Simmons (2022); Tabatabaeepour et al. (2022).
69. Stone (2015).
70. Poland et al. (1993); see also Murphy and Rosenbaum (1999); Flavin (2008); Paltrow and Flavin (2013); Flavin and Paltrow (2010); Roberts et al. (2017); Roberts, Thompson, and Taylor (2021); Patrick et al. (2017); Schroedel and Fiber (2001); and Coleman and Miller (2006).
71. Murphy and Rosenbaum (1999, 4, 6).
72. Roberts (1997, 174).
73. Case record on file with author.
74. Calhoun (2012).

75. Murphy and Rosenbaum (1999); Flavin (2008); Paltrow and Flavin (2013); Flavin and Paltrow (2010); Roberts et al. (2017); Roberts, Thompson, and Taylor (2021).

76. Case record on file with author.

77. Case record on file with author.

78. Original interview on file with author; original interview on file with author.

79. Original interview on file with author. James Palmer is a pseudonym.

80. Case record on file with author.

81. Original interview on file with author; Della Bricker is a pseudonym.

82. Archived news article on file with author.

83. Boone and McMichael (2021, 497).

84. Tabatabaeepour et al. (2022).

85. Meinhofer et al. (2022).

86. Subbaraman et al. (2018).

87. Case record on file with author.

88. Case record on file with author. Angela Waters is a pseudonym.

89. Case record on file with author.

90. T. Johnson (2023). In the United States, instead of actually going to trial before a jury, most of the time the defendants and their attorney will make a deal with the prosecutor where, in exchange for a lower penalty or less serious charge, the defendant will admit their guilt and forgo a jury trial.

91. Yurkanin (2022c).

92. Case record on file with author; Yurkanin (2022c).

93. Yurkanin (2022c).

94. Case record on file with author; Yurkanin (2022c).

95. Yurkanin (2022c).

96. "Lee County Mom" (2020).

97. Case record on file with author; "Lee County Mom" (2020); Yurkanin (2022c).

98. Lester (2020).

99. Case record on file with author; Yurkanin (2022c).

100. Case records on file with author.

101. Archived news article on file with author.

102. Santos (2020).

103. Laube v. Haley, 234 F. Supp. 2d 1227 (M.D. Ala. 2002) at 1245, 1247.

104. "Tutwiler Prison" (n.d.).

105. Samuels (2014, 27).

106. Stein (2014).

107. Quoted in Ridgeway and Casella (2013).

108. Shelburne (2017); "Deterring Staff Sexual Abuse" (2005).

109. Shelburne (2017).
110. Maruschak (2008).
111. Quoted in Yurkanin (2022b).
112. Sufrin (2017, 126).
113. Case record on file with author.
114. Case record on file with author.
115. Case record on file with author.
116. Santos (2020).
117. Quoted in archived news article on file with author.
118. Kenny (2018).
119. Murphy and Rosenbaum (1999, 129).
120. Roberts (2022, xvii).
121. Case record on file with author.
122. Martin (2015).
123. Case record on file with author.
124. Goldkamp, White, and Robinson (2001); Drug Policy Alliance (2011).
125. Drug Policy Alliance (2011, 2).
126. García-Sayán and Dainius Pūras (2019, 1).
127. "Neither Justice nor Treatment" (2017, 3, 2).
128. Phillippi et al. (2021); Goodman, Saunders, and Wolff (2020).
129. Mark, Dowd, and Council (2020).
130. Sung et al. (2009, 392, 393).
131. "Hosanna Home" (n.d.).
132. "Program" (2020).
133. Case record on file with author.
134. Case record on file with author.
135. Bach (2022b, 1).
136. Case record on file with author.
137. Roberts and Pies (2011, 336).
138. Joshi et al. (2021).
139. Case record on file with author.
140. Case record on file with author.
141. Case record on file with author.
142. Archived news article on file with author.
143. Stone (2015, 9).
144. Phillippi et al. (2021, 455).
145. Roberts (1997, 189).
146. Dosani (2014).
147. Winkelman et al. (2020).
148. Phillippi et al. (2021, 458, 459).
149. Stone (2015, 9).
150. Shapiro and Farmer (2015).

151. Nowell (2022).
152. Yurkanin (2022a).
153. Nowell (2022).
154. Case record on file with author.
155. Case record on file with author.
156. Martin (2015).
157. Thirteen-year-olds cannot legally consent to sex, meaning that, at least as a child, she was trafficked and sexually assaulted as a means of survival.
158. Bullock (2022).
159. Case record on file with author.
160. Archived news article on file with author.
161. Case record on file with author.
162. Archived news article on file with author.
163. Case record on file with author.
164. Davis et al. (2022, 112).

CHAPTER 6

1. Bridges (2019a, 812).
2. Grella et al. (2020); Azbel et al. (2017); Belenko, Hiller, and Hamilton (2013); Brinkley-Rubinstein et al. (2018); Friedmann and Schwartz (2012); Mitchell et al. (2016); Polonsky et al. (2015); Petrocelli et al. (2014); Green et al. (2013); Beletsky, Macalino, and Burris (2005).
3. Levy and Goldensohn (2014).
4. Archived news article on file with author.
5. Kackley (2016).
6. Archived news article on file with author.
7. Original interview on file with author. Julia Graham is a pseudonym.
8. Archived news article on file with author.
9. Archived news article on file with author.
10. Archived news article on file with author.
11. Archived news article on file with author.
12. Archived news article on file with author.
13. Archived news article on file with author.
14. Archived news article on file with author.
15. Archived news article on file with author.
16. Archived news article on file with author.
17. Archived news article on file with author.
18. Archived news article on file with author; original interviews on file with author.
19. Archived news article on file with author.

20. Calhoun (2012).
21. House Criminal Justice Subcommittee (2013, 1:03:24).
22. Archived news article on file with author.
23. Archived news article on file with author.
24. Archived news article on file with author.
25. Archived news article on file with author.
26. Murphy and Rosenbaum (1999, 9).
27. Case record on file with author.
28. Case record on file with author.
29. Case record on file with author. Rosemary Cleveland is a pseudonym, and "grandy" is her grandmother.
30. Case record on file with author.
31. Case record on file with author.
32. Case record on file with author. Dorothy Blackburn is a pseudonym.
33. Case record on file with author.
34. Archived news article on file with author.
35. Poehlmann-Tynan (2022, 94–95).
36. Metcalfe et al. (2022, 334).
37. Case record on file with author.
38. Brundrett (2005); archived news media on file with author.
39. Case record on file with author.
40. House Criminal Justice Committee (2013, 26:50).
41. Original interview on file with author. George Lester is a pseudonym.
42. Archived news article on file with author.
43. Original interview on file with author. Rob McBurney is a pseudonym.
44. Archived news article on file with author.
45. Archived news article on file with author.
46. House Criminal Justice Subcommittee (2016, 2:30:03).
47. Archived news article on file with author.
48. Archived news article on file with author.
49. Levy and Goldensohn (2014).
50. Archived news article on file with author.
51. Archived news article on file with author.
52. Archived news article on file with author.
53. Original interview on file with author.
54. Archived news article on file with author.
55. Original interview on file with author. David Campbell is a pseudonym.
56. Archived news article on file with author.
57. Original interview on file with author. Michael Miller is a pseudonym.
58. Original interview on file with author.
59. Archived news article on file with author.
60. Archived news article on file with author.

61. Case record on file with author.
62. Archived news article on file with author.
63. Archived news article on file with author.
64. Archived news article on file with author.
65. Original interview on file with author.
66. Archived news article on file with author.
67. Archived news article on file with author.
68. Archived news article on file with author.
69. Original interviews on file with author. George Lester and David Campbell are pseudonyms.
70. Original interview on file with author.
71. Original interview on file with author. Matthew Payne is a pseudonym.
72. Original interview on file with author.
73. Levy and Goldensohn (2014). Suboxone is another medication used in MOUD.
74. Archived news article on file with author.
75. Archived news article on file with author.
76. Knight (2015, 160).
77. Archived news article on file with author.
78. Archived news article on file with author.
79. Archived news article on file with author.
80. Archived news article on file with author.
81. Archived news article on file with author.
82. Egan (2018).
83. American Nurses Association (n.d.); Egan (2018).
84. "Medications for Substance Use" (2023).
85. Case record on file with author.
86. Yurkanin (2016).
87. Case record on file with author.
88. Yurkanin (2016).
89. Case record on file with author. There were eight other pregnant people being held at the Bessemer County Jail at that time.
90. Yurkanin (2016).
91. C. Robinson (2017).
92. Original interview on file with author.
93. Original interview on file with author.
94. Case record on file with author.
95. Case record on file with author. James Palmer is a pseudonym.
96. Original interview on file with author.
97. Original interview on file with author.
98. Archived news article on file with author.
99. Archived news article on file with author.

100. Archived news article on file with author. James McMahon is a pseudonym.

101. Archived news article on file with author.

102. Archived news article on file with author; original interview on file with author.

103. Original interview on file with author; case record on file with author.

104. Archived news article on file with author.

105. Archived news article on file with author.

106. Archived news article on file with author.

107. Original interview on file with author.

108. Original interview on file with author.

109. Archived news article on file with author.

110. Original interview on file with author.

111. Original interview on file with author.

112. Original interview on file with author.

113. Archived news article on file with author.

114. Reed et al. (2023); Melemis (2015); Ouimette and Brown (2003); Dass-Brailsford and Myrick (2010); Brown and Wolfe (1994).

115. Atkins and Durrance (2020); Kozhimannil et al. (2019); Meinhofer et al. (2022); Poland et al. (1993); Roberts and Nuru-Jeter (2010); Austin, Naumann, and Simmons (2022); Tabatabaeepour et al. (2022); Stone (2015); see also Murphy and Rosenbaum (1999); Flavin (2008); Paltrow and Flavin (2013); Flavin and Paltrow (2010); Roberts et al. (2017); Roberts, Thompson, and Taylor (2021); Patrick et al. (2017); Schroedel and Fiber (2001); and Coleman and Miller (2006).

116. Baughman et al. (2021); Miller and Alexander (2015); Roberts (2014); Roberts (2022); Roberts (2011).

117. Poland et al. (1993); Roberts and Pies (2011); Schempf and Strobino (2009).

118. American Medical Association (1990, 2667).

119. Roberts and Pies (2011, 338).

120. "Data by State" (n.d.).

121. Trivedi (2019).

122. Gielen et al. (2012); Keyser-Marcus et al. (2015); Mills et al. (2006); Covington (2008).

123. Original interview on file with author. Della Bricker and Maureen Gimlet are pseudonyms.

124. Original interview on file with author. Peter Hermann is a pseudonym.

125. Original interview on file with author.

126. Original interview on file with author.

127. Original interview on file with author.

128. Original interview on file with author.
129. Calhoun (2012).
130. Original interview on file with author.

CONCLUSION

1. The criminalization of drug *using* is separate from, say, possessing, selling, manufacturing, and operating a vehicle under the influence of drugs, which *are* prosecutable offenses for nonpregnant people.
2. Jacobs (2014); S. Brown (2015); Bell, McNaughton, and Salmon (2009); Goodwin (2014); Oaks (2015); Ladd-Taylor and Umansky (1998); Feldstein (2018).
3. Davis et al. (2022, 110, 111–12).
4. Ingraham (2020).
5. Baughman et al. (2021); Miller and Alexander (2015); Roberts (2014, 2022, 2011).
6. Roberts (2022).
7. Klibanoff (2023).
8. Paltrow (2022, 1313).
9. Singh et al. (2017).
10. Mizelle and Boyette (2023).
11. Peter Hermann is a pseudonym.
12. Caravan (2014).

APPENDIX 1

1. Greene, Caracelli, and Graham (1989).
2. Quoted in Onwuegbuzie and Leech (2005, 384).
3. Willems and Raush (1969).
4. The search terms included *fetus, fetal, embryo, ovum, zygote, unborn, pregnant, pregnancy, feticide, stillbirth, stillborn, miscarriage, gestation,* and *gestate.*
5. I did not include arrest cases involving alleged drug transmission via breast milk, though such cases share similarities with pregnancy-related arrests and are worthy of study.
6. Key terms for the Google alert searches were *fetus, fetal, embryo, ovum, zygote, unborn, feticide, stillbirth, miscarriage, gestation, gestate, pregnant,* and *pregnancy.*
7. Because these types of cases are usually considered medical crimes, "relevant" medical records are frequently included in the publicly available case file.

8. For South Carolina the 1997 decision in the *Whitner* case serves as the moment of criminalization. For Alabama the 2013 *Ankrom* case marks formal criminalization. For Tennessee the implementation of the fetal assault law marks formal criminalization.

9. Wright et al. (2012).

References

"2010 Tennessee Code 39-13-107." 2010. Justia US Law. Accessed November 23, 2023. https://law.justia.com/codes/tennessee/2010/title-39/chapter-13/part-1/39-13-107.

Adams, Sarah F., Mary B. Mahowald, and Janet Gallagher. 2003. "Refusal of Treatment during Pregnancy." *Clinics in Perinatology* 30 (1): 127–40.

"Alabama Epidemiological Profile: Alcohol, Tobacco, Other Drugs Usage and Abuse, 2018." 2018. Mental Health and Substance Abuse Services Division, Office of Prevention. Accessed November 23, 2023. https://mh.alabama.gov/wp-content/uploads/2019/07/Epi_Profile_2018_Final.pdf.

"Alabama State Policy Information." n.d. Sex Education Collaborative. Accessed November 23, 2023. https://sexeducationcollaborative.org/states/alabama.

"Ala. Code 1975, § 26-15-3.2: Chemical Endangerment of a Child." 2006. Alabama Judicial System. Accessed November 23, 2023. https://judicial.alabama.gov/docs/library/docs/26-15-3.2.pdf.

"Alcohol Use during Pregnancy." 2022. Centers for Disease Control and Prevention. Accessed November 23, 2023. www.cdc.gov/ncbddd/fasd/alcohol-use.html.

Alexander, Michelle. 2020. *The New Jim Crow: Mass Incarceration in the Age of Colorblindness*. New York: New Press.

Alhusen, Jeanne L., Ellen Ray, Phyllis Sharps, and Linda Bullock. 2015. "Intimate Partner Violence during Pregnancy: Maternal and Neonatal Outcomes." *Journal of Women's Health* 24 (1): 100–106.

Altekruse, Sean F., Candace M. Cosgrove, William C. Altekruse, Richard A. Jenkins, and Carlos Blanco. 2020. "Socioeconomic Risk Factors for Fatal Opioid Overdoses in the United States: Findings from the Mortality Disparities in American Communities Study (MDAC)." *PLoS One* 15 (1): e0227966. doi: 10.1371/journal.pone.0227966. PMID: 31951640; PMCID: PMC6968850.

Amereh, Fatemeh, Nooshin Amjadi, Anoushiravan Mohseni-Bandpei, Siavash Isazadeh, Yadollah Mehrabi, Akbar Eslami, Zahra Naeiji, and Mohammad Rafiee. 2022. "Placental Plastics in Young Women from General Population Correlate with Reduced Foetal Growth in IUGR Pregnancies." *Environmental Pollution* 314: 120174.

America Counts Staff. 2021. *Alabama Population Grew 5.1% since 2010, Surpassing 5 Million.* Washington, DC: United States Census Bureau.

American Medical Association Board of Trustees. 1990. "Legal Interventions during Pregnancy." *JAMA* 264 (20): 2663–70.

American Nurses Association. n.d. "Medication-Assisted Treatment (MAT) for Opiate Dependence—It's Not 'Giving Drugs to Drug Addicts.'" Accessed November 26, 2023. www.nursingworld.org/~4af5f1/globalassets/practiceandpolicy/work-environment/health--safety/ana-paw_medication-assisted-therapy.pdf.

Andrade, C. 2018. "Risk of Major Congenital Malformations Associated with the Use of Methylphenidate or Amphetamines in Pregnancy." *Journal of Clinical Psychiatry* 79 (1): e1–4.

Anglin, Mary. 2016. "Toward a New Politics of Outrage and Transformation: Placing Appalachia within the Global Political Economy." *Journal of Appalachian Studies* 22 (1): 51–56.

Appalachian Land Ownership Task Force. 1983. *Who Owns Appalachia? Land Ownership and Its Impact.* Lexington: University Press of Kentucky.

Armstrong, Elizabeth G. 2007. "Moral Panic over Meth." *Contemporary Justice Review* 10 (4): 427–42.

Armstrong, Elizabeth M. 2003. *Conceiving Risk, Bearing Responsibility: Fetal Alcohol Syndrome and the Diagnosis of Moral Disorder.* Johns Hopkins University Press.

Arthur, Stacey L. 1992. "The Norplant Prescription: Birth Control, Woman Control, or Crime Control." *UCLA Law Review* 40:1.

Asmussen, Nicole. 2004. "'Unborn Victims' Bill Doesn't Affect Right to Choose." *Iowa State Daily,* April 2, 2004. https://iowastatedaily.com/192212/opinion/column-unborn-victims-bill-doesnt-affect-right-to-choose/.

"As Search for Killer Continues, Brandy and Brody Parker's Legacy Is Strong." 2014. WHNT News 19. July 20, 2014. https://whnt.com/news/northeast-alabama/as-search-for-killer-continues-brandy-and-brody-parkers-legacy-is-strong/.

Atkins, Danielle N., and Christine Piette Durrance. 2020. "State Policies That Treat Prenatal Substance Use as Child Abuse or Neglect Fail to Achieve Their Intended Goals." *Health Affairs* 39 (5): 756–63.

Austin, Anna E., Rebecca B. Naumann, and Elizabeth Simmons. 2022. "Association of State Child Abuse Policies and Mandated Reporting Policies with Prenatal and Postpartum Care among Women Who Engaged in Substance Use during Pregnancy." *JAMA Pediatrics* 176 (11): 1123–30.

Azbel, Lyuba, Julia Rozanova, Ingo Michels, Frederick L. Altice, and Heino Stöver. 2017. "A Qualitative Assessment of an Abstinence-Oriented Therapeutic Community for Prisoners with Substance Use Disorders in Kyrgyzstan." *Harm Reduction Journal* 14:1–9.

Bach, Wendy A. 2022a. "Memorandum: Study of TN-ST 39-13-107 Prosecutions, 2014–16." Harvard Law School Library.

———. 2022b. *Prosecuting Poverty, Criminalizing Care.* Cambridge: Cambridge University Press.

Bada, Henrietta S., Abhik Das, Charles R. Bauer, Seetha Shankaran, Barry M. Lester, Charlotte C. Gard, Linda L. Wright, Linda LaGasse, and Rosemary Higgins. 2005. "Low Birth Weight and Preterm Births: Etiologic Fraction Attributable to Prenatal Drug Exposure." *Journal of Perinatology* 25 (10): 631–37.

Baer, Judith A. 1999. *Our Lives before the Law: Constructing a Feminist Jurisprudence.* Princeton, NJ: Princeton University Press.

Balmer, Randall. 2022. "The Religious Right and the Abortion Myth." *Politico,* May 10, 2022. www.politico.com/news/magazine/2022/05/10/abortion-history-right-white-evangelical-1970s-00031480.

Baughman, C., T. Coles, J. Feinberg, and H. Newton. 2021. "The Surveillance Tentacles of the Child Welfare System." Columbia Academic Commons. https://doi.org/10.7916/e0de-de42.

Bearak, Jonathan, Anna Popinchalk, Bela Ganatra, Ann-Beth Moller, Özge Tunçalp, Cynthia Beavin, Lorraine Kwok, and Leontine Alkema. 2020. "Unintended Pregnancy and Abortion by Income, Region, and the Legal Status of Abortion: Estimates from a Comprehensive Model for 1990–2019." *Lancet Global Health* 8 (9): e1152–e1161.

Beckett, Katherine. 1995. "Fetal Rights and 'Crack Moms': Pregnant Women in the War on Drugs." *Contemporary Drug Problems* 22 (4): 587–612.

Behnke, Marylou, Vincent C. Smith, Committee on Substance Abuse, and Committee on Fetus and Newborn. 2013. "Prenatal Substance Abuse: Short- and Long-Term Effects on the Exposed Fetus." *Pediatrics* 131 (3): e1009–e1024.

Belenko, Steven, Matthew Hiller, and Leah Hamilton. 2013. "Treating Substance Use Disorders in the Criminal Justice System." *Current Psychiatry Reports* 15:1–11.

Beletsky, Leo, Grace E. Macalino, and Scott Burris. 2005. "Attitudes of Police Officers towards Syringe Access, Occupational Needle-Sticks, and Drug Use: A Qualitative Study of One City Police Department in the United States." *International Journal of Drug Policy* 16 (4): 267–74.

Bell, Kristen, Darlene McNaughton, and Amy Salmon. 2009. "Medicine, Morality and Mothering: Public Health Discourses on Foetal Alcohol Exposure, Smoking around Children and Childhood Overnutrition." *Critical Public Health* 19 (2): 155–70.

Belluck, Pam. 2022. "They Had Miscarriages, and New Abortion Laws Obstructed Treatment." *New York Times,* July 18, 2022. www.nytimes .com/2022/07/17/health/abortion-miscarriage-treatment.html.

Betancourt, Laura M., Wei Yang, Nancy L. Brodsky, Paul R. Gallagher, Elsa K. Malmud, Joan M. Giannetta, Martha J. Farah, and Hallam Hurt. 2011. "Adolescents with and without Gestational Cocaine Exposure: Longitudinal Analysis of Inhibitory Control, Memory and Receptive Language." *Neurotoxicology and Teratology* 33 (1): 36–46.

Bindman, Jay, Azze Ngo, Sophia Zamudio-Haas, and Jae Sevelius. 2022. "Health Care Experiences of Patients with Nonbinary Gender Identities." *Transgender Health* 7 (5): 423–29.

Blake, Mariah. 2004. "The Damage Done: Crack Babies Talk Back." *Columbia Journalism Review* 43 (3): 10–12.

Blakeslee, Sandra. 1989. "Crack's Toll among Babies: A Joyless View, Even of Toys." *New York Times,* September 17, 1989.

Blauner, Robert. 1969. "Internal Colonialism and Ghetto Revolt." *Social Problems* 16 (4): 393–408.

Blondel, Beatrice, and Monique Kaminski. 2002. "Trends in the Occurrence, Determinants, and Consequences of Multiple Births." *Seminars in Perinatology* 26 (4): 239–49.

Bollinger, Michele. 2005. "Why Did Gabriela Flores Go to Jail?" *Socialist Worker,* May 20, 2005. https://socialistworker.org/2005-1/544/544_02_ GabrielFlores.php.

Boone, Meghan, and Benjamin J. McMichael. 2020. "State-Created Fetal Harm." *Georgetown Law Journal* 109:475–522.

Brake, Deborah L., and Joanna L. Grossman. 2013. "Unprotected Sex: The Pregnancy Discrimination Act at 35." *Duke Journal of Gender Law and Policy* 21:67.

Bray, Stephanie R., and Monica R. McLemore. 2021. "Demolishing the Myth of the Default Human That Is Killing Black Mothers." *Frontiers in Public Health* 9:630.

Bridges, Khiara. 2017. *The Poverty of Privacy Rights.* Stanford, CA: Stanford University Press.

———. 2019a. "Race, Pregnancy, and the Opioid Epidemic: White Privilege and the Criminalization of Opioid Use during Pregnancy." *Harvard Law Review* 133:770–851.

———. 2019b. "White Privilege and White Disadvantage." *Virginia Law Review* 105:449–82.

———. 2020. "Racial Disparities in Maternal Mortality." *New York University Law Review* 95:1229.

Brinkley-Rubinstein, Lauren, Nickolas Zaller, Sarah Martino, David H. Cloud, Erin McCauley, Andrew Heise, and David Seal. 2018. "Criminal Justice Continuum for Opioid Users at Risk of Overdose." *Addictive Behaviors* 86:104–10.

Brown, Melissa. 2019. "Alabama DA to Drop Fetal Manslaughter Charges against Marshae Jones." *Montgomery Advertiser,* July 3, 2019. www.montgomeryadvertiser.com/story/news/2019/07/03/alabama-da-drops-charges-against-marshae-jones-manslaughter-case/1639097001/.

Brown, Pamela J., and Jessica Wolfe. 1994. "Substance Abuse and Post-traumatic Stress Disorder Comorbidity." *Drug and Alcohol Dependence* 35 (1): 51–59.

Brown, Sally. 2015. "The Wrong Type of Mother: Moral Panic and Teenage Parenting." In *Gender and Family,* edited by Viviene E. Cree, 43–54. Bristol: Policy Press https://doi.org/10.51952/9781447366676.ch004.

Brundrett, Rick. 2005. "Woman's Abortion Is Unique." *State,* May 1, 2005.

Buklijas, Tatjana, and Nick Hopwood. 2014. "Making Visible Embryos." Accessed November 23, 2023. www.sites.hps.cam.ac.uk/visibleembryos/s7_4.html.

Bullock, Matt. 2022. "Remembering Hurricane Hugo 33 Years after It Devastated South Carolina." WMBF News. September 22, 2022. www.wmbfnews.com/2022/09/22/this-day-history-33-years-ago-hurricane-hugo-devastated-south-carolina/.

Byram, C. 1998. "State Gets $600,000 to Fight Meth Problem." *Deseret News,* May 31, 1998. www.deseret.com/1998/6/1/19383339/state-gets-600-000-to-fight-meth-problem.

Byrd, W. Carson. 2019. "Hillbillies, Genetic Pathology, and White Ignorance: Repackaging the Culture of Poverty within Color-Blindness." *Sociology of Race and Ethnicity* 5 (4): 532–46.

Caldwell, J. A., and C. L. Brown. 2003. "Running on Empty? 'Go Pills,' Fatigue and Aviator Safety." *Flying Safety* 59 (3): 4–11.

Calhoun, Ada. 2012. "The Criminalization of Bad Mothers." *New York Times,* April 25. 2012. www.nytimes.com/2012/04/29/magazine/the-criminalization-of-bad-mothers.html.

Cantor, Julie D. 2012. "Court-Ordered Care: A Complication of Pregnancy to Avoid." *New England Journal of Medicine* 366 (24): 2237–40. doi:10.1056/NEJMp1203742.

Caravan, Gary. 2014. "'There's Nothing New / Under the Sun, / But There Are New Suns': Recovering Octavia E. Butler's Lost Parables." Accessed December 5, 2023. https://lareviewofbooks.org/article/theres-nothing-new-sun-new-suns-recovering-octavia-e-butlers-lost-parables/.

Carey, B. 2014. "Prescription Painkillers Seen as a Gateway to Heroin." *New York Times,* February 10, 2014. www.nytimes.com/2014/02/11/health/prescription-painkillers-seen-as-a-gateway-to-heroin.html.

Carpenter, Tracy R. 2012. "Construction of the Crack Mother Icon." *Western Journal of Black Studies* 36 (4): 264.

Carroll, Linda. 2019. "In Many States, Pregnancy Invalidates a Woman's DNR." Reuters. April 23, 2019. www.reuters.com/article/us-health-pregnancy-advance-directives/in-many-states-pregnancy-invalidates-a-womans-dnr-idUSKCN1RZ1P4.

Chasnoff, Ira J. 1989. "Drug Use and Women: Establishing a Standard of Care." *Annals of the New York Academy of Sciences* 562 (1): 208–10.

Chasnoff, Ira J., William J. Burns, Sidney H. Schnoll, and Kayreen A. Burns. 1985. "Cocaine Use in Pregnancy." *New England Journal of Medicine* 11:666–69.

Chasnoff, Ira J., Harvey J. Landress, and Mark E. Barrett. 1990. "The Prevalence of Illicit Drug or Alcohol Use during Pregnancy and Discrepancies in Mandatory Reporting in Pinellas County, Florida." *New England Journal of Medicine* 322 (17): 1202–6.

Cherry, April. 2007. "The Detention, Confinement, and Incarceration of Pregnant Women for the Benefit of Fetal Health." *Columbia Journal of Gender and Law* 16 (1): 147–97.

Chitwood, Dale D., Sheigla Murphy, and Marsha Rosenbaum. 2009. "Reflections on the Meaning of Drug Epidemics." *Journal of Drug Issues* 39 (1): 29–39.

"Chronicle." 2012. *New York Times,* November 24, 2023. https://nytlabs.com/projects/chronicle.html.

Cicero, Theodore J., Matthew S. Ellis, Hilary L. Surratt, and Steven P. Kurtz. 2014. "The Changing Face of Heroin Use in the United States: A Retrospective Analysis of the Past 50 Years." *JAMA Psychiatry* 71 (7): 821–26.

Cleary, Brian J., Jean M. Donnelly, Judith D. Strawbridge, Paul J. Gallagher, Tom Fahey, Mike J. White, and Deirdre J. Murphy. 2011. "Methadone and Perinatal Outcomes: A Retrospective Cohort Study." *American Journal of Obstetrics and Gynecology* 204 (2): 139.e1–9.

Cleary, Brian J., Maeve Eogan, Michael P. O'Connell, Tom Fahey, Paul J. Gallagher, Tom Clarke, Martin J. White, et al. 2012. "Methadone and

Perinatal Outcomes: A Prospective Cohort Study." *Addiction* 107 (8): 1482–92.

Cohen, Adam. 2016. *Imbeciles: The Supreme Court, American Eugenics, and the Sterilization of Carrie Buck*. New York: Penguin.

Colb, Sherry F. 2011. "New York Woman Is Arrested for Self-Induced Abortion: What Does This Tell Us about Abortion Law?" *Verdict*, December 30, 2011. https://verdict.justia.com/2011/12/30/a-new-york-woman-is-arrested-for-self-induced-abortion.

Coleman, E. 2007. "Pregnant Mom's Slaying Could Help Change Fetal Homicide Law." June 30, 2007. WRAL News. www.wral.com/amp/news/local/story/1547056/.

Coleman, Elizabeth E., and Monica K. Miller. 2006. "Assessing Legal Responses to Prenatal Drug Use: Can Therapeutic Responses Produce More Positive Outcomes Than Punitive Responses?" *Journal of Law and Health* 20:35.

Combating Methamphetamine Proliferation in America. 1999. Senate Hearing 106-715. Washington, DC: US Government Publishing Office, 1999. www.govinfo.gov/content/pkg/CHRG-106shrg67479/html/CHRG-106shrg67479.htm.

Committee on Obstetric Practice. 2017."Smoking Cessation during Pregnancy." *Obstetrics and Gynecology* 130 (4): e200–e204.

"Contraceptive Deserts." n.d. Power to Decide. Accessed November 23, 2023. https://powertodecide.org/contraceptive-deserts.

Corey, Elizabeth, Stephanie Frazin, Samantha Heywood, and Sadia Haider. 2020. "Desire for and Barriers to Obtaining Effective Contraception among Women Experiencing Homelessness." *Contraception and Reproductive Medicine* 5 (12): 1–7. https://doi.org/10.1186/s40834-020-00113-w.

Covington, Stephanie S. 2008. "Women and Addiction: A Trauma-Informed Approach." Supplement, *Journal of Psychoactive Drugs* 40 (S5): 377–85.

Cox, Lauren. 2008. "Some Worry Underground Abortions Are Still a Reality." ABC News. August 22, 2008. https://abcnews.go.com/Health/WomensHealth/story?id = 5628977andpage = 1.

"Crack Mom in Prison to Appeal to Supreme Court." 1998. *Chicago Tribune*, March 19, 1998.

Crear-Perry, Joia, Rosaly Correa-de-Araujo, Tamara Lewis Johnson, Monica R. McLemore, Elizabeth Neilson, and M. Wallace. 2021. "Social and Structural Determinants of Health Inequities in Maternal Health." *Journal of Women's Health* 30 (2): 230–35.

Crenshaw, Kimberlé. 1989. "Demarginalizing the Intersection of Race and Sex: A Black Feminist Critique of Antidiscrimination Doctrine, Feminist Theory and Antiracist Politics." *University of Chicago Legal Forum* 1989 (1): 139.

Daniels, Cynthia. 1996. *At Women's Expense: State Power and the Politics of Fetal Rights*. Cambridge, MA: Harvard University Press.

———. 1997. "Between Fathers and Fetuses: The Social Construction of Male Reproduction and the Politics of Fetal Harm." *Signs: Journal of Women in Culture and Society* 22 (3): 579–616.

———. 2008. *Exposing Men: The Science and Politics of Male Reproduction*. Oxford: Oxford University Press.

Dass-Brailsford, Priscilla, and Amie C. Myrick. 2010. "Psychological Trauma and Substance Abuse: The Need for an Integrated Approach." *Trauma, Violence, and Abuse* 11 (4): 202–13.

"Data by State." n.d. Children's Bureau. Accessed November 23, 2023. https://cwoutcomes.acf.hhs.gov/cwodatasite/byState.

Davis, Angela. 1981. *Women, Race and Class*. New York: Random House.

Davis, Angela Y., Gina Dent, Erica R. Meiners, and Beth E. Richie. 2022. *Abolition. Feminism. Now*. Vol. 2. Chicago: Haymarket Books.

Davis, Dána-Ain A. 2019a. "Obstetric Racism: The Racial Politics of Pregnancy, Labor, and Birthing." *Medical Anthropology* 38 (7): 560–73.

———. 2019b. *Reproductive Injustice*. New York: New York University Press.

———. 2020. "Reproducing While Black: The Crisis of Black Maternal Health, Obstetric Racism and Assisted Reproductive Technology." *Reproductive Biomedicine and Society Online* 11:56–64.

Davis, Devra L., Gladys Friedler, Donald Mattison, and Robert Morris. 1992. "Male-Mediated Teratogenesis and Other Reproductive Effects: Biologic and Epidemiologic Findings and a Plea for Clinical Research." *Reproductive Toxicology* 6 (4): 289–92.

Denbow, Jennifer M. 2015. *Governed through Choice: Autonomy, Technology, and the Politics of Reproduction*. New York: New York University Press.

"Deterring Staff Sexual Abuse of Federal Inmates." 2005. Office of the Inspector General. April 2005. https://oig.justice.gov/sites/default/files/archive/special/0504/index.htm.

Dickens, Charles. 2004. *The Annotated Christmas Carol: A Christmas Carol in Prose*. Edited by Michael Patrick Hearn. New York: Norton.

Dignam, Brett, and Eli Y. Adashi. 2014. "Health Rights in the Balance: The Case against Perinatal Shackling of Women behind Bars." *Health and Human Rights Journal* 16:13.

Dolan, Irene J., Penelope Strauss, Sam Winter, and Ashleigh Lin. 2020. "Misgendering and Experiences of Stigma in Health Care Settings for Transgender People." *Medical Journal of Australia* 212 (4): 150–51.

Dosani, Sanya. 2014. "Should Pregnant Women Addicted to Drugs Face Criminal Charges?" *Al Jazeera America*, September 4, 2014. http://america.aljazeera.com/watch/shows/312merica-tonight/articles/2014/9/4/should-pregnant-womenaddictedtodrugsfacecriminalcharges.html.

Doyle, Pat. 1996. "The Outcome of Multiple Pregnancy." Supplement, *Human Reproduction* 11 (S4): 110–20.

"Drug Crimes." n.d. Crime.Alabama.Gov. Accessed November 28, 2023. https://crime.alabama.gov/Data/TwentyTwentyStatewideDrugCrime.

"Drug Overdose Deaths." 2023. Centers for Disease Control and Prevention. August 22, 2023. www.cdc.gov/drugoverdose/deaths/index.html.

Drug Policy Alliance. 2011. *Drug Courts Are Not the Answer: Toward a Health-Centered Approach to Drug Use.* New York: Drug Policy Alliance.

Duggan, Eliza. 2016. "A Velvet Hammer: The Criminalization of Motherhood and the New Maternalism." *California Law Review* 104:1299.

Egan, Jennifer. 2018. "Children of the Opioid Epidemic." *New York Times Magazine,* May 9, 2018. www.nytimes.com/2018/05/09/magazine/children-of-the-opioid-epidemic.html.

Einarson, Adrienne, and Sara Riordan. 2009. "Smoking in Pregnancy and Lactation: A Review of Risks and Cessation Strategies." *European Journal of Clinical Pharmacology* 65:325–30.

Eisenstein, Zillah R. 1988. *The Female Body and the Law.* Berkeley: University of California Press.

Elofson, Matt. 2010. "Chemical Endangerment Charge Questioned." *Dothan Eagle,* October 23, 2010. https://dothaneagle.com/news/chemical-endangerment-charge-questioned/article_f1bb8be5-f5e0-5c38-94be-838b865fe38d.html.

Erickson, Patricia E. 2000. "Federal Child Abuse and Child Neglect Policy in the United States since 1974: A Review and Critique." *Criminal justice Review* 25:77-92.

"Excessive Alcohol Use." 2013. *Prevention Status Reports.* Centers for Disease Control and Prevention. March 17, 2014. www.cdc.gov/psr/2013/alcohol/index.html.

"Family Members of Unborn Victims Go to Washington to Help Pass Bill." 2004. National Right to Life. April 5, 2004. www.nrlc.org/federal/unbornvictims/familyprofiles/.

"The Farm Maid's Tale: Jailed for Her Own Abortion." 2005. Daily Kos. May 2, 2005.www.dailykos.com/stories/2005/05/02/111144/-The-Farm-Maid-s-Tale-Jailed-for-Her-Own-Abortion.

Faulk, Kent. 2013. "Alabama Supreme Court: Unborn Children Protected under State's Chemical Endangerment Law." January 11, 2013. AL.com. www.al.com/spotnews/2013/01/alabama_supreme_court_unborn_c.html.

Feldstein, Ruth 2018. *Motherhood in Black and White: Race and Sex in American Liberalism, 1930–1965.* Ithaca, NY: Cornell University Press.

Fellner, Jamie. 2009. "Race, Drugs, and Law Enforcement in the United States." *Stanford Law and Policy Review* 20:257–92.

"Fentanyl." 2023. Centers for Disease Control and Prevention. August 8, 2023. www.cdc.gov/opioids/basics/fentanyl.html.

Fentiman, Linda C. 2006. "The New 'Fetal Protection': The Wrong Answer to the Crisis of Inadequate Health Care for Women and Children." *Denver University Law Review* 84 (2): 537–99.

———. 2009. "Pursuing the Perfect Mother: Why America's Criminalization of Maternal Substance Abuse Is Not the Answer—A Comparative Legal Analysis." *Michigan Journal of Gender and Law* 15:389–424.

Fineman, Martha L. 1991. "Images of Mothers in Poverty Discourses." *Duke Law Journal* 1991 (2): 274–95.

Finnegan, Loretta P. n.d. "Modified Finnegan Neonatal Abstinence Score (NAS)." Accessed November 23, 2023. www.mdcalc.com/calc/10048/modified-finnegan-neonatal-abstinence-score-nas#use-cases.

FitzGerald, Susan. 2013. "'Crack Baby' Study Ends with Unexpected but Clear Result." *Philadelphia Inquirer*, July 21, 2013. www.inquirer.com/philly/health/20130721__Crack_baby__study_ends_with_unexpected_but_clear_result.html.

Fixmer-Oraiz, Natalie, and Shui-yin Sharon Yam. 2021. "Queer(ing) Reproductive Justice." *Oxford Research Encyclopedia of Communication*. Accessed November 23, 2023. https://doi.org/10.1093/acrefore/9780190228613.013.1195.

Flavin, Jeanne. 2008. *Our Bodies, Our Crimes: The Policing of Women's Reproduction in America*. New York: New York University Press.

Flavin, Jeanne, and Lynn M. Paltrow. 2010. "Punishing Pregnant Drug-Using Women: Defying Law, Medicine, and Common Sense." *Journal of Addictive Diseases* 29 (2): 231–44.

"Forced Sterilization of Disabled People in the United States." 2022. National Women's Law Center. November 23, 2023. https://nwlc.org/wp-content/uploads/2022/01/%C6%92.NWLC_SterilizationReport_2021.pdf.

Forray, Ariadna 2016. "Substance Use during Pregnancy." F1000 Research, https://pubmed.ncbi.nlm.nih.gov/27239283/.

Forray, Ariadna, and Dawn Foster. 2015. "Substance Use in the Perinatal Period." *Current Psychiatry Reports* 17:1–11.

Friedman, Ann. 2006. "Mail-Order Abortions: Pfizer's Little Secret." *Nation*, November–December 2006. www.motherjones.com/politics/2006/11/mail-order-abortions-cytotec/.

Friedmann, Peter D., and Robert P. Schwartz. 2012. "Just Call It 'Treatment.'" *Addiction Science and Clinical Practice* 7:1–3.

Gallagher, Janet. 1987. "Prenatal Invasions and Interventions: What's Wrong with Fetal Rights?" *Harvard Women's Law Journal* 10:9–58.

Galton, Francis. 1883. *Inquiries into the Human Faculty*. New York: MacMillan.

———. 1904. "Eugenics: Its Definition, Scope, and Aims." *American Journal of Sociology* 10 (1): 1–25.

García-Sayán, and Dainius Pūras. 2019. "Drug Courts Pose Dangers of Punitive Approaches Encroaching on Medical and Health Care Matters, UN Experts

Say." United Nations Human Rights Special Procedures. March 20, 2019. www.unodc.org/documents/commissions/CND/2019/Contributions/UN_Entities/InfoNote20March2019.pdf.

General Assembly. 2020. "Chapter 46B of the *Code of Virginia* § 1095h–m (1924)." *Encyclopedia Virginia.* Virginia Humanities. December 7, 2020. https://encyclopediavirginia.org/entries/chapter-46b-of-the-code-of-virginia-%C2%A7-1095h-m-1924.

George, Marie-Amelie. 2020. "Queering Reproductive Justice." *University of Richmond Law Review* 54 (3): 671–704.

Gielen, Nele, Remco Havermans, Mignon Tekelenburg, and Anita Jansen. 2012. "Prevalence of Post-traumatic Stress Disorder among Patients with Substance Use Disorder: It Is Higher Than Clinicians Think It Is." *European Journal of Psychotraumatology* 3 (1): 17734.

Giuffrè, Mario, Ettore Piro, and Giovanni Corsello. 2012. "Prematurity and Twinning." Supplement, *Journal of Maternal-Fetal and Neonatal Medicine* 25 (S3): 6–10.

Goldkamp, John S., Michael D. White, and Jennifer B. Robinson. 2001. "Do Drug Courts Work? Getting Inside the Drug Court Black Box." *Journal of Drug Issues* 31 (1): 27–72.

Goldstein, Amy. 2004. "Bush Signs Unborn Victims Act." *Washington Post,* April 2, 2004.

Goldstick, Jason E., Rebecca M. Cunningham, and Patrick M. Carter. 2022. "Current Causes of Death in Children and Adolescents in the United States." *New England Journal of Medicine* 386 (20): 1955–56.

Gomez, Anu Manchikanti, Liza Fuentes, and Amy Allina. 2014. "Women or LARC First? Reproductive Autonomy and the Promotion of Long-Acting Reversible Contraceptive Methods." *Perspectives on Sexual and Reproductive Health* 46 (3): 171.

Gómez, Laura E. 1997. *Misconceiving Mothers: Legislators, Prosecutors, and the Politics of Prenatal Drug Exposure.* Philadelphia: Temple University Press.

González-Rojas, Jessica. 2016. "The First of Many Victims of Hyde." *Conscience* 37 (1): 70.

Good, Meadow M., Ido Solt, Joann G. Acuna, Siegfried Rotmensch, and Matthew J. Kim. 2010. "Methamphetamine Use during Pregnancy: Maternal and Neonatal Implications." Pt. 1. *Obstetrics and Gynecology* 116 (2): 330–34.

Goodman, Daisy J., Elizabeth C. Saunders, and Kristina B. Wolff. 2020. "In Their Own Words: A Qualitative Study of Factors Promoting Resilience and Recovery among Postpartum Women with Opioid Use Disorders." *BioMed Central Pregnancy and Childbirth* 20:1–10.

Goodman, Jessica. 2022. "Scott Peterson Moved Off California's Death Row More Than Two Years since Death Sentence Overturned." KIRO7 News.

October 24, 2022. www.kiro7.com/news/trending/scott-peterson-moved-off-californias-death-row-more-than-2-years-since-death-sentence-overturned/S3ECJ7QTJVFNXGSN4G4R6UZ3QE/.

Goodwin, Michele. 2014. "Fetal Protection Laws: Moral Panic and the New Constitutional Battlefront." *California Law Review* 102: 781–875.

———. 2020. *Policing the Womb: Invisible Women and the Criminalization of Motherhood.* Cambridge University Press.

———. 2021. "Pregnancy and the New Jane Crow." *Connecticut Law Review* 53:543–69.

Gorman, Margaret C., Kaebah S. Orme, Nancy T. Nguyen, Edward J. Kent III, and Aaron B. Caughey. 2014. "Outcomes in Pregnancies Complicated by Methamphetamine Use." *American Journal of Obstetrics and Gynecology* 211 (4): 429.e1–7.

Goshin, Lorie S., Gina Sissoko, Grace Neumann, Carolyn Sufrin, and Lorraine Byrnes. 2019. "Perinatal Nurses' Experiences with and Knowledge of the Care of Incarcerated Women during Pregnancy and the Postpartum Period." *Journal of Obstetric, Gynecologic and Neonatal Nursing* 48 (1): 27–36.

Gould, Stephen Jay. 1985. "Carrie Buck's Daughter." *Constitutional Commentary* 2:331–39.

"Governor Denies Gentry's Pardon in Killing of Young Mother and Unborn Baby." 2018. KAKE ABC.com. June 19, 2018. www.kake.com/story/38461294/governor-denies-gentrys-pardon-in-killing-of-young-mother-and-unborn-baby.

Green, Traci C., Nickolas Zaller, Wilson R. Palacios, Sarah E. Bowman, Madeline Ray, Robert Heimer, and Patricia Case. 2013. "Law Enforcement Attitudes toward Overdose Prevention and Response." *Drug and Alcohol Dependence* 133 (2): 677–84.

Greene, Jennifer C., Valerie J. Caracelli, and Wendy F. Graham. 1989. "Toward a Conceptual Framework for Mixed-Method Evaluation Designs." *Educational Evaluation and Policy Analysis* 11 (3): 255–74.

Grella, Christine E., Ericka Ostile, Christy K. Scott, Michael Dennis, and John Carnavale. 2020. "A Scoping Review of Barriers and Facilitators to Implementation of Medications for Treatment of Opioid Use Disorder within the Criminal Justice System." *International Journal of Drug Policy* 81:1–21.

Grogger, Jeff, and Michael Willis. 2000. "The Emergence of Crack Cocaine and the Rise in Urban Crime Rates." *Review of Economics and Statistics* 82 (4): 519–29.

Grossman, Matthew R., Adam K. Berkwitt, and Rachel R. Osborn. 2020. "Racial Association and Pharmacotherapy in Neonatal Opioid Withdrawal Syndrome: Thinking beyond Genetics." *Journal of Perinatology* 40 (4): 689–90. https://link-gale-com.libaccess.sjlibrary.org/apps/doc/A618522131/AONE?u = csusjandsid = bookmark-AONEandxid = 0eb007d1.

Hale, Steven. 2014. "Haslam Makes Tennessee a Battleground over the Rights of Pregnant Women and Prosecutorial Bounds." Nashville Scene. May 8, 2014. www.nashvillescene.com/news/by-signing-the-controversial-sb-1391-gov-bill-haslam-makes-tennessee-a-battleground-over-the/article_f71715c8-640e-5b9c-a691-49928c42c97e.html.

Hancock, Ange-Marie. 2004. *The Politics of Disgust: The Public Identity of the Welfare Queen.* New York: New York University Press.

Harrison, Laura. 2022. *Losing Sleep: Risk, Responsibility, and Infant Sleep Safety.* New York: New York University Press.

Hart, Carl L., Caroline B. Marvin, Rae Silver, and Edward E. Smith. 2012. "Is Cognitive Functioning Impaired in Methamphetamine Users? A Critical Review." *Neuropsychopharmacology* 37 (3): 586–608.

Hartigan, John. 2005. *Odd Tribes: Toward a Cultural Analysis of White People.* Durham, NC: Duke University Press.

Hegeman, Roxana. 2006. "Wichita Family Mourns Pregnant Teen's Death." *Lawrence Journal-World,* June 18, 2006. www2.ljworld.com/news/2006/jun/18/wichita_family_mourns_pregnant_teens_death/.

Herbert, Bob. 2001. "In America: Stillborn Justice." *New York Times,* May 24. 2001. www.nytimes.com/2001/05/24/opinion/in-america-stillborn-justice.html.

Hobbes, Thomas. 2010. *Leviathan.* Rev. ed. Peterborough: Broadview.

"Hosanna Home." n.d. Harvest Evangelism. Accessed November 24, 2023. www.harvestevangelism.org/hosanna-home.

House Criminal Justice Subcommittee. 2013. Tennessee General Assembly. March 19, 2013. https://tnga.granicus.com/player/clip/7499?view_id=269&meta_id=140901&redirect=true&h=d0a51db2aa83c7a9f5b41e5e05b66b51.

———. 2016. Tennessee General Assembly. March 15, 2016. https://tnga.granicus.com/player/clip/12002?view_id=278&meta_id=246661&redirect=true&h=14d599016f467cafd9d26ef3d5d79561.

House Hearing: Unborn Victims of Violence Act of 2003, or Laci and Connor's Law. 2003. Washington, DC: US Government Publishing Office, 2003. www.congress.gov/event/108th-congress/house-event/LC15442/text.

Howard, Grace 2013. "The Limits of Pure White: Raced Reproduction in the Methamphetamine Crisis." *Women's Rights Law Reporter* 35:373.

———. 2019. "The Pregnancy Police: Surveillance, Regulation, and Control." *Harvard Law and Policy Review* 14:347.

Hoyert, Donna L. 2022. "Maternal Mortality Rates in the United States, 2020." Centers for Disease Control and Prevention. February 23, 2022. https://dx.doi.org/10.15620/cdc:113967.

Hulse, G. K., E. Milne, D. R. English, and C. D. J. Holman. 1997. "Assessing the Relationship between Maternal Cocaine Use and Abruptio Placentae." *Addiction* 92 (11): 1547–51.

Hunt, Dana E., Sarah Kuck, and Linda Truitt. 2006. *Methamphetamine Use: Lessons Learned.* Cambridge, MA: Abt Associates.

Hurt, Hallam, Laura M. Betancourt, Elsa K. Malmud, David M. Shera, Joan M. Giannetta, Nancuy L. Brodsky, and Martha J. Farah. 2009. "Children with and without Gestational Cocaine Exposure: A Neurocognitive Systems Analysis." *Neurotoxicology and Teratology* 31 (6): 334–41.

Huss, Laura. 2022. "Self-Managed Abortion Is Not Illegal in Most of the Country, but Criminalization Happens Anyway." If/When/How. August 9, 2022. www.ifwhenhow.org/abortion-criminalization-new-research/.

Huybrechts, Krista F., Gabriella Bröms, Lotte B. Christensen, Kristjana Einarsdóttir, Anders Engeland, Kari Furu, Brian T. Bateman, et al. 2018. "Association between Methylphenidate and Amphetamine Use in Pregnancy and Risk of Congenital Malformations: A Cohort Study from the International Pregnancy Safety Study Consortium." *JAMA Psychiatry* 75 (2): 167–75.

Ikemoto, Lisa C. 1998. "Forced Cesareans." *Current Opinion in Obstetrics and Gynecology* 10 (6): 465–68.

Ingraham, Christopher 2020. "U.S. Spends Twice as Much on Law and Order as It Does on Cash Welfare, Data Show." *Washington Post,* June 4, 2020. www.washingtonpost.com/business/2020/06/04/us-spends-twice-much-law-order-it-does-social-welfare-data-show/

Isenberg, Nancy 2017. *White Trash: The 400-Year Untold History of Class in America.* New York: Penguin.

Jacobs, Liezille. 2014. "'Bad' Mothers Have Alcohol Use Disorder: Moral Panic or Brief Intervention?" *Gender and Behaviour* 12 (1): 5971–79.

James, Lois, David Brody, and Zachary Hamilton. 2013. "Risk Factors for Domestic Violence during Pregnancy: A Meta-analytic Review." *Violence and Victims* 28 (3): 359–80.

Jansson, Lauren M. n.d. "Prenatal Substance Exposure and Neonatal Abstinence Syndrome: Management and Outcomes." UpToDate. Accessed November 24, 2023. www.uptodate.com/contents/neonatal-abstinence-syndrome.

Jarlenski, Marian, Jay Shroff, Mishka Terplan, Sarah C. M. Roberts, Brittany Brown-Podgorski, and Elizabeth E. Krans. 2023. "Association of Race with Urine Toxicology Testing among Pregnant Patients during Labor and Delivery." *JAMA Health Forum* 4 (4): e230441. doi:10.1001/jamahealthforum.2023.0441.

Johnson, Douglas. 2004. "New Front in the Abortion Debate Unborn Are Victims, Too." National Right to Life. March 30, 2004. www.nrlc.org/federal/unbornvictims/twovictims/sanfranchronicleoped/.

Johnson, Thea. n.d. "Plea Bargain Task Force Report." Criminal Justice Section, American Bar Association. Accessed November 24, 2023. www.americanbar.org/content/dam/aba/publications/criminaljustice/plea-bargain-tf-report.pdf.

Jordan-Zachery, Julia S. 2009. *Black Women, Cultural Images and Social Policy*. New York: Routledge.

Joshi, Chandi, Margie R. Skeer, Kenneth Chui, Gagan Neupane, Reecha Koirala, and Thomas J. Stopka. 2021. "Women-Centered Drug Treatment Models for Pregnant Women with Opioid Use Disorder: A Scoping Review." *Drug and Alcohol Dependence* 226:108855. https://doi.org/10.1016/j.drugalcdep.2021.108855.

Kackley, Rod. 2016. *Drug-Addicted Mothers No Longer Fear Prosecution*. PJ Media. April 13, 2016. https://pjmedia.com/rod-kackley/2016/04/13/drug-addicted-mothers-no-longer-fear-prosecution-n103306.

Kaye, Julia, Brigitte Amiri, Louise Melling, and Jennifer Dalven. 2016. "Health Care Denied." ACLU. April 13, 2016. www.aclu.org/sites/default/files/field_document/healthcaredenied.pdf.

Kennedy, David M. 2011. *Don't Shoot: One Man, a Street Fellowship, and the End of Violence in Inner-City America*. New York: Bloomsbury.

Kenny, Kathleen S. 2018. "Mental Health Harm to Mothers When a Child Is Taken by Child Protective Services: Health Equity Considerations." *Canadian Journal of Psychiatry* 63 (5): 304–7.

Keveney, Bill. 2022. "After Roe v. Wade, Abortion Bans from the 1800s Became Legal Matters in These States." *USA Today*, October 1, 2022. www.usatoday.com/story/news/nation/2022/10/01/abortion-laws-1800-s-became-legal-issue-after-supreme-court-ruling/10454537002/.

Keyser-Marcus, Lori, Anika Alvanzo, Traci Rieckmann, Leroy Thacker, Allison Sepulveda, Alyssa. Forcehimes, Dace S. Svikis, et al. 2015. "Trauma, Gender, and Mental Health Symptoms in Individuals with Substance Use Disorders." *Journal of Interpersonal Violence* 30 (1): 3–24.

Kim, Juliana. 2022. "3 More States Are Poised to Enact Abortion Trigger Bans This Week." NPR. August 22, 2022. www.npr.org/2022/08/22/1118635642/abortion-trigger-ban-tennessee-idaho-texas.

Kinnard, Meg. 2022. "'A Scary Time': Fear of Prosecution Forces Doctors to Choose between Protecting Themselves or Their Patients." Stat News. July 5, 2022. www.statnews.com/2022/07/05/a-scary-time-fear-of-prosecution-forces-doctors-to-choose-between-protecting-themselves-or-their-patients/.

Kirkpatrick, Matthew G., Erik W. Gunderson, Chris-Ellyn Johanson, Frances R. Levin, Richard W. Foltin, and Carl L. Hart. 2012. "Comparison of Intranasal Methamphetamine and D-Amphetamine Self-Administration by Humans." *Addiction* 107 (4): 783–91.

Klautke, Egbert. 2016. "'The Germans Are Beating Us at Our Own Game': American Eugenics and the German Sterilization Law of 1933." *History of the Human Sciences* 29 (3): 25–43.

Klibanoff, Eleanor. 2023. "Three Texas Women Are Sued for Wrongful Death after Allegedly Helping Friend Obtain Abortion Medication." *Texas Tribune,* March 10, 2023. www.texastribune.org/2023/03/10/texas-abortion-lawsuit/.

Knight, Kelly Ray. 2015. *Addicted. Pregnant. Poor.* Durham, NC: Duke University Press.

Kolbert, Kathryn, and Julie F. Kay. 2021. *Controlling Women: What We Must Do Now to Save Reproductive Freedom.* New York: Hachette Books.

Kolder, Veronika E., Janet Gallagher, and Michael T. Parsons. 1987. "Court-Ordered Obstetrical Interventions." *New England Journal of Medicine* 316 (19): 1192–96. doi:10.1056/NEJM198705073161905.

Koren, Gideon, Heather Shear, Karen Graham, and Tom Einarson. 1989. "Bias against the Null Hypothesis: The Reproductive Hazards of Cocaine." *Lancet* 334 (8677): 1440–42.

Kozhimannil, Katy B., William N. Dowd, Mir M. Ali, Priscilla Novak, and Jie Chen. 2019. "Substance Use Disorder Treatment Admissions and State-Level Prenatal Substance Use Policies: Evidence from a National Treatment Database." *Addictive Behaviors* 90:272–77.

Krauthammer, Charles. 1989. "Children of Cocaine." *Washington Post,* July 30 1989. www.washingtonpost.com/archive/opinions/1989/07/30/childrenof-cocaine/41a8b4db-dee24906-a686-a8a5720bf52a/.

Ladd-Taylor, Molly, and Lauri Umansky, eds. 1998. *"Bad" Mothers: The Politics of Blame in Twentieth-Century America.* New York: New York University Press.

Ladhani, Noor Niyar N., Prakesh S. Shah, Kellie E. Murphy, and Knowledge Synthesis Group on Determinants of Preterm/LBW Births. 2011. "Prenatal Amphetamine Exposure and Birth Outcomes: A Systematic Review and Metaanalysis." *American Journal of Obstetrics and Gynecology* 205 (3): 219.e1–7.

Lang, Gregory, Edwin A. Farnell IV, and Jeffrey D. Quinlan. 2021. "Out-of-Hospital Birth." *American Family Physician* 103 (11): 672–79.

"Last Five Years Account for More Than One-Quarter of All Abortion Restrictions Enacted since Roe." 2016. Guttmacher Institute. January 13, 2016. www.guttmacher.org/article/2016/01/last-five-years-account-more-one-quarter-all-abortion-restrictions-enacted-roe.

Lawn, Rebecca B., and Karestan C. Koenen. 2022. "Homicide Is a Leading Cause of Death for Pregnant Women in US." *BMJ* 2022 (379): o2499.

"Lee County Mom Sentenced to 18 Years for Baby's Meth Death." 2020. WRBL News 3. July 8, 2020. www.wrbl.com/alabama-news-2/lee-county-mom-sentenced-to-18-years-for-babys-meth-death/.

Lester, Hannah. 2020. "Jury Says Woman's Meth Use Killed Baby." *Opeka-Auburn News*, March 4, 2020. www.oanow.com/news/crime_courts/jury-says-woman-s-meth-use-killed-baby/article_8655d70e-8821-5265-b564-1aa196de22b7.html.

Levy, Rachael, and Rosa Goldensohn. 2014. "The State Where Giving Birth Can Be Criminal." *Nation*, December 15, 2014. www.typeinvestigations.org/investigation/2014/12/15/the-state-where-giving-birth-can-be-criminal/.

Lewis, Helen M., Linda Johnson, and Donald Askins, eds. 1978. *Colonialism in Modern America: The Appalachian Case*. Boone, NC: Appalachian Consortium.

Lind, Jennifer N., Julia D. Interrante, Elizabeth C. Ailes, Suzanne M. Gilboa, Sara Khan, Meghan T. Frey, Cheryl S. Broussard, et al. 2017. "Maternal Use of Opioids during Pregnancy and Congenital Malformations: A Systematic Review." *Pediatrics* 139 (6): e20164131. 10.1542/peds.2016-4131

Lindbohm, Marja-Liisa, Kari Hemminki, Michele G. Bonhomme, Ahti Anttila, Kaarina Rantala, Piejo Heikkilä, and Michael J. Rosenberg. 1991. "Effects of Paternal Occupational Exposure on Spontaneous Abortions." *American Journal of Public Health* 81 (8): 1029–33.

Linnemann, Travis, and Tyler Wall. 2013. "'This Is Your Face on Meth': The Punitive Spectacle of 'White Trash' in the Rural War on Drugs. *Theoretical Criminology* 17 (3): 315–34.

Lipton, Jack P., and Colin F. Campbell. 1988. "The Constitutionality of Court-Imposed Birth Control as a Condition of Probation." *New York Law School Journal of Human Rights* 6:271.

Lombardo, Paul A. 2008. *Three Generations, No Imbeciles: Eugenics, the Supreme Court, and Buck v. Bell*. Johns Hopkins University Press.

———. 2022. "'We Who Champion the Unborn': Racial Poisons, Eugenics, and the Campaign for Prohibition." *Journal of Law, Medicine and Ethics* 50 (1): 124–38.

López, Iris Ofelia 2008. *Matters of Choice: Puerto Rican Women's Struggle for Reproductive Freedom*. Brunswick, NJ: Rutgers University Press.

Lovell, Rachel, Misty Luminais, and Karen Coen Flynn. 2018. "Structural Misgendering of Transgender Sex Workers in Chicago via Mug Shots? A Case Study of Practicing in the Social Sciences." *Practicing Anthropology* 40 (1): 48–52.

Luker, Kristin. 2007. *When Sex Goes to School: Warring Views on Sex—and Sex Education—since the Sixties*. New York: Norton.

MacKinnon, Catherine A. 2007. *Women's Lives, Men's Laws*. Cambridge, MA: Harvard University Press.

Manian, Maya. 2020. "Immigration Detention and Coerced Sterilization: History Tragically Repeats Itself." ACLU. 2020. www.aclu.org/news/immigrants-rights/immigration-detention-and-coerced-sterilization-history-tragically-repeats-itself.

"Man Who Partied after Killing Pregnant Wife Gets 50 Years." 2004. *Sun Journal,* July 24, 2004. www.sunjournal.com/2004/07/25/man-partied-killing-pregnant-wife-gets-50-years/.

Margerison, Claire E., Meaghan H. Roberts, Alison Gemmill, and Sidra Goldman-Mellor. 2022. "Pregnancy-Associated Deaths Due to Drugs, Suicide, and Homicide in the United States, 2010–2019." *Obstetrics and Gynecology* 139 (2): 172–80. doi: 10.1097/AOG.0000000000004649.

Mark, Nicholas D. E., and Lawrence L. Wu. 2022. "More Comprehensive Sex Education Reduced Teen Births: Quasi-experimental Evidence." *Proceedings of the National Academy of Sciences* 119 (8): e2113144119.

Mark, Tami L., William N. Dowd, and Carol L. Council. 2020. *Tracking the Quality of Addiction Treatment over Time and across States: Using the Federal Government's "Signs" of Higher Quality [Internet].* Research Triangle Park, NC: RTI.

Marshall, Mary Faith 2016. "An Incautious Tale of Biomedical Ethics, Abortion Politics and Political Expediency." *Narrative Inquiry in Bioethics* 6 (1): 28–31.

Martin, Joyce A., and Michelle J. Osterman. 2023. "Changes in Prenatal Care Utilization: United States, 2019–21." *National Vital Statistics Reports* 72 (4): 1–14. www.cdc.gov/nchs/data/nvsr/nvsr72/nvsr72-04.pdf.

Martin, Nina. 2014. "A Stillborn Child, a Charge of Murder and the Disputed Case Law on 'Fetal Harm.'" ProPublica. March 18, 2014. www.propublica.org/article/stillborn-child-charge-of-murder-and-disputed-case-law-on-fetal-harm.

———. 2015. "Take a Valium, Lose Your Kid, Go to Jail." Salon. September 29, 2015. www.salon.com/2015/09/29/take_a_valium_lose_your_kid_go_to_jail_partner/.

Martinez, Gladys M. 2020. "Trends and Patterns in Menarche in the United States: 1995 through 2013–17." *National Health Statistics Reports.* No. 146. September 10, 2020. https://stacks.cdc.gov/view/cdc/93643.

Maruschak, Laura M. 2008. "Medical Problems of Prisoners." Bureau of Justice Statistics. April 1, 2008. https://bjs.ojp.gov/library/publications/medical-problems-prisoners.

McCabe, Sean E., J. R. Knight, C. J. Teter, and H. Wechsler. 2005. "Non-medical Use of Prescription Stimulants among US College Students: Prevalence and Correlates from a National Survey." *Addiction* 100 (1): 96–106.

McCann, Allison, Amy Schoenfeld Walker, Ava Sasani, Taylor Johnston, Larry Buchanan, and Jon Huang. 2022. "Tracking the States Where Abortion Is Now Banned." *New York Times,* September 23, 2022. www.nytimes.com/interactive/2022/us/abortion-laws-roe-v-wade.html.

McClintock, Anne. 1993. "Family Feuds: Gender, Nationalism and the Family." *Feminist Review* 44 (1): 61–80.

"Medical Management of Abortion." 2018. World Health Organization. November 24, 2023. https://apps.who.int/iris/bitstream/handle/10665/278968/9789241550406-eng.pdf.

"Medications for Substance Use Disorder." 2023. Substance Abuse and Mental Health Services Administration. October 3, 2023. www.samhsa.gov/medications-substance-use-disorders.

Meinhofer, Angelica, Allison Witman, Johanna Catherine Maclean, and Yuhua Bao. 2022. "Prenatal Substance Use Policies and Newborn Health." *Health Economics* 31 (7): 1452–67.

Melemis, Steven M. 2015. "Relapse Prevention and the Five Rules of Recovery." *Yale Journal of Biology and Medicine* 88 (3): 325.

Metcalfe, Robyn E., Luke D. Muentner, Claudia Reino, Maria L. Schweer-Collins, Jean M. Kjellstrand, and J. Mark Eddy. 2022. "Witnessing Parental Arrest as a Predictor of Child Internalizing and Externalizing Symptoms during and after Parental Incarceration." *Journal of Child and Adolescent Trauma* 16 (2): 329–38.

"Methamphetamine Abuse in Women of Reproductive Age." 2011. *Obstetrics and Gynecology* 117 (3): 751–55.

Miller, Lisa L. 2015. "What's Violence Got to Do with It? Inequality, Punishment, and State Failure in US Politics." *Punishment and Society* 17 (2): 184–210.

Miller, Reuben Jonathan, and Amanda Alexander. 2015. "The Price of Carceral Citizenship: Punishment, Surveillance, and Social Welfare Policy in an Age of Carceral Expansion." *Michigan Journal of Race and Law* 21:291.

Miller, Ryan W. 2021. "Scott Peterson Gets New Life Sentence in Wife's Murder after Years on Death Row." *USA Today,* December 8, 2021. www.usatoday.com/story/news/nation/2021/12/08/scott-peterson-life-sentence-laci-peterson-murder-case/6431016001/.

Mills, Katherine L., Maree Teesson, Joanne Ross, and Lorna Peters. 2006. "Trauma, PTSD, and Substance Use Disorders: Findings from the Australian National Survey of Mental Health and Well-Being." *American Journal of Psychiatry* 163 (4): 652–58.

Mink, Gwendolyn. 1998. *Welfare's End.* Ithaca, NY: Cornell University Press.

Mitchell, Gary. 2006. "Unborn Now Have Voice, Supporters of New Alabama Law Say." Christian Post. April. 14, 2006. www.christianpost.com/news/unborn-now-have-voice-say-supporters-of-new-ala-law.html.

Mitchell, Monique B. 2016. *The Neglected Transition: Building a Relational Home for Children Entering Foster Care.* New York: Oxford University Press.

Mitchell, Shannon Gwin, Jennnifer Willet, Laura B. Monico, Amy James, Danielle S. Rudes, Jill Viglioni, Peter D. Friedmann, et al. 2016. "Community Correctional Agents' Views of Medication-Assisted Treatment:

Examining Their Influence on Treatment Referrals and Community Supervision Practices." *Substance Abuse* 37 (1): 127–33.

Mizelle, Shawna, and Chris Boyette. 2023. "Alabama Attorney General Says People Who Take Abortion Pills Could Be Prosecuted." CNN. January 12, 2023. www.cnn.com/2023/01/12/politics/alabama-abortion-women-prosecution/index.html.

Mohapatra, Seema 2011. "Unshackling Addiction: A Public Health Approach to Drug Use during Pregnancy." *Wisconsin Journal of Law, Gender and Society* 26:241.

Morgan, John P., and Lynn Zimmer. 1997. "The Social Pharmacology of Smokeable Cocaine: Not All It's Cracked Up to Be." *Crack in America: Demon Drugs and Social Justice,* edited by Craig Reinarman and Harry G. Levine, 131–70. Berkeley: University of California Press.

Morone, James A. 1997. "Enemies of the People: The Moral Dimension to Public Health." *Journal of Health Politics, Policy and Law* 22 (4): 993–1020.

———. 2004. *Hellfire Nation: The Politics of Sin in American History.* New Haven, CT: Yale University Press.

Morris, J. K., N. J. Wald, and H. C. Watt. 1999. "Fetal Loss in Down Syndrome Pregnancies." *Prenatal Diagnosis* 19 (2): 142–45.

Motion for Leave and Brief of Amici Curiae in Support of Petition of Amanda Helaine Kimbrough. n.d. Pregnancy Justice. Accessed December 2, 2023. www.pregnancyjusticeus.org/wp-content/uploads/2019/10/Kimbrough-20Motion20for20Leave20to20File20and2020Final20Brief20fdt.pdf.

"Mug Shot Match-Up." n.d. Montana Meth Project. Accessed November 23, 2023. www.methproject.org/answers/will-using-meth-change-how-i-look.html#Mug-Shot-Match-Up.

Murakawa, Naomi. 2011. "Toothless: The Methamphetamine 'Epidemic,' 'Meth Mouth,' and the Racial Construction of Drug Scares." *Du Bois Review: Social Science Research on Race* 8 (1): 219–28.

Murch, Donna. 2015. "Crack in Los Angeles: Crisis, Militarization, and Black Response to the Late Twentieth-Century War on Drugs." *Journal of American History* 102 (1): 162–73.

Murphy, Sheigla, and Marsha Rosenbaum. 1999. *Pregnant Women on Drugs: Combating Stereotypes and Stigma.* Brunswick, NJ: Rutgers University Press.

Nash, Elizabeth, and Isabel Guarnieri. 2022. "13 States Have Abortion Trigger Bans: Here's What Happens When Roe Is Overturned." Guttmacher Institute. June 6, 2022. www.guttmacher.org/article/2022/06/13-states-have-abortion-trigger-bans-heres-what-happens-when-roe-overturned.

"National Unintended Pregnancy." n.d. Americas Health Rankings. Accessed November 24, 2023. www.americashealthrankings.org/explore/health-of-women-and-children/measure/unintended_pregnancy/state/SC.

Navarro, Elisa. 2022. "Kings County Woman Speaks Out after Being Prosecuted for Murder after Stillbirth." ABC 30. October 3, 2022. https://abc30.com/kings-county-woman-chelsea-becker-stillbirth-murder-charge-meth-use-during-birth/12292327/.

"Neither Justice nor Treatment: Drug Courts in the United States." 2017. Physicians for Human Rights. June 2017. https://phr.org/wp-content/uploads/2017/06/phr_drugcourts_executivesummary.pdf.

Nelson, Lawrence J., and Mary Faith Marshall. 1998. *Ethical and Legal Analyses of Three Coercive Policies Aimed at Substance Abuse by Pregnant Women*. Charleston, SC: Medical University of South Carolina.

Netherland, Jules, and Helena B. Hansen. 2016. "The War on Drugs That Wasn't: Wasted Whiteness, 'Dirty Doctors,' and Race in Media Coverage of Prescription Opioid Misuse." *Culture, Medicine, and Psychiatry* 40 (4): 664–86.

Neuspiel, Daniel R. 1996. "Racism and Perinatal Addiction." *Ethnicity and Disease* 6 (1–2): 47–55.

Newman, Amie. 2010a. "Pregnant? Don't Fall Down the Stairs." Rewire News Group. February 15, 2010. https://rewirenewsgroup.com/2010/02/15/pregnant-dont-fall-down-stairs/.

———. 2010b. "When Getting Baked Means More Than Just a Bun in the Oven." *Rewire*. December 20, 2010. https://rewirenewsgroup.com/2010/12/20/when-getting-baked-doesnt-refer-oven/

Nowell, Cecelia. 2022. "Kim Blalock Took Lawfully Prescribed Pain Killers during Pregnancy—and Was Charged with a Felony." *Elle*, April 6, 2022. www.elle.com/culture/a39541235/kim-blalock-took-lawfully-prescribed-pain-killers-during-pregnancyand-was-charged-with-a-felony/.

Nussbaum, Martha. 2004. "What's Privacy Got to Do with It?" In *Women and the US Constitution: History, Interpretation, and Practice*, edited by Sibyl A. Schwarzenbach and Patricia Smith, 153–75. New York: Columbia University Press, 2004.

Oaks, Laury. 2015. *Giving Up Baby: Safe Haven Laws, Motherhood, and Reproductive Justice*. New York: New York University Press.

Ocen, Priscilla A. 2017. "Birthing Injustice: Pregnancy as a Status Offense." *George Washington Law Review* 85:1163.

Ogawa, Yusuke, Nozomi Takeshima, and Toshi A. Furukawa. 2018. "Maternal Exposure to Benzodiazepine and Risk of Preterm Birth and Low Birth Weight: A Case-Control Study Using a Claims Database in Japan." *Asia-Pacific Psychiatry* 10 (3): e12309.

Olshan, Andrew F., and Elaine M. Faustman. 1993. "Male-Mediated Developmental Toxicity." *Reproductive Toxicology* 7 (3): 191–202.

Onwuegbuzie, Anthony J., and Nancy L. Leech. 2005. "On Becoming a Pragmatic Researcher: The Importance of Combining Quantitative and

Qualitative Research Methodologies." *International Journal of Social Research Methodology* 8 (5): 375–87.

"The Opioid Epidemic: By the Numbers." 2016. Department of Health and Human Services. Accessed November 24, 2023. www.nmhealth.org/data/view/substance/1914/.

Ouimette, Paige E., and Pamela J. Brown. 2003. *Trauma and Substance Abuse: Causes, Consequences, and Treatment of Comorbid Disorders.* Washington, DC: American Psychological Association.

"Our View: Revisit Chemical Endangerment Law?" *Gadsden Times,* November 24, 2015. www.gadsdentimes.com/story/opinion/editorials/2015/11/24/our-view-revisit-chemical-endangerment-law/32090083007/.

"Overdose Prevention Strategy." n.d. Department of Health and Human Services. Accessed November 23, 2023. www.hhs.gov/overdose-prevention/.

Owens, Deirdre C., and Sharla M. Fett. 2019. "Black Maternal and Infant Health: Historical Legacies of Slavery." *American Journal of Public Health* 109 (10): 1342–45.

Page, Jared. 2011. "Utah Family's Tragedy Leads to Change in North Carolina Law." *Deseret News,* September 25. 2011. www.deseret.com/2011/9/25/20387795/utah-family-s-tragedy-leads-to-change-in-north-carolina-law.

Paltrow, Lynn M. 2022. "Roe v Wade and the New Jane Crow: Reproductive Rights in the Age of Mass Incarceration." *American Journal of Public Health* 112 (9): 1313–17.

Paltrow, Lynn, and Jeanne Flavin. 2013. "Arrests of and Forced Interventions on Pregnant Women in the United States, 1973–2005: Implications for Women's Legal Status and Public Health." *Journal of Health Politics, Policy and Law* 38 (2): 299–343.

Paltrow, Lynn M., and Hillary Fox. 1992. *Criminal Prosecutions against Pregnant Women: National Update and Overview.* New York: Reproductive Freedom Project/American Civil Liberties Union Foundation.

Paltrow, Lynn M., and Kathrine Jack. 2010. "Pregnant Women, Junk Science, and Zealous Defense." *Champion* 30:30.

Patrick, Megan E., Patrick Wightman, Robert F. Schoeni, and John E. Schulenberg. 2012. "Socioeconomic Status and Substance Use among Young Adults: A Comparison across Constructs and Drugs." *Journal of Studies on Alcohol and Drugs* 73 (5): 772–82.

Patrick, Stephen W., Davida M. Schiff, Sheryl A. Ryan, Joanna Quigley, Pamela K. Gonzalez, and Leslie R. Walker. 2017. "A Public Health Response to Opioid Use in Pregnancy." *Pediatrics* 139 (3): e20164070.

Patterson, Blake. 2019. "Alabama Woman Charged in Fetal Death, Her Shooter Goes Free." Keloland News. June 27, 2019. www.keloland.com/news/national-world-news/alabama-woman-charged-in-fetal-death-her-shooter-goes-free/.

"PDA: Historical Perspective." n.d. US Legal. Accessed November 24, 2023. https://pregnancydiscriminationact.uslegal.com/pda-historical-perspective/.

Perera, Frederica P., Virginia Rauh, Wei-Yann Tsai, Patrick Kinney, David Camann, Dana Barr, Tom Bernert, et al. 2003. "Effects of Transplacental Exposure to Environmental Pollutants on Birth Outcomes in a Multiethnic Population." *Environmental Health Perspectives* 111 (2): 201–5.

Perera, Frederica P., Robin M. Whyatt, Wieslaw Jedrychowski, Virginia Rauh, David Manchester, Regina M. Santella, and Ruth Ottman. 1998. "Recent Developments in Molecular Epidemiology: A Study of the Effects of Environmental Polycyclic Aromatic Hydrocarbons on Birth Outcomes in Poland." *American Journal of Epidemiology* 147 (3): 309–14.

Pérez, Miriam Zoila. 2007. "Queering Reproductive Justice." Rewire News Group. May 31, 2007. https://rewirenewsgroup.com/2007/05/31/queering-reproductive-justice/.

Perrotte, Violette, Arun Chaudhary, and Annekathryn Goodman. 2020. "'At Least Your Baby Is Healthy': Obstetric Violence or Disrespect and Abuse in Childbirth Occurrence Worldwide: A Literature Review. *Open Journal of Obstetrics and Gynecology* 10 (11): 1544–62.

Petrelli, G., I. Figa-Talamanca, R. Tropeano, M. Tangucci, C. Cini, S. Aquilani, L. Gasperini, and P. Meli. 2000. "Reproductive Male-Mediated Risk: Spontaneous Abortion among Wives of Pesticide Applicators." *European Journal of Epidemiology* 16:391–93.

Petrocelli, Matthew, Trish Oberweis, Michael R. Smith, and Joseph Petrocelli. 2014. "Assessing Police Attitudes toward Drugs and Drug Enforcement." *American Journal of Criminal Justice* 39:22–40.

Pfohl, Stephen. 1977. "The 'Discovery' of Child Abuse." *Social Problems* 24 (3): 310–23.

———. 1981. "Labeling Criminals." In *Law and Deviance,* edited by H. Laurence Ross, 65–97. Beverly Hills: Sage.

Phillippi, Julia C., Rebecca Schulte, Kemberlee Bonnet, David D. Schlundt, William O. Cooper, Peter R. Martin, Katy B. Kozhimannil, and Stephen W. Patrick. 2021. "Reproductive-Age Women's Experience of Accessing Treatment for Opioid Use Disorder: 'We Don't Do That Here.'" *Women's Health Issues* 31 (5): 455–61. https://doi.org/10.1016/j.whi.2021.03.010.

Pilkington, Ed. 2015. "Alone in Alabama: Dispatches from an Inmate Jailed for Her Son's Stillbirth." *Guard,* October 7, 2015. www.theguardian.com/us-news/2015/oct/07/alabama-chemical-endangerment-pregnancy-amanda-kimbrough.

Poehlmann-Tynan, Julia. 2022. "Parental Incarceration and Young Children's Development: Pathways to Resilience." In *Parent-Child Separation,* edited by Jennifer Glick, Valarie King, and Susan M. McHale. 87–107. Cham, Switzerland: Springer.

Poland, Marilyn L., Mitchell P. Dombrowski, Joel W. Ager, and Robert J. Sokol. 1993. "Punishing Pregnant Drug Users: Enhancing the Flight from Care. *Drug and Alcohol Dependence* 31 (3): 199–203.

Polonsky, M., L. Azbel, J. A. Wickersham, F. S. Taxman, E. Grishaev, S. Dvoryak, and F. L. Altice. 2015. "Challenges to Implementing Opioid Substitution Therapy in Ukrainian Prisons: Personnel Attitudes toward Addiction, Treatment, and People with HIV/AIDS." *Drug and Alcohol Dependence* 148:47–55.

"Prenatal Drug and Alcohol Exposure: Science Refutes Media Hype and Enduring Myths." 2022. Pregnancy Justice. August 17, 2022. www.pregnancyjusticeus.org/resources/prenatal-drug-and-alcohol-exposure-science-refutes-media-hype-and-enduring-myths/.

Price, K. 2018. "Queering Reproductive Justice in the Trump Era: A Note on Political Intersectionality." *Politics and Gender* 14 (4D): 581–601. doi:10.1017/S1743923X18000776.

"Principles of Harm Reduction." 2020. National Harm Reduction Coalition. Accessed November 24, 2023. https://harmreduction.org/about-us/principles-of-harm-reduction/.

"The Program." 2020. New Life for Women. Accessed November 24, 2023. www.newlifeforwomen.org/the-program.html.

"Public Chapter No. 1006." 2011. State of Tennessee. Accessed November 24, 2023. https://publications.tnsosfiles.com/acts/109/pub/pc1006.pdf.

"QuickFacts: Coffee County, Alabama." n.d. United States Census Bureau. Accessed November 24, 2023. www.census.gov/quickfacts/fact/table/coffeecountyalabama/HCN010217.

"Quickfacts: South Carolina." n.d. United States Census Bureau. Accessed November 27, 2023. www.census.gov/quickfacts/fact/table/SC#.

Quinnell, Kenneth. 2021. "Pathway to Progress: The Pregnancy Discrimination Act of 1978." AFL-CIO. April 15, 2021. https://aflcio.org/2021/4/15/pathway-progress-pregnancy-discrimination-act-1978.

Ragusa, Antonio, Alessandro Svelato, Criselda Santacroce, Piera Catalano, Valentina Notarstefano, Oliana Carnevali, Fabrizio Papa, et al. 2021. "Plasticenta: First Evidence of Microplastics in Human Placenta." *Environment International* 146: 106274.

Rawls, Phillip. 2008. "Alabama Targets Drug-Using Mothers." *Tuscaloosa News*, August 3, 2008. www.tuscaloosanews.com/story/news/2008/08/03/alabama-targets-drug-using-mothers/27759814007/.

Reed, Megan K., Kelsey R. Smith, Francesca Ciocco, Richard W. Hass, Avery, Lin Cox, Erin L. Kelly, and Lara C. Weinstein. 2023. "Sorting through Life: Evaluating Patient-Important Measures of Success in a Medication for Opioid Use Disorder (MOUD) Treatment Program." *Substance Abuse*

Treatment, Prevention, and Policy 18 (4): 4–12. https://doi.org/10.1186/s13011-022-00510-1.
Reeves, Jeff. 2017. "10 Years Later, Jenna Nielsen's Brutal Murder Still Unsolved." CBS 17. November 1, 2017. www.cbs17.com/news/10-years-later-jenna-nielsens-brutal-murder-still-unsolved/.
"Reproductive Justice." n.d. In Our Own Voice, National Black Women's Reproductive Justice Agenda. Accessed November 24, 2023. https://blackrj.org/our-issues/reproductive-justice/.
"Results from the 2009 National Survey on Drug Use and Health: Detailed Tables." 2010. U.S. Department of Health and Human Services. September 2010. www.samhsa.gov/data/sites/default/files/cbhsq-reports/2009%20NSDUH%20Detailed%20Tables/2009%20NSDUH%20substance%20use%20detailed%20tables.pdf.
"Results from the 2015 National Survey on Drug Use and Health: Detailed Tables." 2016. U.S. Department of Health and Human Services. September 8, 2016. www.samhsa.gov/data/report/results-2015-national-survey-drug-use-and-h.
Ridgeway, James, and Jean Casella. 2013. "America's 10 Worst Prisons: Julia Tutwiler." *Mother Jones*, May 9, 2013. www.motherjones.com/politics/2013/05/americas-10-worst-prisons-julia-tutwiler/.
Riley, Edward P., M. Alejandra Infante, and Kenneth R. Warren. 2011. "Fetal Alcohol Spectrum Disorders: An Overview." *Neuropsychology Review* 21:73–80.
Roberts, Dorothy E. 1990. "Punishing Drug Addicts Who Have Babies: Women of Color, Equality, and the Right of Privacy." *Harvard Law Review* 104:1419.
———. 1991. *Women, Pregnancy, and Substance Abuse.* Washington, DC: Center for Women Policy Studies.
———. 1992. "Crime, Race, and Reproduction." *Tulane Law Review* 67:1945.
———. 1995. "Motherhood and Crime." *Social Text* 42:99–123.
———. 1996. "Unshackling Black Motherhood." *Michigan Law Review* 95:938.
———. 1997. *Killing the Black Body: Race, Reproduction, and the Meaning of Liberty.* New York: Pantheon.
———. 2000a. "Creating and Solving the Problem of Drug Use during Pregnancy."
———. 2000b. "Misconceiving Mothers: Legislators, Prosecutors, and the Politics of Prenatal Drug Exposure." *Journal of Criminal Law and Criminology* 90 (4): 1353.
———. 2011. "Prison, Foster Care, and the Systemic Punishment of Black Mothers." *UCLA Law Review* 59:1474.
———. 2014. "Child Protection as Surveillance of African American Families." *Journal of Social Welfare and Family Law* 36 (4): 426–37.

———. 2022. *Torn Apart: How the Child Welfare System Destroys Black Families—and How Abolition Can Build a Safer World.* New York: Basic Books.

Roberts, Sarah C., and Amani Nuru-Jeter. 2010. "Women's Perspectives on Screening for Alcohol and Drug Use in Prenatal Care." *Women's Health Issues* 20 (3): 193–200.

———. 2012. "Universal Screening for Alcohol and Drug Use and Racial Disparities in Child Protective Services Reporting." *Journal of Behavioral Health Services and Research* 39:3–16.

Roberts, Sarah C., and Cheri Pies. 2011. "Complex Calculations: How Drug Use during Pregnancy Becomes a Barrier to Prenatal Care." *Maternal and Child Health Journal* 15 (3): 333–41.

Roberts, Sarah C., Sue Thomas, Ryan Treffers, and Laurie Drabble. 2017. "Forty Years of State Alcohol and Pregnancy Policies in the USA: Best Practices for Public Health or Efforts to Restrict Women's Reproductive Rights?" *Alcohol and Alcoholism* 52 (6): 715–21.

Roberts, Sarah C., Terri-Ann Thompson, and Kimá J. Taylor. 2021. "Dismantling the Legacy of Failed Policy Approaches to Pregnant People's Use of Alcohol and Drugs." *International Review of Psychiatry* 33 (6): 502–13.

Robertson, Katie 2022. "Facts Were Sparse on an Abortion Case, but That Didn't Stop the Attacks." *New York Times,* July 14, 2022. www.nytimes.com/2022/07/14/business/media/10-year-old-girl-ohio-rape.html.

Robinson, Carol. 2017. "Heroin-Addicted Mom Gives Birth to Second Baby: Lawyers Seek Bond, Treatment." AL.com. January 25, 2017. www.al.com/news/birmingham/2017/01/heroin_dependent_mom_has_secon.html.

Robinson, Richard Knox. 2022. "From the Kallikaks to the Kallikaks: Hillbilly Elegy and the Legacy of Eugenics." *Film Criticism* 46 (2): doi: https://doi.org/10.3998/fc.3610.

The Role of Purdue Pharma and the Sackler Family in the Opioid Epidemic. 2021. Washington, DC: U.S. Government Publishing Office. 2021. www.congress.gov/event/116th-congress/house-event/LC65831/text?s = 1andr = 10.

Romo, Vanessa. 2019. "Woman Indicted for Manslaughter after Death of Her Fetus, May Avoid Prosecution." NPR KQED. June 28, 2019. www.npr.org/2019/06/28/737005113/woman-indicted-for-manslaughter-after-death-of-her-fetus-may-avoid-prosecution.

Ross, Loretta. 2006. "What Is Reproductive Justice?" *Reproductive Justice Briefing Book: A Primer on Reproductive Justice and Social Change.* Accessed November 24, 2023. www.law.berkeley.edu/php-programs/courses/fileDL.php?fID=4051.

———. 2020. "Understanding Reproductive Justice." In *Feminist Theory Reader: Local and Global Perspectives,* edited by Carole McCann, Seung-kyung Kim, and Emek Ergun, 77–82. New York: Routledge.

Ross, Loretta, and Rickie Solinger. 2017. *Reproductive Justice: An Introduction*. Vol. 1. Oakland: University of California Press.

Roth, Rachel, and Sara L. Ainsworth. 2015. "'If They Hand You a Paper, You Sign It': A Call to End the Sterilization of Women in Prison." *Hastings Women's Law Journal* 26:7.

Rudd, Rose A., Noah Aleshire, Jon E. Zibbell, and R. Matthew Gladden. 2016. "Increases in Drug and Opioid Overdose Deaths: United States, 2000–2014." *American Journal of Transplantation* 16 (4): 1323–27.

Samuels, Jocelyn. 2014. "Tutwiler Prison Report." Civil Rights Division, U.S. Department of Justice. January 17, 2014. www.documentcloud.org/documents/1031449-tutwiler-prison-report.html.

Samuels, Terri-Ann A., Howard Minkoff, Joseph Feldman, Awoniyi Awonuga, and Tracey E. Wilson. 2007. "Obstetricians, Health Attorneys, and Court-Ordered Cesarean Sections." *Women's Health Issues* 17 (2): 107–14.

Santos, Alysia. 2020. "The Separation." Marshall Project. May 6, 2020. www.themarshallproject.org/2020/05/06/the-separation.

Savitz, David A. 1994. "Paternal Exposures and Pregnancy Outcome: Miscarriage, Stillbirth, Low Birth Weight, Preterm Delivery." In *Male-Mediated Developmental Toxicity*, edited by Andrew F. Olshan and Donald R. Mattison, 177–84. New York: Plenum.

Schempf, Ashley H., and Donna M. Strobino. 2009. "Drug Use and Limited Prenatal Care: An Examination of Responsible Barriers." *American Journal of Obstetrics and Gynecology* 200 (4): 412.e1–10.

Schoen, Johanna. 2005. *Choice and Coercion: Birth Control, Sterilization, and Abortion in Public Health and Welfare*. Chapel Hill: University of North Carolina Press.

Schroedel, Jean R., and Pamela Fiber. 2001. "Punitive versus Public Health-Oriented Responses to Drug Use by Pregnant Women." *Yale Journal of Public Health Policy and Ethics* 1:217–36.

Seely, Natalee. 2021. "Reporting on Transgender Victims of Homicide: Practices of Misgendering, Sourcing and Transparency." *Newspaper Research Journal* 42 (1): 74–94.

Senate Judiciary Committee. 2014. Tennessee General Assembly. March 18, 2014. https://tnga.granicus.com/player/clip/9050?view_id=269&meta_id=168824&redirect=true&h=c834e15f8eeee7a6f3aae1a9a6c9ce94.

Shah, Prakesh S., Taiba Balkhair, and Knowledge Synthesis Group on Determinants of Preterm/LBW Births. 2011. "Air Pollution and Birth Outcomes: A Systematic Review." *Environment International* 37 (2): 498–516.

Shah, Rizwan, Sabrina D. Diaz, Amelia Arria, Linda L. LaGasse, Chris Derauf, Elana Newman, Lynne M. Smith, et al. 2012. "Prenatal Methamphetamine Exposure and Short-Term Maternal and Infant Medical Outcomes." *American Journal of Perinatology* 29 (5): 391–400.

Shanker, T. and M. Duenwald. 2003. "Bombing Error Puts a Spotlight on Pilots' Pills." *New York Times,* January 19, 2003. www.nytimes.com/2003/01/19/us/threats-and-responses-military-bombing-error-puts-a-spotlight-on-pilots-pills.html.

Shapiro, Ari, and Blake Farmer. 2015. "Drug Treatment Slots Are Scarce for Pregnant Women." *All Things Considered.* November 19, 2015. www.npr.org/2015/11/19/456693703/drug-treatment-slots-are-scarce-for-pregnant-women.

Shelburne, Beth. 2017. "On Your Side Investigation: Big Changes Made at Tutwiler Prison for Women under Settlement with US Dept. of Justice." 6 WBRC. May 16, 2017. www.wbrc.com/story/35441776/on-your-side-investigation-big-changes-made-at-tutwiler-prison-for-women-under-settlement-with-us-dept-of-justice/.

Shoblock, James R., Eric B. Sullivan, Isabelle M. Maisonneuve, and Stanley D. Glick. 2003. "Neurochemical and Behavioral Differences between D-Methamphetamine and D-Amphetamine in Rats." *Psychopharmacology* 165 (4): 359–69.

SIA Legal Team. n.d. "Criminalization for Use of Drugs and Pregnancy: Regina McKnight Case Study." CUNY School of Law. Accessed November 23, 2023. www.ohchr.org/sites/default/files/Documents/Issues/Women/WG/DeprivedLiberty/Others/Human_Rights_and_Gender_Justice_Clinic_at_CUNY_School_of_Law_and_others-3.pdf.

Sichel, Dana L. 2007. "Giving Birth in Shackles: A Constitutional and Human Rights Violation." *American University Journal of Gender, Social Policy and the Law* 16:223.

Siegel, Reva B. 2010. "*Roe*'s Roots: The Women's Rights Claims That Endangered *Roe.*" *Boston University Law Review* 90:1875–901.

Silva, Daniella. 2017. "Anna Yocca, Tennessee Woman in Coat-Hanger Abortion Case, Released from Jail a Year Later." NBC News. January 10, 2017. www.nbcnews.com/news/us-news/anna-yocca-tennessee-woman-coat-hanger-attempted-abortion-case-released-n705416.

Singh, Susheela, Lisa Remez, Gilda Sedgh, Lorraine Kwok, and Tsuyoshi Onda. 2017. "Abortion Worldwide, 2017: Unequal Progress and Unequal Access." Guttmacher Institute. Accessed November 24, 2023. www.guttmacher.org/sites/default/files/report_pdf/abortion-worldwide-2017.pdf.

Smith, Ada. 2016. "Appalachian Futurism." *Journal of Appalachian Studies* 22 (1): 73–75.

Smith, Andrea. 2015. *Conquest: Sexual Violence and American Indian Genocide.* Durham, NC: Duke University Press.

Smith, Kelley, and Rachel Lipari. 2017. "The CBHSQ Report." Substance Abuse and Mental Health Services Administration. January 17, 2017. www.samhsa.gov/data/sites/default/files/report_2724/ShortReport-2724.pdf.

Smith, Richard M. 1986. "The Plague among Us." *Newsweek* 107 (24): 15.

Solotaroff, Paul 2003. "Crystal Meth: Plague in the Heartland." *Rolling Stone*, January 23, 2003. www.rollingstone.com/culture/culture-news/crystal-meth-plague-in-the-heartland-38456/.

"South Carolina Crime Statistics." n.d. South Carolina Law Enforcement Division. Accessed November 25, 2023. https://beyond2020.sled.sc.gov/tops/.

"South Carolina State Policy Information." n.d. Sex Education Collaborative. Accessed November 24, 2023. https://sexeducationcollaborative.org/states/south-carolina.

Stack, Liam. 2017. "Woman Accused of Coat-Hanger Abortion Pleads Guilty to Felony." *New York Times*, January 11, 2017. www.nytimes.com/2017/01/11/us/tennessee-abortion-crime.html.

"Statewide Drug Crimes." n.d. Crime.Alabama.Gov. Accessed November 28 2023. https://crime.alabama.gov/Data/StatewideDrugCrime.

Stein, Kelsey. 2014. "Over Two Decades, 'Sexual Abuse and Harassment Have Only Worsened' at Julia Tutwiler Prison." Al.com. January 20, 2014. www.al.com/wire/2014/01/over_two_decades_sexual_abuse.html.

Stellman, Steven D., Jeanne Mager Stellman, and John F. Sommer Jr. 1988. "Health and Reproductive Outcomes among American Legionnaires in Relation to Combat and Herbicide Exposure in Vietnam." *Environmental Research* 47 (2): 150–74.

Stern, Alexandra Minna. 2001. *Eugenic Nation: Faults and Frontiers of Better Breeding in Modern America*. Berkeley: University of California Press.

———. 2005. "Sterilized in the Name of Public Health: Race, Immigration, and Reproductive Control in Modern California." *American Journal of Public Health* 95 (7): 1128–38.

———. 2022. "From 'Race Suicide' to 'White Extinction': White Nationalism, Nativism, and Eugenics over the Past Century." *Journal of American History* 109 (2): 348–61.

Stern, Alexandra Minna, Nichole L. Novak, Natalie Lira, Kate O'Connor, Siobán Harlow, and Sharon Kardia. 2017. "California's Sterilization Survivors: An Estimate and Call for Redress." *American Journal of Public Health* 107 (1): 50–54.

Stevenson, Amanda Jean, Leslie Root, and Jane Menken. 2022. "The Maternal Mortality Consequences of Losing Abortion Access." *SocArXiv*, June 29, 2022. https://doi.org/10.31235/osf.io/7g29k

St. George, Donna. 2004. "Many New or Expectant Mothers Die Violent Deaths." *Washington Post*, December 19, 2004. www.washingtonpost.com/wp-dyn/articles/A10074-2004Dec18.html.

Stone, R. 2015. "Pregnant Women and Substance Use: Fear, Stigma, and Barriers to Care." *Health and Justice* 3 (2): 1–15. https://doi.org/10.1186/s40352-015-0015-5.

Stroud, Hernandez D. 2016. "Our Opioid Crisis Reveals Deep Racial Bias in Addiction Treatment." *Time,* July 15, 2016. https://time.com/4385588/crack-babies-heroin-crisis/.

Subbaraman, Meenakshi S., Sue Thomas, Ryan Treffers, Kevin Delucchi, William C. Kerr, Priscilla Martinez, and Sarah C. M. Roberts. 2018. "Associations between State-Level Policies Regarding Alcohol Use among Pregnant Women, Adverse Birth Outcomes, and Prenatal Care Utilization: Results from 1972 to 1973; Vital Statistics." *Alcoholism: Clinical and Experimental Research* 42 (8): 1511–17.

Sufrin, Carolyn. 2017. *Jailcare: Finding the Safety Net for Women behind Bars.* Oakland: University of California Press.

"Summary of the HIPAA Privacy Rule." 2022. U.S. Department of Health and Human Services. Accessed November 24, 2023. www.hhs.gov/hipaa/for-professionals/privacy/laws-regulations/index.html.

Sung, Hung-En E., Doris Chu, Linda Richter, and Amy Shlosberg. 2009. "Treatment Philosophy and Service Delivery in a Network of Faith-Based Substance Abuse Treatment." *Families in Society* 90 (4): 390–98.

Supreme Court of the United States. 2021. *Dobbs v. Jackson Women's Health.* December 1, 2021. Heritage Reporting Corporation. www.supremecourt.gov/oral_arguments/argument_transcripts/2021/19-1392_4425.pdf.

Sussman, Dana. 2008. "Bound by Injustice: Challenging the Use of Shackles on Incarcerated Pregnant Women." *Cardozo Journal of Law and Gender* 15:477.

Szekely, Peter. 2019. "Alabama Prosecutor Drops Charges against Woman Who Lost Foetus after Being Shot." Reuters. July 3, 2019. www.reuters.com/article/uk-alabama-crime-idUKKCN1TY2QU.

Tabatabaeepour, Nadia, Jake R. Morgan, Ali Jalali, Shashi N. Kapadia, and Angélica Meinhofer. 2022. "Impact of Prenatal Substance Use Policies on Commercially Insured Pregnant Females with Opioid Use Disorder." *Journal of Substance Abuse Treatment* 140:108800.

Talvi, Silja J. A. 2003. "Criminalizing Motherhood." *Nation,* December 3, 2003. www.thenation.com/article/archive/criminalizing-motherhood/.

Tantibanchachai, Chanapa. 2014. "Whitner v. South Carolina (1997)." *Embryo Project Encyclopedia.* November 30, 2014. http://embryo.asu.edu/handle/10776/8266.

Taylor, Caroline M., Jean Golding, and Alan M. Emond. 2015. "Adverse Effects of Maternal Lead Levels on Birth Outcomes in the ALSPAC Study: A Prospective Birth Cohort Study." *BJOG: An International Journal of Obstetrics and Gynaecology* 122 (3): 322–28.

"Tennessee Senate Bill 0459." 2013. Legiscan. Accessed November 24, 2023. https://legiscan.com/TN/bill/SB0459/2013.

"Tennessee Senate Bill 3412." 2021. Tennessee General Assembly. Accessed November 24, 2023. https://capitol.tn.gov/bills/107/Bill/SB3412.PDF.

"Tennessee State Policy Information." n.d. Sex Education Collaborative. Accessed November 24, 2023. https://sexeducationcollaborative.org/states/tennessee.

"Texas Criminal Code Section 1.07.26." 2021. Texas Constitution and Statutes. Accessed November 24, 2023. https://statutes.capitol.texas.gov/Docs/PE/htm/PE.1.htm#1.07.

Thompson, Ian E. 1979. "The Nature of Confidentiality." *Journal of Medical Ethics* 5 (2): 57–64.

Thomsen, Carly. Forthcoming. *Queering Reproductive Justice.* Oakland: University of California Press.

Thomsen, Carly, and Grace Tacherra Morrison. 2020. "Abortion as Gender Transgression: Reproductive Justice, Queer Theory, and Anti-crisis Pregnancy Center Activism." *Signs: Journal of Women in Culture and Society* 45 (3): 703–30.

Todd, Patricia. 2013. "Brief Amicus Curiae on Behalf of Petitioner, *Ex Parte Ankrom.*" No. 1110176, Ala. January 11, 2013.

Tonry, Michael 1994. "Race and the War on Drugs." *University of Chicago Legal Forum* 1994 (1): 25–82.

"Treatment Episode Data Sets (TEDS): 2001–2011." 2013. Substance Abuse and Mental Health Services Administration. Accessed November 24, 2023. www.samhsa.gov/data/sites/default/files/TEDS2011St_Web/TEDS2011St_Web/TEDS2011St_Web.pdf.

"Treatment Episode Data Sets (TEDS): 2005–2015." 2017. Substance Abuse and Mental Health Services Administration. Accessed November 24, 2023. www.samhsa.gov/data/sites/default/files/2015%20TEDS_State%20Admissions.pdf.

Trivedi, Shanta. 2019. "The Harm of Child Removal." *NYU Review of Law and Social Change* 43:523.

Trost, Cathy. 1989. "Born to Lose: Babies of Crack Users Crowd Hospitals, Break Everybody's Heart." *Wall Street Journal,* July 18, 1989.

"Tutwiler Prison for Women." n.d. Equal Justice Initiative. Accessed November 23, 2023. https://eji.org/cases/tutwiler/.

"Understanding the Opioid Overdose Epidemic." 2023. Centers for Disease Control and Prevention. August 8, 2023. www.cdc.gov/opioids/basics/epidemic.html.

Waggoner, Miranda R. 2017. *The Zero Trimester: Pre-pregnancy Care and the Politics of Reproductive Risk.* Oakland: University of California Press.

Wai, Kyi M., Ohn Mar, Satoko Kosaka, Mitsutoshi Umemura, and Chiho Watanabe. 2017. "Prenatal Heavy Metal Exposure and Adverse Birth Outcomes in Myanmar: A Birth-Cohort Study." *International Journal of Environmental Research and Public Health* 14 (11): 1339.

Wakeman, Jessica. 2017. "Laci Peterson Murder: Everything You Need to Know." *Rolling Stone*, August 15, 2017. www.rollingstone.com/culture/culture-news/laci-peterson-murder-everything-you-need-to-know-199774/.

Warner, Margaret, James P. Trinidad, Brigham A. Bastian, Arialdi M. Miniño, and Holly Hedegaard. 2016. "Drugs Most Frequently Involved in Drug Overdose Deaths: United States, 2010–2014." *National Vital Statistics Reports* 65:10.

Warren, Graham W., Anthony J. Alberg, Andrew S. Kraft, K. Michael Cummings. 2014. "2014 Surgeon General's Report: The Health Consequences of Smoking; 50 Years of Progress." *Cancer* 120 (13): 1914–16.

Weir, Lorna. 2006. *Pregnancy, Risk and Biopolitics: On the Threshold of the Living Subject*. London: Routledge.

Weller Andrew E., Richard C. Crist, Benjamin C. Reiner, Glenn A. Doyle, and Wade H. Berrettini. 2021. "Neonatal Opioid Withdrawal Syndrome (NOWS): A Transgenerational Echo of the Opioid Crisis." *Cold Spring Harbor Perspectives in Medicine* 11 (3): a039669. doi: 10.1101/cshperspect.a039669. PMID: 32229609; PMCID: PMC7919394.

Welle-Strand, Gabrielle K., Svetlana Skurtveit, Lauren M. Jansson, Brittelise Bakstad, Lisa Bjarkø, and Edle Ravndal. 2013. "Breastfeeding Reduces the Need for Withdrawal Treatment in Opioid-Exposed Infants." *Acta Paediatrica* 102 (11): 1060–66.

"West Virginia Senate Bill 146." 2005. West Virginia Legislature. Accessed November 24, 2023. www.wvlegislature.gov/Bill_Status/bills_history.cfm?INPUT=146&year=2005&sessiontype=RS.

"Who Do Fetal Homicide Laws Protect? An Analysis for a Post-Roe America." 2022. National Advocates for Pregnant Women. August 18, 2022. www.pregnancyjusticeus.org/resources/who-do-fetal-homicide-laws-protect-an-analysis-for-a-post-roe-america/.

Widra, Emily, and Tiana Herring. 2021. "States of Incarceration: The Global Context, 2021." Prison Policy Initiative. September 2021. www.prisonpolicy.org/global/2021.html

Willems, Edwin P., and Harold L. Raush. 1969. *Naturalistic Viewpoints in Psychological Research*. New York: Holt, Rinehart and Winston.

Wilson, Duff, and John Shiffman. 2015. "Helpless and Hooked." Reuters. December 7, 2015. www.reuters.com/investigates/special-report/baby-opioids/.

Winerip, Michael. 2013. "Crack Babies: A Tale from the Drug Wars." *New York Times Retro Report*, May 20, 2013. www.nytimes.com/video/booming/100000002226828/crack-babies-a-tale-from-the-drug-wars.html.

Winkelman, Tyler N., Becky R. Ford, Rebecca J. Shlafer, Anna McWilliams, Lindsay K. Admon, and Stephen W. Patrick. 2020. "Medications for Opioid Use Disorder among Pregnant Women Referred by Criminal Justice Agencies before and after Medicaid Expansion: A Retrospective Study of

Admissions to Treatment Centers in the United States." *PLoS Medicine* 17 (5): e1003119.

Wong, Lo, Angel Hoi Wan Kwan, So Ling Lau, Wing To Angela Sin, and Tak Yeung Leung. 2021. "Umbilical Cord Prolapse: Revisiting Its Definition and Management." *American Journal of Obstetrics and Gynecology* 225 (4): 357–66.

Wood, Frank, April Carrillo, and Elizabeth Monk-Turner. 2022. "Visibly Unknown: Media Depiction of Murdered Transgender Women of Color." *Race and Justice* 12 (2): 368–86.

Wray, Matt. 2006. *Not Quite White: White Trash and the Boundaries of Whiteness*. Durham, NC: Duke University Press.

Wright, Tricia E., Renee Schuetter, Eric Fombonne, Jessica Stephenson, and William F. Haning. 2012. "Implementation and Evaluation of a Harm-Reduction Model for Clinical Care of Substance Using Pregnant Women." *Harm Reduction Journal* 9 (1): 1–10.

Wright, Tricia E., Renee Schuetter, Jacqueline Tellei, and Lynnae Sauvage. 2015. "Methamphetamines and Pregnancy Outcomes." *Journal of Addiction Medicine* 9 (2): 111–17.

Wurst, Keele E., Barbara K. Zedler, Andrew R. Joyce, Maciek Sasinowski, and E. Lenn Murrelle. 2016. "A Swedish Population-Based Study of Adverse Birth Outcomes among Pregnant Women Treated with Buprenorphine or Methadone: Preliminary Findings." *Substance Abuse: Research and Treatment* 10:89–97.

Young, Thelathia "Nikki." 2012. "Queering "the Human Situation," *Journal of Feminist Studies in Religion* 28 (1): 126–31.

Yurcaba, Jo. 2022. "Law Professor Khiara Bridges Calls Sen. Josh Hawley's Questions about Pregnancy 'Transphobic.'" NBC News. July 13, 2022. www.nbcnews.com/nbc-out/out-politics-and-policy/law-professor-khiara-bridges-calls-sen-josh-hawleys-questions-pregnanc-rcna38015.

Yurkanin, Amy. 2016. "Pregnant Addict Tests Limits of Alabama's Harsh Drug Laws." AL.com. October 2, 2016. www.al.com/news/birmingham/2016/10/whats_best_for_baby_law_enforc.html.

———. 2022a. "Charge Dropped against Alabama Woman Who Renewed Pain Pill Prescription While Pregnant." AL.com. February 23, 2022. www.al.com/news/2022/02/charge-dropped-against-alabama-woman-who-renewed-pain-pill-prescription-while-pregnant.html.

———. 2022b. "Pregnant Women Held for Months in Order to Protect Fetuses from Drugs." AL.com. September 8, 2022. www.al.com/news/2022/09/pregnant-women-held-for-months-in-one-alabama-jail-to-protect-fetuses-from-drugs.html.

———. 2022c. "She Lost Her Baby, Then Her Freedom: 'When the Judge Said 18 Years, I Couldn't Believe It.'" AL.com. September 2, 2022. www.al.com

/news/2022/09/she-lost-her-baby-then-her-freedom-alabama-gets-tough-on-moms-in-the-war-on-drugs.html.

Zwink, Nadine, and Ekkehart Jenetzky. 2018. "Maternal Drug Use and the Risk of Anorectal Malformations: Systematic Review and Meta-analysis." *Orphanet Journal of Rare Diseases* 13 (1): 1–23.

Index

Founded in 1893,
UNIVERSITY OF CALIFORNIA PRESS
publishes bold, progressive books and journals on topics in the arts, humanities, social sciences, and natural sciences—with a focus on social justice issues—that inspire thought and action among readers worldwide.

The UC PRESS FOUNDATION
raises funds to uphold the press's vital role as an independent, nonprofit publisher, and receives philanthropic support from a wide range of individuals and institutions—and from committed readers like you. To learn more, visit ucpress.edu/supportus.

www.ingramcontent.com/pod-product-compliance
Lightning Source LLC
Chambersburg PA
CBHW020841270326
41928CB00006B/503

* 9 7 8 0 5 2 0 3 9 1 0 7 9 *